RABBI DR. **S. Z. KAHANA**

LEGENDS OF ZION

Edited by LEO GARTENBERG

Translated from the Hebrew by Rabbi Dr. S. M. LEHRMAN.

RESEARCH CENTRE OF KABBALAH
JERUSALEM — NEW YORK

Rabbi Dr. S. Z. KAHANA

LEGENDS OF ZION

©

Copyright by the Author

133, Yehuda Halevi Str., Tel-Aviv

Research Centre Book of Related Interest
Ask your bookseller for the books you have missed

ENTRANCE TO THE ZOHAR, compiled and edited by Dr. Philip S. Berg
ENTRANCE TO THE TREE OF LIFE, compiled and edited by Dr. Philip S. Berg
KABBALAH FOR THE LAYMAN, by Dr. Philip S. Berg
TEN LUMINOUS EMANATIONS, vol. 1, compiled and edited by R. Levi Krakovsky
TEN LUMINOUS EMANATIONS, vol. 2, compiled and edited by Dr. Philip S. Berg
LIGHT OF REDEMPTION, by Levi Krakovsky
GENERAL PRINCIPLES OF KABBALAH, by R. Moses H. Luzatto
REINCARNATION: THE WHEELS OF A SOUL, by Dr. Philip S. Berg
KABBALAH: A GIFT OF THE BIBLE, by R. Yehuda Ashlag
POWER OF THE ALEPH BETH, by Dr. Philip S. Berg
ASTROLOGY: AN ECHO OF THE FUTURE, by Dr. Philip S. Berg

BOOK IN PRINT

KABBALISTIC MEDITATION, by Dr. Philip S. Berg

Printed in the United States of America

1986

THE SEVEN GATES
(PREFACE)

THE FIFTH GATE

THE SIXTH GATE

THE SEVENTH GATE

THE FIRST GATE

MOUNT ZION

Mount Zion proudly raises its head in the very centre of Jerusalem. It is the mountain on which God has desired to build His habitation. For many centuries it has remained desolate and waste, a hunting-place for foxes until its release in 1948, when the War of Independence was gallantly fought and triumphantly concluded. Our generation has restored to some extent its pristine splendour, with the result that it is gradually being established and crystalized as an important centre of spiritual and cultural life in our day and age. With dignity and pride, the mountain surveys the two sections of Jerusalem — the Old City and the New Suburbs.

Though the Old City was captured, yet miraculously, Mount Zion — which is part and parcel of ancient Jerusalem — remained in our hands, symbolizing for us the site of the Temple and all its holy splendour. On its border, the Kotel Ha'Ma'Aravi keeps a ceaseless vigil since the miraculous victory resulting from the Six Days' War. Without the blinking of an eye-lid, as it were, the Wall gazes down tenderly on the scene below it, always dynamic and effervescent, by day and night. Our valiant Defence Army, which fought for the capture of Old Jerusalem and Mount Zion, has many a miraculous tale to unfold of the wonders attending upon the Six Days' War. Most of the personal accounts of vivid experiences have been recorded in the archives of the Mount.

Mount Zion is endowed with magical charm and is dignified in its bearing and possessed of an old-world beauty and comeliness. In many respects, it is comparable to a royal palace filled with treasures, such as is described by the Psalmist, the "Sweet Singer of Israel. — "Beautiful in its panorama, it is the joy of the whole earth. Mount Zion, on its northern border, resembles the city of a great and mighty King!" In similar strains, it has been described by poet and writer as; "The apotheosis of beauty on which God has appeared." To this very day, the mountain retains its splendour and dignity, gazing down with an air of sympathy and respect on the surrounding wastes of the Judean Hills and of the Moab territory.

The guides and the Elders who have made the Mount their spiritual habitation, have many a tale to reveal about its history, for these legends are deeply engrained in the hearts of the people. They have been fragrantly preserved by stories and accounts which are legion in number. To this countless store, have now been added the discoveries unearthed by the curious spade of the excavator, as well as by scientific research. The Elders of the Mount, however, are most concerned with the traditional and purely religious aspects of the mountain. For this reason, they do not attach so much significance to the bare archaeological finds which emphasize the superficial and the material rather than the ethical and moral character of the place. Mount Zion still remains the centre of gravity, drawing the nations unto itself with cords of reverence which have bound unto it deathless memories of past splendour and dreams of future glory. It is not only the soil itself which is Mount Zion, but the soul of holiness which broods and hovers over it continually. It is national tradition and inner devotion which are the magnets which pull the heart towards it. Such an approach takes pride of place over any academic venture.

As soon as a man ascends the mountain, his heart begins to pound within him. He instinctively senses the sanctity of the place and he feels at once uplifted and exhilarated. One writer, hailing from America, once recorded in the special book kept on the mountain for that purpose, that as soon as he came to the top of the Mount, he was compelled to kiss the rocks and stones of the place and that he experienced an instinctive desire to take off his shoes and walk about the mountain barefoot. This, in fulfilment of the words uttered by God

to Moses, when he beheld the Burning Bush; "Take off thy shoes from
off thy feet, for the ground upon which thou standest is holy soil!"

To climb up the mountain is to be, at the same time, exalted with it.
One seems to ascend it effortlessly, as if propelled by some hidden
power, sparked-off by immotral longings of the soul, while one's heart
reverberates with the "Song of the Mountain" which, according to
a current legend, keeps on humming endlessly. It is heard mostly among
the branches of the trees on the mountain which, so runs the legend,
are relics of the fabled Harp of David which was suspended above the
couch on which he rested. The strings of this Harp emitted wondrous
strains and harmonies as the midnight breeze rippled across them; thus
arousing the Psalmist from his sleep in order to pour out his deathless
supplications to his Creator.

In the early days, ascending the mountain was quite an adventure. The
climbers had to be helped up with the aid of stout ropes. Despite this,
they were not weary. On the contrary, as they climbed, and especially
when they reached the summit, they burst forth into song: "My lot
has fallen in pleasant places!" For they saw in this climb a reflection
of the travails to be experienced in the Messianic Age, when ropes,
will be used to bind King David, Israel's Messiah, unto his children,
so that they may march together, with pain and joy, through the
splendid past to the glorious, hopeful future.

A new road has now been constructed to the mountain, one which
makes walking and climbing thereon a delight. Those who ascend, seem
to have been endowed with the wings of a dove and with a melody
of the heart!

A large notice was posted at the gate leading up to Mount Zion, on
which was inscribed in bold square letters the words of the Psalmist:
"Who will ascend the Mount of the Lord; and who will remain standing in His Holy Place?" One day, the notice was found to have been
turned upside down and no one knew how this had come about. A
legend then began to spread that it was the mountain itself which had
reversed the notice, for it did not wish to exclude anyone who wished

to ascend. On the contrary, it was the wish of the mountain that all should climb up and be inspired by its panorama and the heavenly music with which it reverberates. Since then, the notice has been permanently removed and the Mount extends the warmest of welcomes to all who wish to brave the ascent.

On both sides of the steps leading up to the mountain, there used to be large stones on which were inscribed Scriptural verses which spoke in praise of the Mount. These were: "Cry aloud and shout, thou inhabitant of Zion! For great is the Holy One of Israel in the midst of thee!" (Isaiah XII.6)"And they shall come and sing in the height of Zion !" (Jer. XXXI. 12); "And the ransomed of the Lord shall return and come with singing unto Zion and everlasting joy shall be upon their heads. They shall obtain gladness and joy, and all sorrow and sighing shall flee away!" (Isaiah. XXXV. 10.) When the new road was constructed, these rocks, bearing these biblical notes of rapture, were removed and buried in the soil of the mountain. Thus the entire mountain was converted into one endless paean of praise to the Almighty.

The mountain has a square place, in which the priests can fulfil their benedictions in comfort and spaciousness. During the early years of 'the establishment of Medinat Israel, it was in this square that the priests stood, wrapped in the prayer-shawls (Taliyot), blessing with uplifted hands the people who stood in their tens of thousands at the foot of the mountain.

It happened once, that the sentries of the Arab Legion who kept watch from the top of the Old City Wall opposite, were terrified at the sight of the assembled throngs and began to shoot into their midst, under the impression that they had come to storm Arab positions. At the sound of shooting, the assembled multitudes of Jewish pilgrims began to flee, helter-skelter, in an attempt to save their lives. Since that episode, it was decided to do away with the custom of the Priestly Blessing from the top of Mount Zion as a precautionary measure.

On the top of the mountain, there stands a giant Menorah — the symbol of the Jewish State and Mount Zion, as well as of the spirit of the Jewish Nation. According to our sages, God said to Israel; "My people and I will go together and illuminate Zion... "Arise and shine, for now her light has come!"

This mountain has been hallowed throughout the generations, as the place of the Shechinah and the venue of the Messiah, the Son of David. This tradition is based on the words of the Psalmist, "...And I have anointed my King on My Holy Mountain, Zion."

It is difficult to pin-point the exact site of the place called Mount Zion, or "The Hills of Zion" as we read in the verse. "...As the dew of (Mount) Hermon, which descends on the Hills of Zion..." A variety of opinions as to its exact location had already existed in the biblical and talmudic periods. In our own day, "Mount Zion" designates the mount which stretches southwards from the Old City, facing Yemin Mosheh and prolonging its way between the Valley of Hinnom and the Kidron Brook.

Both the Bible and the Talmud regard Mount Zion as a very sacred mountain, identifying it with Mount Moriah and as the place described in the verses : "...unto the place of the Lord of Hosts, Mount Zion — the mount on which Thou dost dwell." "...The Mount Zion which He loved." "He dwelleth in Zion, on My Holy Mountain." "Mount Zion, on the northern borders of the City of the Great King."

The Talmud refers to Mount Zion as the "Blessed Mountain", whence blessings proceed for the entire human race; as it is written : "May the Lord bless thee from Zion," "For it is from there, that the Lord commandest blessing to come forth to the world."

In popular tradition, Mount Zion is regarded as the "Mountain of Song". This is on account of the belief that the Sepulchre of King David is to be found there. It is also now the depository of the Cave of the Holocaust, which grimly commemorates the Six Million Martyrs who laid down their lives in order to hallow the Name of Heaven in hymn and with heroism.

In fact, the entire mountain resounds and reverberates with the beloved

11

music composed by the Divine Psalmist. At night, especially, when the world is quiet and composed in rest and sleep, one seems to catch strains of the melodies which rippled across the Harp suspended above the couch of David and which awakened him to the service of God, (Berachot 4a). At the same bewitching hour — midnight, one seems to recapture the tunes heard by King David. These same tunes continue to resound on Mount Zion to this day and will continue to do so until Redemption will dawn for the House of Israel in the Time to Come.

During the period 1948-1967, that is, in the twenty years preceding the Six Day's War, Mount Zion was the most holy and important place in Medinat Israel to which winding processions would wend their way in order to be united in spirit with Jerusalem in general and the Old City in particular. Especially thrilling to the pilgrims was the fleeting glimpse they obtained from the crest of Mount Zion, of the Western Wall (Kotel Ha'ma'aravi) — a fleeting glimpse, which has never ceased to be an abiding vision in the hearts of loyal Jews.

Mount Zion was always designated to be the centre of joy, being situated in a beautiful landscape and panorama which held all those who frequented it in breathless and joyous adoration. Across the years, however, and even down to the present day and age, it also became the focal point of much grief and lamentation, for it harbours the tomb of King David.

He who ascends the Mount becomes filled with a sense of charm and majesty. He seems to be girded with strength as he climbs the narrow steps leading to the Mizpeh Ha'bayit, filled with ancient secrets and eternal mysteries. From there, he can cast his gaze in complete adoration across the spacious wastes. His soul becomes sublime and elated, his body seems emancipated from its human desires and passions. He feels uplifted and transported into a realm of limitless horizons gazing down on deathlessness. Indeed, he imagines he is now out of the world of sorrow, trials and errors altogether, dwelling in the eternal regions above.

The outstanding value of the place which Mount Zion occupies in the realms of legend and mystical experience, awakens praise whenever its "Zion, My Holy Mountain" awakens magic in the mind. Hassidim tell that they awakened the people from their heavy slumber just by loudly proclaiming the name "Zion!" — a Name which penetrated into their heart of hearts, so that those who heard it immediately bestirred themselves to spiritual exercises.

When descending from the mountain, one senses a surcharge of mighty, emotional experience. In order to perpetuate these transient memories and powerful feelings, those who superintend the affairs of the Mount present to each visitor, a beautifully prepared Certificate which records his visit and shows forth the verse of the Psalmist. "It is from there that the Lord hath commanded the blessing of Everlasting Life;" They also decorate the visitor with a brooch on which are engraved the Kotel Ha'ma'arvi and the Harp of David.

Mount Zion was never regarded as a substitute for the Wall, but merely as an approach to it; a kind of vestibule leading to the "Dining-Hall". The light it shed may have been weaker than that reflected by the Wall; a kind of shadowy light sparked forth from the great light which one day will corruscate and scintillate from the "Dining-Hall" itself. The main value of Mount Zion consists in the fact that it is situated exactly facing the Temple Mount, as well as it being the path directly leading to it. The nearest approach to the Wall is by way of the Gate of Mount Zion.

When we stood on the Mitzpeh Ha'Bayit prior to the Six Days' War, we looked down with nostalgic yearning too deep for words, but voicing inwardly the question: "When will the gate be opened, so that he shall be enabled once more to approach the Wall direct?" For we are far from being the first to be deprived of the Wall. Throughout the winding procession of the generations, whenever a direct approach to the Wall was impossible, spiritual centres were arranged on one of the hills in the closest vicinity to the Temple Mount. In the Gaonic period, the Mount of Olives — which has been transformed in our days into

13

a burial-place — used to serve as a spiritual centre and religious focal point. Facing the Temple Mount, it became the stage of the most important undertakings — religious and communal — of that period. It was the scene of festive, religious ceremonies and observances which bore a general and national character.

Unto Mount Scopus, festival pilgrims would wend their way in throngs numbering myriads, accompanying their eager steps with joyous hymns. On this mountain, also stood the great Yeshivah "Ga'Onei Ya'Akob", where on Hoshana Rabba, the most impressive and happy services, Hakkafot with Etrog and Lulav would take place. This was in fulfilment of the Psalmist's advice: "Surround Zion and encircle it!"

On this mountain, Sukkot was a most jubilant experience; especially so, were the impressive gatherings and from which also the important proclamations were made, especially those relating to the Calendar and those national days which linked Jews of the Diaspora with their brethren in Israel. The parallel and example of the Mount of Olives and the role it played in Gaonic times, served as a model and a pattern to the Executive Council of Mount Zion when they drew up the programme of their activities.

THE CRUMB

In one of his talks, Reb Zanvill once explained that Mount Zion is only one "crumb" from the "Royal Table", but a crumb which was carried by the faithful of our nation throughout their wanderings. He unfolded before his interested listeners the well-known story of the Besht about a rich man who invited his friends to his wedding, presenting them with a royal feast When they were about to depart, the host requested his guests to take home with them some crumbs from the cakes, for these could serve for them as "food for the way" which was so long and distant. The guests, however, full of surprise at his words, paid no heed to his wise counsel. One of them, however, being wiser then the others did translate this invitation into practical effect and filled his bag with as many morsels of the choice food as it could countain.

As they proceeded on their journey, robbers attacked them and deprived them of all their possessions leaving them only with the few morsels of food with which their wise companion had filled his bag,

The result was that the others almost suffered starvation.

When the Temple still stood, Mount Moriah was the main religious Center. After the destruction Mt. Zion became a crumb of Moriah It was this "scrap and crumb" however, which the faitful remnant took with them throughout their nomadic journeyings in the diaspora. It was this "crumb" of spiritual food that they placed in all their supplications and religious observancees. Those who robbed us of our spiritual and national treasures paid no heed to this "scrap" of "sanctified food", thus allowing us to retain it across the countless ages.

It is this "scrap of food" upon which we have feasted when spiritually hungry and with which we shall regale ourselves until "the Day" will come when the Temple will once again be rebuilt on its original site and with all its pristine glory.

Reb Zanwill presented this story written on a parchament to his friend Beni the "collector of crumbs. Beni has a good Jewish heart and lives in the Galuth. Every year he makes a pilgrimage to the Holy Land and takes little stones from the historial shrines as "crumbs" for his mental food. By this, he gets a feeling of safety and Jewish identity. They call him therefore Beni Stein' strong as a stone.

After the Six Days' War (1967), when Jerusalem was unified, Mount Zion was no longer the corridor to the Wall and the Temple Mount but an integral part of it, as it always had been. The main claim for this "sense of belonging" being the presence of David's mortal remains on the mountain. David was the real Founder of the Temple built by his son Solomon, as well as being the traditional Messianic King.

MOTHER ZION

The ascent to the Tomb of David on Mount Zion where all the Kings of the Davidic dynasty have been laid to rest rewards with longevity these who dwell in Zion. Why? Reb Zanwill gave this reason : because a visit to the Tomb betokens the respect paid to parents and teachers and the rewards for such paying of respect is the promise of length of years on earth. Is it not written in the Fifth Commandment of the Decalogue : "Honour thy father and thy mother, so that thy days on earth may be prolonged!" Zion is regarded as a "Mother" in Jewish life and thought.

The following is the secret once revealed to Reb Zanwill by an old man, who was so eager to reach the Tomb of David that he ran the whole way up the stone steps leading to the top, without once stopping for breath! This is exactly how it happened : One day, as Reb Zanwill was standing on top of the mountain, he espied from a distance a very old man, to all appearances a tourist from the Diaspora, hurriedly climbing up the mountain. He was breathing heavily and seemed fatigued, yet his hurried pace showed no signs of slackening. It was evident that he could not reach his "Journey's End" quickly enough. The higher he climbed, the more violent seemed his hurry. He ran as if he had mobilized every ounce of strength within him for this purpose. Reb Zanwill was filled with pity for him, so he descended with the intention of asking the aged climber to slow down his speed They met half-way and exchanged greetings, but the old man did not stop for further conversation. Gathering his legs under him, as it were, he continued to run up the slopes.

Reb Zanwill again intercepted the panting climber and spoke to him, as a doctor does a to a patient, telling him that such haste for one of his advanced years could bode no good for his health. He asked the old man : "Why are you in such a great hurry to get to the top?" The old man stared at him in open-eyed amazement. "Why am I in such violent haste?", he said. "Of course, I am in a hurry! You see, I am very anxious to see my mother again, not having seen her for so many years."

Reb Zanwill gazed upon the old man in surprise and wonder. He could not get over the words which had escaped from the other's lips. What ? This aged climber was in desperate haste to meet his mother who was waiting for him at the top of the mountain ? The stranger looked like a man of eighty and yet he talked glibly of his mother. So how old could his mother be? Reb Zanwil could hardly believe his ears. In order to ascertain whether he had heard correctly, he again asked the old man : "Did you say that your mother was waiting for you at the top ?" "Yes, of course," the other replied eagerly. "She is sitting right at the top and is waiting most yearningly for me to embrace and greet her."

Reb Zanwill rejoiced to hear this answer and said to the aged stranger: "You have, indeed, chosen a most beautiful place for such a meeting with your old mother whom you have not seen for so long. Please let me accompany you, for I wish to see how you will greet her."

The two mounted silently, saving their breath for the steep climb still ahead of them. When they reached the summit, the old man burst out into heartfelt sobs and tears of joy, kissing the earth he trod.

As he continued in this prostrate position for some long time, Reb Zanwill ran towards him in order to help him to rise, being under the impression that the other had collapsed out of sheer fatigue. Yes, he would help him on his way to meet his old mother!

When he approached the prone figure who was still kissing the holy soil, he heard the old man mumbling : "Here she is ! Here she is!" Then, looking up and seeing the expression of astonishment on Reb Zanwill's face, he began to explain what he had meant by his rendez-vous with his old mother : "You see, my mother is not on the mountain. It is the mountain itself that is my mother!"

He then related the story told of Jeremiah, who once went up to Jerusalem after its destruction by Nebuchadnezzar, King of Babylon.

17

When the Prophet came to Mount Zion, he burst forth in lamentation :"Woe is me for you, Mother Zion! I have yearned to prophesy only good and comforting things about you; but, alas, it has been my mournful duty to foretell only retribution and destruction!"

On another occasion, when Jeremiah went up to Jerusalem, he saw a woman sitting on the top of the mountain, dressed in black garments with hair dishevelled and crying piteously, as if asking all around "Who can comfort me ?" The Prophet said to her, "Surely you are not better than your Mother Zion ?" The woman replied, "No, but I am thy Mother Zion !" "Here is my mother," said the old man, and here is my native home. Happy am I that I have been able to fall upon the bosom of my mother!"

From the days of Jeremiah onwards, the people have symbolized Mount Zion as their mother, to whom they pour out their tears and emotions of heart and soul.

TRUTH CREATES

When Reb Zanwill began to care for Mt. Zion, many archaeologists approached him with the question : 'Is it true that you wish to develop Mt. Zion when, in reality, this is not the historical Mt. Zion?". The answers he gave them were many, explaining to them that history was not all that mattered in this case. What was more important, was a tradition of more than a thousand years which assigns this Mt. to be Mt. Zion. In addition, he told them the story of how the mountain leaped from its place when the soldiers of Israel were compelled to abandon the Old City. It was then that Mt. Zion jumped from its place, in order to be included in the part which belonged to Israel.

When the archaeologists greeted this story with derision, rejecting its veracity, the Director told them of what had happened at the creation of man, a legend related in the name of R. Simon :

"When G-D was about to create man, He took counsel with four angels. The angel Hesed (Kindness) pleaded that man should be created, for he would dispense charity; whereas Truth (Emet) opposed his creation, on the ground that he would utter falsehoods. The angel Zedek (Righteousness) argued in man's favor, for he would do righteous things; but the angel Shalom opposed this, complaining that man would be full of strife and quarrels. So God was faced with an equal vote, two against two. So what did God do? He hurled Truth to the ground and decided to create man after all.

The story of R. Simon caused a stir in the academy. When he had finished the tale, he was attacked with the cry: "Is it possible that Truth should be attacked because it told the truth?". To this, R. Simon replied: "From here, you can learn that when Truth says not to create, it is not telling the truth but falsehood". He then showed them the secret of truth in the verse: "In the beginning, God created, etc. The last Hebrew letters of the first three Hebrew words form the word E-M-T, "Truth". A similar combination is in the last letters of the three Hebrew words "G-D created to do" (Bara Elohim La'asot-E-M-T) Why is this formation? To teach you that truth is in the area of creation and practical action, not in the area of negation and inactivity.

Reb Zanwill vindicated his plans for Mt. Zion by telling the archaeologists: "If you will tell me in the name of truth how and what to create, I will listen to you; but if you tell me not to create, though you claim to speak in the name of truth, I will copy the example of the divine Architect of the universe and cast so-called Truth to the ground".

THE FAITHFUL MOUNTAIN

Walking towards Mount Zion, the path leads by the desolate Valley of Hinnom where the refuse of the City had been cast out for hundreds of years. This was where, in the days in which Jeremiah the Prophet lamented and bewailed so loudly his foretelling of doom and destruction upon those who had fallen into benighted, heathen worship and sacrificed their children to Moloch, thrusting them into the hideous iron arms, whence they rolled down into the fierce furnace, kept burning in the brazen body of the idol.

This stricken vale had, also, for many years, been the dwelling-place of bands of lepers, those pitiful outcasts of society. Legend has it that, on the Day of Atonement, when the High Priest drove out the Scapegoat laden with the sins of the People of Israel, from the Temple, it was through the Valley of Hinnom that the poor bewildered beast wandered, carrying its lonely burden.

As the path climbs up towards the summit, it passes the ruins of the Sultan's Pool and an old mulberry tree, rivalling the ancient olive-trees with its great old age. The way winds upwards from ridge to ridge until at last the top is reached and the traveller has scaled the heights of holy Mount Zion.

There are always those who will dispute and query the authenticity of sacred places; there are even those who will doubt that this is the real Mount Zion and who maintain that the true one is somewhere else ! But all who have true faith, rest secure in the knowledge that this is, indeed Mount Zion, the Holy Mountain, the most sacred among all the peaks of Judea, the best-loved by God as filling Him with greater joy than any other place in His Creation.

As with all their greatly-loved and hallowed shrines however, many, many generations of Jews have spun wonderful and heroic legends about Mount Zion where King David prayed, where he lies in his Tomb and where surely, in good and due time, the Messiah will ap-

20

pear. Rabbi Zanwill, the Custodian, tells us: "One of these epic stories concerns not of long, past ages ago, but of our own day. When the War of Independence was at its height, the Jewish soldiers were desperately battling, fiercely disputing, foot by foot, every inch of the way to hold the Old City against the far greater numbers of the Arab invaders. Slowly, inexorably, the Jewish troops were forced back in retreat. As darkness fell, their Commander gathered together the women and children and hastened them all, as far away as possible, into the country where they would be safe. Then, he and his exhausted men bitterly retreated to positions far away on the western slopes of the Judean hills.

"Then the great heart of Mount Zion began to beat and throb with grief and sorrow. "My People have gone from me!", it mourned. "How can I be separated from my People? When their feet no more ascend and descend my slopes, when they walk no more with their eyes full of wondering love and their hearts beating with devotion, then I shall be alone, deserted, abandoned..."

"It was then, that the great heart lifted itself up. "I will go to my People!", it cried. "I will be there with my heroic, desperate soldiers! Their hearts shall beat anew in mine!". With mighty strength, Mount Zion gathered itself in one great, earth-shaking convulsion, and lo! it appeared upon the other side of the ridge and stood among the encampments of the soldiers. To retreat with its own people, this was the glorious victory of the Mountain!"

"The mountains skipped like rams, and the hills like young sheep!", sang the Psalmist, when the Lord rescued his people and brought them forth from the land of Egypt. Surely, that glorious spirit lived on when Mount Zion leaped to the side of its own people in their dire need, so many centuries later!"

THE LAND OF THE DEER

On the day of Israel's Independence (Iyar 5th) the custom prevails of hanging up flags to commemorate the restoration of ancient Israel to statehood and to rejoice over the first steps of the messianic age and the liquidation of the Galut. Do we not pray thrice daily : "And raise an ensign with which to gather our exile?" One of the flags which flutters on Mt. Zion is named "the flag of the assembly of the Exiles" and it has the picture of a deer in its centre. These flags first appeared when the first million Jews, from every corner of the globe, settled in Israel and which fluttered from every Israeli ship that sailed the ocean, in the hope of attracting other Jews from the Diaspora to make their permanent home in Israel.

In searching for the best illustration, for Israel is resembled to many animals in the Bible, many of these came to stake a claim. The hind came and quoted : "I found Israel like a hind in the wilderness'. Those responsible for the choice, opted for the deer. This was her claim for recognition as the fitting emblem : "If your intention is to gather the Exiles, then none is more qualified so to do than I. Were it not for me, the land would not have been able to absorb all those seeking entry. It is for this reason, that the Land is called "Eretz Hatsvi", the second word meaning both "deer" and "beauty". Morever, just as the skin of the deer expands when the flesh it covers waxes larger, so will Eretz-Israel expand with each large immigration. It is this that Jeremiah intended when he said : "And I will give you a pleasant land, a beautiful inheritance" (Tsvi)

The decision was unanimous and the deer was adopted as the most apposite emblem. A deer was embroidered in the centre of the flag with its head turned backwards. At the base of the picture was the inscription : "Flee, my beloved, and be like the deer (Tsvi"). For just as the deer always returns to the place from which it had escaped, so will Israel one day return to their place of origin -- Eretz Israel.

It is the custom of Reb Zanvil to draw the attention of all those who ascend the Mount to the flag. When he has finished his remarks, he is fond of asking them whether they resemble the deer and whether their heads are turned backwards; that is, whether it is their intention to return to the Land from which they had departed.

GOD'S HAND PROTECTS

The expression, "The Hand of God" is one of the most beautiful similies for protection and shelter. The loving power of the Creator is outstretched over His People to guard and shield them from spiritual evil and physical harm. We are told that Aaron lifted up his hands and blessed the people; but since the words written in Leviticus are in the singular, it is a benediction from the Hand of God through his instrument, Aaron.

Long, long ago, the benediction from the Hand of God was seen when Moses led the Chosen People out of Egypt. It was the same Blessing which, thousands of years later, shielded the people of Jerusalem on a miraculous occasion during the War of Independence.

It was on the Feast of Shavuot and a devout multitude of Jews were climbing Mount Zion. On the holy summit, clothed in their white ceremonial robes and with upstretched arms, the Priests were waiting to bless them. The Arab forces, however, keeping anxious watch from the other side of the mountain, were filled with panic. They thought that this was an invading army that had come to capture Mount Zion, with the result that they instantly began shooting at random into the very heart of the crowd.

It was then that the Hand of God wrought a miracle to shield His People. Not one bullet found its mark and not a single pilgrim met death that day, even amid the hail of Arab rifle-fire. For the hands of the Priest were the Hand of God. The rain of death from the bullets was turned aside and brought to naught.

23

THE SECOND GATE

THE TOMB OF KING DAVID

The most central object of interest on Mount Zion is the grave which
tradition has assumed to be that of King David. Mystics believe that
the mortal remains of David have long since been transferred to
Heaven and that earth has no power over him. But popular tradition
claims that he is still entombed there as "the King bound in fetters"
awaiting his redemption. This personal redemption will also usher in
the National Redemption for which every observant Jew prays thrice
daily. Countless are the popular legends which cluster round the tomb
of this royal Messiah who lies in his grave, open-eyed, hoping, waiting
and listening intently to the supplications of all those who pray at his
sepulchre. Elsewhere, worshippers raise their eyes heavenwards during
their prayers. On Mount Zion, at the side of David's Tomb, they
lower their eyes earthwards, their lips muttering a silent prayer to the
Messianic King, expressing their wish to be linked with him in hope
and longing for the long awaited day to dawn soon.

The Sepulchre, assigned as that of David, is not in a room. It takes
the form of a memorial catafalque. Actually, it is deep, deep down in
the nethermost parts of the Mount, hidden away and concealed from
human gaze, so that none can approach it too near. The famous me-
dieval traveller, Rabbi Benjamin of Tudella, records in his travelogue
that it once happened that men penetrated right inside the cave where
the grave is. As they were almost on the threshhold of the place and
sought to enter therein, a violent storm broke out, from the midst of
which they heard a loud voice raised in warning tones : "Get out
quickly from this place, for God does not wish to show Himself to
n..an !"

24

The Tomb of David is the gem of the Mount, and still magnetically draws tens of thousands to pray by its side and to be allied in memory with him who sleeps therein. The memorial stone is bedecked with ornamental, embroidered coverings bearing designs displaying royal crowns. Near it, has been placed a Sefer Torah, called Kommamiut (Independence), for it was written exclusively in memory of those gallant defenders of our ancestral Homeland who made the supreme sacrifice during the War of Independence (1948).

Those who enter the place where the Tomb is to be found, do so with bowed head and reverent mien, as befits the deference due before our royal Messiah. A Psalm or two is recited, so as to be linked with its author and a light is-kindled to symbolize the Light which will one day shine forth from Zion. There is no clear evidence as to the exact location of King David's grave. What is clear is that he lies buried in Jerusalem, or quite nearby. Nothing else can be stated with certainty. The men of the Mount base their belief mainly on the tradition which has identified this as the place for close on a thousand years. Hence do they disregard the hypotheses of expert archaeologists who cast doubt on this tradition. Their scepticism is founded on tendentious theories, on political issues, or theological considerations.

Reb Zanwill is of the opinion that there should be an authorized revision of all the suppositions lately advanced by archaeologists. It is essential to conduct a thorough research to be made by scholars expert in their knowledge of Bible, Talmud, Tosefta and Midrashim. This research should be conducted not from translations or anthologies, but direct from the original source. He further emphasizes that the main significance of the Tomb and the Mount will best be revealed in a study of the tales and legends which are enshrined in the books compiled by travellers to Eretz-Israel in the Middle Ages. It is from these accounts, that past generations fostered their love and longing for our ancestral Home land and by which love and pride will be strengthened in Jewish hearts. Reb Zanwill is of the opinion that it is correct to designate this site as David's Tomb, because it helps the bystander to be linked King David. Moreover, it is here either where David is actually buried or where his royal palace stood and where the Ark of God lodged after it had been brought from Kiryat Ye'arim, as is stated by Rabbi Ya'akob, the Messenger, the Disciple of Rabbi Yehiel of Paris. Reb Zanwill does not actually regard this Tomb as the grave wherein lie the mortal remains of David. In fact, his followers quote him as having voiced his belief that the body of King David had long ago been removed to the heavenly realms. They are fond of telling the story which we shall tell later on in this book, of the archaeologist who came to excavate the Sepulchre in order to come across the actual mortal remains of Kind David!

With the establishment of Medinat Israel, the Tomb became a spiritual centre where believers were fortified in their Jewish ties with the past and received support in their belief that the Messianic era will dawn in the Time to Come. The grave became a wonderful link between the present and the future. For this approach, they found support in the Midrash (on Samuel XIX) which states: "When the King-Messiah will eventually come, he will be asked : 'Where do you wish to live ?' His reply will be. "On Zion, my holy mountain; for just as it requires to be partitioned when it is built, so must it be partitioned when it is laid waste". The leaders on Mount Zion do not believe that the Sepulchre actually holds the mortal remains of King David. They merely regard it as a monument of his Kingship which still lives. The Tomb on Mount Zion recalls the splendours of King David, in which the people have deposited the royal crown which toppled down from his head but which will one day be placed again on his royal brow. Hence the current custom to place crowns on the Sepulchre and to connect those crowns with Yom Ha'Atzmaut, the Festival of Redemption. On this day, a royal crown is placed on the Tomb, amounting now to twenty-two, equating with the twenty-two monarchs of the Davidic dynasty. Near the Tomb, a palm-tree, symbolizing the House of David, has been planted; for in Psalm XCI we read that : "The righteous shall flourish like the palm-tree!" The Harp of David has also been renewed.

26

The pilgriamges on the occasion of the three Pilgrim Festivals are majestic scenes enacted by tens of thousands of joyous pilgrims with songs on their lips and deep faith in their hearts. When they approach the Sepulchre, they pray to King David to beseech God to transform the beginnings of the Redemption which we have merited to witness in our own day into perfect and lasting Salvation. The most important point on the Mount next to the Sepulchre, was that called "Mizpeh Ha'Bayit" (The Watch-Tower), and it is there that the crowds throng on the festivals. From this Mizpeh, they looked down on the Temple Mount, the Kotel Ha'Ma'Aravi, Mount Scopus, the mountains of Judea and the Old City of Jerusalem. Mizpeh Ha'Bayit connects the pilgrims with that part of Eretz-Israel which is the most holy and historical and which is now, thanks to the Six Days' War miracle, again in our possession. May it be so always, with no power on earth to separate us therefrom ! It is at this point where Old Jerusalem meets the new part of the City, where one faces the other with prayer and longing, deep calling unto deep nostalgically, with silent sighs and heartfelt sobs...

DUE TO THE MERIT OF DAVID

The main aim of Mt. Zion is to inspire heartfelt prayer. This was also the most important contribution to prayer made by King David, "the sweet singer of Israel". Although, according to the talmudic sages, Mt. Zion has become the lynch-pin and the main meeting-place it, was the patriarchs who instituted our three daily statutory prayers, King David is regarded as the main pillar of divine worship. For this is the point of human worship and it is before David's Tomb that they come to praise and supplicate and to express gratitude for having been delivered from the jaws of the enemy and have survived as Jews.

When discussion took place soon after the War of Independence (1948), when the first "rays of the dawn of salvation" began to appear, it was decided to welcome the re-establishment of Medinat Israel, at first, with the possession of every part of Eretz Israel, allowing the Kotel Ha'Ma'Ravi and the Temple Mount to remain, for the time being, in the hands of the enemy. Divergence of opinion existed, however, with regard to Mt. Zion. Those who opposed the idea of retaining Mt. Zion in our hands, contended that the holiness of the Mount equated with the sanctity of the Temple itself and was, accordingly, part of the Temple Mount. Hence was it only logical that Mt. Zion should share the fate of the Temple Mount and be left in hostile possession. This argument was opposed by those who averred that Mt. Zion is linked with King David, by whom it was designated to be the venue of prayer and worship. Jewish tradition avers that "the gates of prayer have never been locked." For this reason, they maintained, was it not right or proper to allot this "gate of tears" into the possession of hostile strangers, thus barring the way of Jewish worship there.

Arguments, pro and con, ensued during the heated discussion, without having reached any definite conclusion. It was settled only after King David had himself appeared, staking a claim that Mt. Zion be maintained in Jewish hands on account of his share in its status. He expained :

"When I first expressed my wish to build the Temple on Mt. Zion, I was told that I was not the right one to do so, and so my wish was thrust aside. I accepted the verdict and arranged that Mt. Zion takes its place as a substitute for prayer and song; that it is Prayer which is the substitute for sacrifice. "A broken spirit, in lieu of sacrifice." Now that you are discussing the place of my prayer as the place of the Temple and wish to include the Mount as part of the territory of the Temple Mount, is it your intention to link it with retribution and not with the benefits to come thereon? Has the sense of Justice been smitten in your eyes ?"

After much reflection and further discussion, it was then unanimously agreed that justice was on the side of David. Mt. Zion must remain in their hands at the abode of prayer. The enemy must not be allowed to serve as a barrier between Israel and their Heavenly Father. Thus, they must be allowed to pour out their supplications without let or hindrance.

THE PILGRIM OF THE GRAVES

It is not only a visit to David's sepulchre that draws the pilgrims, for the same attraction is enjoyed by all the graves of the saints and martyrs in Israel. The legends of Reb Zanwill cover all these graves. The ambition of these narratives is to make the visits to them instinctive as well as interesting and also to make familiar the ideas and lessons connected with these holy and historic sites. It must be confessed that not all grasp the educational facet of these visits. The majority go on pilgrimages to them on the accepted festivals, when their visit assumes the characteristic of a popular rite which militates somewhat against the non-supersititious nature of Judaism. Instead of engaging in study at the graveside, they utter supplications and pour out petitions — acts which are not always in accordance with the *halacha*. Such is the custom operating among many, that each visitor brings to his pilgrimage an emotion in conformity wtih his own spirit and understanding. This visit to the graves is a custom that has been followed for many generations, stretching back to the hoary past. Already of Joshua we read, that he used to prostrate himself at the graves of the patriarchs. So did Jeremiah and later generations of our ancestors. This custom became prevalent especially after the destruction of the Temple when the entire country became desolate and lay in ruins. It was then these graves became the only places which remained as relics of a glorious past. Around these isolated graves, pilgrimages were organized and lovely settlements in Galilee sprang up, as well as in Jerusalem and Hebron.

Generally speaking, these pilgrimages to the graves fulfilled an important mission in Jewish life, despite the fact that many good people,

29

at all times, took a rooted objection to such visits on the ground that they savoured too much of superstition and pagan practices. Latterly, especially, they have dwindled in importance because of the general tendency to enage in the upbuilding of the Jewish State. With the result that the holy graves have been somewhat neglected, thus being deprived of much of their practical and actual value and interest.

Those who are opposed to Mt. Zion, are those also who are against visits being paid to the graves. They ridicule the preoccupations of Reb Zanwill and his colleagues in this sphere of activity, even referring to them in terms that are as slighting as they are totally undeserved, calling them "grave-watchers," and other nomenclatures even less dignified and respectful.

THE BUILDER OF THE TEMPLE

It happened once that an archaeologist came to Mount Zion, and asked Reb Zanwill for permission to dig beneath the Sepulchre which is believed to contain the mortal remains of King David which he wished to discover for himself. He came armed with a detailed map of the entire site and with all the essentials requisite for this digging venture; as well as with instruments necessary to record his excavations in accordance with the practice of Archaeology.

Reb Zanwill stared at him in blank amazement. and asked him flatly: "Whom exactly do you wish to find — David, or the King?" It was now the turn of the archaeologist to express surprise, "What do you mean by asking me: "Whom exactly do you wish to find, David or the King?' Are they not both one and the same — not two separate persons?". Reb Zanwill retorted: "True they are both one and the same individual; yet they are, nevertheless, two separate and distinct persons; that is, they are two persons who have become merged into one, yet who can nevertheless be divided and separated into two distinct units. For this is what hapened: whereas David

30

soared to the azure realms above, his Kingdom remains buried here below. For this reason, it is idle on your part to try to find the body of David. which has been transported heavenwards."

Reb Zanwill then unfolded before him the story concerning the transportation of David's body above the shadow of our earth. Actually, there are two separate versions of this story : some connect this legend with the desire of David to build the Temple — a desire which he could not fulfil on account of the many bloody wars in which he was forced to engage; while others link it with his Harp with which he poured forth his emotion in hymns and praise to God. When God's Temple was destroyed, the world was laid waste and the Shechinah wandered through the wide places of the world, unable to find for Itself a dwelling-place. As a result, the Shechinah was filled with pain and sighing. When the Angels on High beheld His concern and the homelessness of the Divine Spirit, they were filled with grief on His behalf and searched high and low to find a fitting abode for His Illustrious Presence They then arrived at the momentous decision that, since His Temple on earth had been razed to the ground, they would construct a Temple on High. They decided to go down to the ruins of the Earthly Temple and search for the Keys and the Plans, so that they could model themselves on its pattern, and use these as their "blue-prints".

Their first port-of-call was Solomon, who had built the Temple and they asked him to supply them with all the desired particulars. The answer he gave them was : "True, I built the Temple, but it was my father who actually drew up all the plans for its construction; and he still possesses the Keys. For well-known reasons, he was not actually allowed to build it, yet the idea was his and hence the Keys are in his possession." So to David, the Angels resorted, and asked him for the Keys. The countenance of the King went white with pain and he said : "I have always wished to raise a Temple *ad gloriam Dei,* for the honour and glory of God; but the wars in which I was forced to engage precluded me from fulfilling this cherished desire. Even

31

now, you wish to build a Heavenly Temple without my help, thrusting me aside, even though now I lie peacefully in my Tomb, no longer engaged in battles!" Hearing this, the Angels bowed their heads and immediately decided to transport David heavenwards, where he could construct the Celestial Temple. David rejoiced at this decision and handed over the Keys to the Angels; he was then borne heavenwards.

We have the words of Psalm XXX.1-2 : "A Psalm; a Song at the Dedication of the House of David! 'I will extol Thee, O Lord, for Thou hast raised me up'" Which House did David dedicate ? It was the Heavenly Temple; hence his words "For Thou hast raised me up (from the grave below").

From that day to this, David stands guard over the Heavenly Temple which he opens and closes daily with his celestial attendant, the Angel Michael.

When the Arachaeologist heard the story of Reb Zanwill, that King David had been borne heavenwards by angels, he asked: "This being so, then what do you have here in the Tomb?" The reply he received was : "There are two things here : firstly, this place where its earthly counterpart was. So when one stands before David's Tomb on Mount Zion, one should raise one's eyes heavenwards towards the place where he now eternally resides amidst heavenly glory."

"Secondly," Reb Zanwill proceeded in his answer to the question posed to him : "In this Sepulchre, where the King lies buried, there is also interred with him, his Kingdom and all the glorious past of his people. For when the enemy came to destroy our land, the princes and leaders of our nation hurriedly hid the national and personal treasures in secluded caves; but the treasures of King David and the possessions of the members of his family were committed to this spot for safe custody. It is in this Sepulchre deep down in the bowels of the earth, that they will safely remain until the time comes when the Shofar of the Messiah will galvanize all dormant objects into effervescent and sparkling life !"

These words of Reb Zanwill made such an impression on the Archaeologist that he could hardly wait another day before he packed up all his belongings, excavation tools and all, and returned to the country from which he hailed. Before going, however, he asked Reb Zanwill another favour: Would he grant him permission to dig into the Grave and below it, in order to find the treasure hidden deep down in the earth ?

Reb Zanwill replied, with his characteristic smile lighting up his face : "If it is your intention to enrich yourself with the material treasures of gold and silver and other precious objects, then you are too late, my friend; for these have already long ago been removed from here — some of them by the heavenly angels' and the rest by robbers and excavators. No! My reference, when speaking of the treasures buried here was to the spiritual riches — to the goldren pages of our past national history. In this Sepulchre, lie stored the mystical pages of our glorious past; records, torn out of the Book of Jewish History in the course of generations by the power of the mountain; but they are inscribed on its stones and clods of earth. They are pages which tell of joy and sorrow, slavery and freedom, subjection and royalty. In fact, deposited below, is a complete Diary, very comprehensive, leaving no record or item of importance unnoticed, from the beginning of time, right down to this very day.

"All that is exalted and wonderful, all that is gladsome or painful. Happy is he who will dig here. But for this purpose none of the earthly tools and implements which you have brought with you, will be of use to you. For it is not with human picks or hoes; not even with my permission, that you can find warm understanding and A Feeling Heart !"

LEGENDS OF THE KINGS BURIED AT THE TOMB OF DAVID

The Tomb of David was not intended for himself alone, but one that he had also prepared for the subsequent Kings who would be his true descendants. In the course of time, these numbered twenty-two, the same number as there are letters in the Hebrew alphabet. Legend tells us that the Almighty had this mystic number in mind when He created the world and the letters with which His Scriptures would be written. In the Tomb, there are two chambers, one above the other. The lower one is the monument of King David, the higher chamber is that of Solomon. Many fascinating legends are told of David and Solomon and, at least, of four of the other Kings who were counted as of true Davidic descent. All these are buried in adjacent caves. So carefully and skilfully was this cluster of royal sepulchres hidden deep in the earth of Mount Zion, that no vandals or evil men could ever discover or violate it. According to legend, a tunnel stretches from Mt. Zion to Mt. Moriah, thus joining both forgotten caves.

Once upon a time, a Turkish Grandee paid a visit to the Tomb and, leaning too far through the aperture in order to see as much as possible, dropped his dagger far down the sepulchre. As it had a hilt richly encrusted with jewels, he immediately caused one of his Moslem servants to be put down with a rope, to retrieve the weapon. After some delay, the man was pulled up again — dead! Three more Mohammedan slaves were were sent down, one after the other, by their Turkish master. Each one, on being pulled up again to the top, was found to be lifeless! Flustered and furious, the Grandee sent an angry message to the Rabbi of Jerusalem, holding him responsible for retaining the dagger.

The Rabbi, first of all, called for three days of prayer and fasting, after which a lottery was drawn to decide who should be sent on the dangerous attempt at recovery. The task fell to the Shammas of the Synagogue, a holy and devout Jew. His friends, with bated breath, waited for him to come up safely out of the Tomb, holding in his hand the dagger which he would at once deliver to its owner. So pleased and gratified was the Turkish Grandee, that his future treatment of the Jews was marked by kindness and courtesy. Later, the Shammas told the Rabbi in secret, that when he reached the bottom of the Tomb, an impressive and venerable old man appeared and handed him the jewelled dagger he was seeking!

Another story is told of the Keeper of the Tomb who, having a spite against a poor and humble Jewish laundress, persuaded her with fair and false words to enter the sacred place. Once she was inside, he locked the door on her and ran off to the Moslem Official to report that a Jewess had entered what was, at that time, regarded as a Mohammedan Shrine. He suggested that she be burnt for her impious behaviour, nothing less than that.

The poor woman, terrified and helpless at finding herself imprisoned and alone, burst into despairing tears and called on the protection of the Almighty. Suddenly, surrounded by a brilliant radiance, a patriarchal figure appeared before her, who gently took her by the hand and drew her after him, down steps and along passages, until she found herself out on the mountain-side. Her saviour bade her go back to her home as swiftly and as silently as possible. Let no one know that she had ever left it.

When the Moslem official arrived, swelling with anger, he could find no presumptuous woman. She was looked for in every corner. The whole place was carefully examined, but there was no sign of any kind that any one had been there. The official, looking very foolish, was exceedingly wrath with the Keeper. All the more, when the spies he had secretly sent to the woman's house returned with the report that she was at home struggling industriously with a huge pile of laundry. She looked dumb-foundeded at their interrogations about her visiting the Tomb.

Making the punishment fit the crime, the Official had the malicious Keeper burnt, in place of the poor victim of his hatred and who he had sought to entrap. For many years, the woman kept her own counsel and told nobody of her secret, but listening silently to the common belief that a miracle had been wrought. Only when she was at point of death, did she reveal her story.

THE SHOES

When the Rabbi of Kaminka, Reb Luzer arrived in Jerusalem, he wore boots that were the peculiar taste of the Russian peasants. They were made with heavy soles and heels, the better to cope with the abundant snows and slush frequent in that part of the world. Naturally, during summer in Israel, they were especially heavy on the feet. Yet he wore them constantly, in heat and cold, rain or glorious sunshine, day and night. Never did he take them off. They could not understand why he wore them even at night when he slept. As he walked along thus shod, he hummed to himself the words of Shir Ha'Shirim (The Songs of Songs): "How comely and graceful are thy feet in shoes."

His close friends advised him to discard these boots both on account of their being burdensome, as well as being most ungainly in appearance; besides they were not in tune with the fasion of boots worn at that time by average Jews. He, however, remained impervious to their good intentions and friendly advice and continued to wear them. The reason for his doing so was kept a close secret, only to be revealed to his son on his death-bed.

Reb Luzer was a very poor man who, all his life, had yearned to go to Israel but did not have the money for such a long trip. Still, he was always hoping that the One Above would accept his prayer and would help him fulfill his dream. If not now, then in his old age, at least.

This help came in a wonderful way. One day, during a fair, a poor man came to his house, one who went around from house begging for donations. He asked for permission to leave a pair of boots in his house because it was too warm to wear them in the city. He showed the man a spot in the house where the old boots could be placed. The poor man promised that toward evening, he would return for his boots.

All that evening the poor man did not show up to claim his boots. Soon, the matter was forgotten. The boots just stood in the corner of the room. A few days before Passover, when the house underwent a thorough cleaning, the boots were discovered. They had been there for a long time with no one ever touching them. He looked into them for there may be Hametz therein.

When the boots were picked up, gold coins fell out and spread all over the floor. The local Rabbi, a great saint, was consulted as to what to do with the money. The Rabbi answered: "You should know that your prayers, made during most of your life, were heard in heaven and answered. You now have enough money to go to Israel. The poor man who came to you was not an ordinary human being of flesh and blood, but God's messenger from above, probably the prophet Elijah." Reb Luzer was amazed to hear the rabbi's words, whom he believed to be a great saint, one endowed with holy vision. He knew his words could be relied upon.

Therefore, he wasted no time. No sooner were the Passover days over, than he left his home for the Holy Land. He took the boots that he found and put then on his feet.

It was not the money with which to buy other boots that mattered here, but the boots themselves that played the dominant part.

He gained the impression that it was the prophet Elijah himself who presented him with these outlandish boots. Moreover, it seemed to him as if they had been made from the leather girdle of the prophet and that it was by the aid of these boots that he will able to reach his desired haven — Jerusalem, more than with the help

37

of money. He tried on these boots on his own feet. Marvellous to relate, they fitted him so expertly as if they had specially been designed for his slender feet and not for the large feet of Polish farmers in which to trudge the muddy slush and the heavy snows. From the money that he found in the boots, he took but little as his legacy, preferring to distribute the bulk of it for charity.

In those days, the trip to Jerusalem was not a simple task. Many hardships had to be experienced before one could reach Israel, or Palestine, as it was then called. When he did arrive, he settled not far from the Kotel Ha'Maaravi (Western Wall), the only place where the Holy Spirit remained after the destruction of the Holy Temple. Twice each day, he went in his worn-out boots to the Wall to pour out his heart and to cry over the exile of the Holy Spirit and the exile of the children of Israel. Always with a small book of the "Tehilim" (Psalms), he would pray to the Holy One, blessed be He, that He have pity on his people and redeem them from exile. From the Holy Wall, he walked to Mount Zion, where he had scheduled a visit to the graves of the Household of David and there complete the entire book of Tehilim every day. As usual, he was not permitted into the actual cave of King David but only to the designated spot where all Jews were permitted to go.

It happened on one day that the Pasha of Jerusalem became dangerously ill. Even the finest doctors could not cure him because no matter what they did, no help seemed to come. In desperation, the Pasha sent a messenger to the Jews of Jerusalem that they pray for his health. In return for their prayers, he promised them that if he recovered, he would reward the Jews with anything they asked for.

When the Jerusalem Jews heard the Pasha's message, they decided to turn over the entire matter to Reb Luzer. He took with him ten Jews and they went to the Holy Wall where they prayed for the ruler's recovery.

The next day, the Pasha felt much better. He had passed through the crisis and was now on his way to full recovery. The Pasha was certain that the Jews of Jerusalem had pulled him through with their prayers. When he learned that Reb Hersh Kaminker's father had led the prayers, he sent for the holy saint and asked him what reward he wanted in payment. Without a moment's hesitatio1., he asked that he be permitted to enter he actual cave of King David, so that he could pray deep in the cave. The Pasha agreed and gave orders that the request of the man be observed immediately.

When the ministers of the Pasha and the Moslems learned of this order, they created a great tumult. It was against their taste that a Jew be permitted such a special privilege. This had never been so permitted before.

The Pasha soon realized that he had made a mistake in being so hasty in fulfilling the wish of a Jew. Now that he had seen the anger of the Arabs, he feared that his order might even cause harm to the Jews, because the Arabs could use any excuse to revenge themselves upon the Jews.

The Pasha was at a loss as to what to do. He called in his advisers, for their opinion. He did not wish to anger the Arab population, but he could not break his word to the Jews. It would be dishonourable for him to do so.

Finally, the Pasha decided that he had an idea. He had given his word to permit a Jew to enter and pray. He had promised nothing about the Jew being allowed to come out of the cave. He could remain there and die from hunger.

And this is what hapened. Reb Luzer came to the cave in his worn out boots with the Tehillim in his hands. The doors were open for him, but no sooner did he enter than the doors were shut tight.

Reb Luzer went down deep into the cave and started reciting Tehillim. He cried a great deal, spilled many tears for the exile of the Holy spirit and the exile of Jews from the Holy Land. He prayed for redemption. Finishing his prayers, he wanted to leave the cave, but noticed that the door had been shut tight. He began to knock, but no one answered. He yelled, but no answer. He knocked with all his might, yelled with all his strength, but his voice remained inside.

Now, he understood what had happened. He returned to the inside of the cave, fell to the ground and cried bitterly until he fell asleep. In his dream, he saw an old man approaching him. The man was dressed in the clothing of a king and had a crown on his head. His face was as radiant as the sun, and a long white beard made his apearance regal and awe-inspiring.

The old man took him by the hand and said: "They think you will die here from hunger, but they are mistaken. Come with me, and I will show you how to get out of this cave. No one knows this passage." Taking his hand, the old man led him through many underground passages and led him out from the cave, emerging near his home.

Suddenly, Reb Luzer raised his eyes and saw that, thanks to the old man, he had been brought safely home. However, to his amazement the old man had disappeared. Never again during his lifetime, did he see him again.

There was no doubt in his mind but that the old man was King David himself, and that he had been saved as a reward for his reciting the holy Tehillim daily. This had saved him from certain death in the cave.

This is the regular legend. But there are others that connect his rescue with the boots. They tell that when Reb Luzer came to pray in affectionate reverence at the Sepulchre of King David, he was asked by the custodians of the Tomb to take off his boots, as the custom obtained on such occasions. He, however, adamantly refused." I wear my boots always day and night, even when I sleep," he told them. A heated discussion then arose as to the course of action to take in this instance, till the decision arrived at was that, under no circumstances would he be allowed to enter the Cave of the Sepulchre with his boots on. Although the Pasha (Governor) was inclined to waive this rule in his case, in defiance of the prevailing custom, the Rabbi did not enter the area of the Tomb but remained standing above the Tomb in a prayerful attitude. It was thus that he was saved from the devilish machinations of the wicked ones intent on killing him.

When the son heard his father's story of the boots, his heart beat fast and an idea was sparked-off in his mind.

He put the boots of his father into his grave near his feet, so that he could go with them on high to the Gan Eden. After all, were they not made from the girdle of Elijah?

THE GUARDIAN OF THE POOR

Beggars at the holy graves constitute a difficult problem, one which has been the theme of many discussions in times past and in the present day. Whereas some see in this practice something meritorious, others opine that it is a shameful exhibition.

Apart from the material urgency to ask for alms which spurs on beggars to frequent these places, where donors of every kind abound, there is also in this habit a personal background. These are some of the very few places where the oppressed and dejected can find some compensation for his inferiority complex and his low place in society. For there he meets with people who have come to supplicate God to relieve them of their dire distress. Like the poor themselves, these petitioners stand with bowed heads and broken hearts; like them, they are laden with suffering and are dissatisfied with their "lot" in life — which is not a "lot."

At the grave-side, there prevails a feeling of equality which is the source of inner satisfaction. Here the poor find comfort; for suffering shared by others itself constitutes a large modicum of comfort. What significance can there be attached to the garments worn by the donors and his personal status, or even in the outward state of his character and emotions? The poor fully realize that the visitors have repaired

41

here not so much because of personal troubles, revealed or hidden. Besides, who can tell whose sorrows, the rich visitors or the poor beggars' are more grievous?

Moreover, the poor man is fully aware that all men, withersoever they may be, are in reality powerless and in need of divine mercy from that same heavenly source in whose sight both the poor and the rich enjoy equal status. For the Lord is their shield!

There exists a very strong affiliation among Jews between visiting graves and the distribution of charity. When man is in the presence of the Divine, he becomes exalted and raises himself nearer to charitable endeavours. "Charity doth exalt a nation." From the Torah standpoint, charity does not fall short of prayer itself; in fact, some deem it even of more surpassing value. Moreover, many prayers stress this concept: "And the Lord has become a stronghold for the poor."

This same phenomenon is also witnessed on Mt. Zion where, from the early hours of the morn, we will find the poor selling candles or begging for alms. Then they wander from synagogue to synagogue, ratting their collection-boxes. At first, Reb Zanwill permitted then so to do, supporting his attitude, despite bitter opposition, on verses culled from Scriptures and rabbinical sources dealing with this theme. According to him, the poor are an integral part of the holy place just as are the priests, readers, overseers, students of the Torah, reciters of the Psalms and the "Ten Impractical Persons" (Asarah Batlanim), and others of a similar turn of mind. Reb Zanwill looks upon them as part of the spiritual decoration of the place, to which they even lend a certain moral value. For this attitude, he finds further support in the rabbinical view that "Israel's redemption will come only on account of charity; for does not the prophet Isaiah assure us that Israel's redemption will come only on account of charity?" (Shabbat 130a). Another Scriptural verse fully supports this assertion: "For the Lord has established Zion, wherein the poor of His people will find shelter." Commenting on this verse, our Sages say: "The ways of God are not equated with those of human beings. For whereas among the latter one finds that the rich alienates himself from being related to a poor kinsman, pretending not to know him, but basking in his friendship should the relative be rich and distinguished. Totally different, however are the ways of God with men. For who are His people? The poor. For when He sees a poor man, He associates Himself with him. A proof? See what is written : "Thus saith the Lord : 'The heavens are My throne... and it is upon the poor, etc. that I will cast my gaze." (9 Isaiah 60.) The Midrash (Exodus Rabba, XXX. I2) adds : "When God will once again favour Zion, His first act of compassion will be on the poor; as it is said : "For the Lord hath founded Zion, wherein the poor of His people will find protection."

KING DAVID'S CROWN

"David, son of Jesse, reigned over all Israel... Seven years reigned he in Hebron and thirty-and-three years reigned he in Jerusalem..." "And David slept with his fathers, and was buried in the City of David." The traditional Tomb of David is up on Mount Zion, in the complex of low, dark, massive vaults, built by the Romans some two thousand years ago and covering much of the old City of David. There, through the centuries, it has been honoured. For during the Moslem possession of Jerusalem, David was revered as one of the greatest Prophets. His Tomb lies within the walls of what was then the Mosque of Nebe Da'ud.

In a chamber, with foundations cut from the living rock and guarded by a screen of wrought-iron, the darkness is lightened and the aura of reverence magnified by the multitude of candles, symbols of eternal love and prayer. For David will usher in the Messianic Age. Until then, every prayer and uplifting of the heart in praise offered at his Tomb, will hasten that time of Redemption ending for ever human anguish and pain throughout the world. The massive bier over the grave is covered with a heavy pall of crimson velvet. On the rock beside it, the epitaph reads: "David, King of Israel who lives for ever!" Behind the Tomb, is a beautiful Scroll of the Torah, flanked on either side with exquisitely wrought silver crowns — not, as might be expected, the royal crowns of the King, but Sifre Torah crowns of the desecrated Scrolls from many of the despoiled and violated Synagogues of Europe. The lovely custom of placing a crown at the Tomb of King David for each year of the free State of Israel, was begun in 1949; since when, many have now been added.

None of these, however, is the crown worn by King David himself. There are many legends about his great humility in refusing a crown of pure gold when the lords of Judah came to him in Hebron and offered him this symbol of majesty. "All Heaven is my Crown," he said, "and all the world of nature and of men is my royal dwelling-place!" He would wear only a Kippah, embroidered with the stars of the firmament; and during all the days of his reign in Hebron, he would wear no other emblem of his kingship.

The time came, however, when all the Tribes of Israel summoned King David to reign over them in Jerusalem. Then the regalia of royalty must be worn to honour the great office to which God had called him. But what form should his crown take? What would be a worthy diadem to be the Crown of Jerusalem? True humility, however, still possessed the innermost heart of the King and, with sudden enlightenment, he cried: "The Law of Moses is the true Diadem of Jerusalem! The Torah is the Coronet which Jerusalem must wear!"

Ever since, the Scrolls of the Torah are furnished with most beautiful Silver Crowns. Such a Scroll, with such a Crown, always formed part of the furnishings around the royal throne. The same symbol adorns him Tomb; for this great and righteous King always governed by the truths of the Torah and its holiness crowned his life and rule.

KING DAVID'S PEARLS

Strange are the innermost secrets of the human heart and only seldom are they revealed even to the most intimate of those around us. Rabbi Zanwill tells a touching legend of the hidden heart and mind of the great King David. Living in great splendour, surrounded by his Court, there was yet one place where none might enter and of which the door was always locked — the King alone having the key. This was the inner chamber where he slept, or rather to which he retired ostensibly to sleep.

Every night, however, when all the world was asleep, the outer guards of the Palace would recognize a solitary, cloaked figure, passing swiftly by them, going no one knew where. The inner guards would tell their comrades that, before he went, they heard the King lock and double-lock his chamber door. Naturally, the guards talked to their wives and friends, the wives talked to their friends and soon, everyone knew of the King's nocturnal pilgrimages. No one knew, however, their object or destination. There was, of course, much talk and gossip behind the King's back, many and varied were the ideas and suggestions discussed. Were there secret meetings with some of his Council ? His friends ? A woman ? The poor and desolate who, ignorant of who he might be, found in him a mysterious wonder-worker, succouring their miseries ? Or, was there some secret in the room itself ?

Speculation was rife; the most profoundly anxious and troubled of all the King's friends was Abishai, who was not only — as Captain of the Guard — responsible for his safety, but was also his oldest and best-loved comrade. At last, driven by his nameless fears, Abishai felt that (albeit the utmost loyal secrecy) he must discover the meaning of David's nightly roamings. So, waiting until all the Palace was dark and silent, he stole one night to a point near the King's door,

45

and waited till, according to his strange habit, the King came out, firmly locked the door and set off on his secret errand. Abishai wrapped his own cloak round him and followed his master.

The King walked swiftly through the sleeping city and along the winding path on the thickly-wooded hillside. In a grove where the trees were thickest, he halted. Abishai, closely shadowing him, stopped also. It was a stormy night and the wind blew through the branches, like the rigging of a ship mingling with the wind, now rising above it, now so low that it was scarcely audible, Abishai heard the voice of the King in prayer. They were all prayers of sorrow and lamentation. — This then was the secret! "My God, my God, why hast Thou forsaken me ? And art far from my help at the words of my cry... O Lord, rebuke me not in Thine anger; neither chasten me in Thy wrath... Give ear, O God, to my prayer, and hide not Thyself from my supplication... Save me, O God, for the waters are come in, even unto my soul..."

Long did the King remain in prayer, his arms outstretched imploringly against the night sky. At last, turning suddenly, he went back as swiftly as he had come. Abishai followed, keeping him in sight until the sleeping-chamber was reached and the door unlocked by the King and bolted behind him. Torn with his deep affection for his old comrade and lord and by the knowledge of his grief, Abishai patiently watched and waited. One day, it chanced that the King did not lock his door. Abishai stealthily went in and there found one very strange thing — the pillow on the royal couch was wet... That same night, he awaited David's return. Creeping to the bolted door, he listened and discovered the other half of the mystery. With anguished tears and passionate remorse for all his sins, the King bedewed his pillow, bitterly acknowledging his transgressions and pleading with the Merciful Almighty for forgiveness.

Overcome with pain at beholding such suffering. Abishai bethought him of the great Prophet Nathan. At daylight, he went to seek him out and tell him of the King's penitential mourning. "Come," said the Prophet, "Let us go to him!" When they approached the royal chamber, by another strange chance, the door was open and the room empty. Nathan and Abishai went in and looked around them and then sought to examine the bed. To their amazement, gathered before them on the pillow, were great clusters of beautiful pearls, shimmering with their own warm and glowing light. The men stood stupified. What was the meaning of this heap of treasure where they had expected to find only a sodden and tumbled pillow ? The guards, however, were taking no risks and, respectfully urging their Captain and the Prophet out of the room, fastened the door, lest their presence so near to such jewels might seem highly suspicious.

The Prophet, walked however, secure in the love and confidence of the King. Seeking an opportunity, he spoke to him gravely and earnestly about leaving unguarded such quantities of pearls, worth a king's ransom. The King then opened his heart to Nathan and told him how, night after night, he prayed and mourned over his sins and wept for sorrow and remorse. Each morning, he found that every tear had become a pearl...!

King David told how he gathered up the pearls and gave them away wherever such wealth could do most good; namely to the pood and the sick, for noble causes, for the care of his soldiers and his labourers and to adorn and beautify the worship of God. "As it is through my sins that this treasure has been found and given to me", he said, "it must be, in reparation for good deeds to my fellow-men that such riches must be spent."

DONATED MEALS AT THE TOMB OF DAVID

None will gainsay that the sepulchre of King David on Mt. Zion should be preserved in a regal state. It is out of the question that it should be the very last word in cleanliness, beautifully decorated and held in the greatest respect. For who deserves greater honour to his memory than the beloved King, builder of Jerusalem of and the sweet singer of Israel whose mortal remains are believed to rest on this holy Mount ?

The Director does his very best that this should always be so, but not always are his meticulous directions successfully implemented. For far too often, whole families gather around the grave in fulfillment of some vow they had taken and take out parcels of packed food and drink and, spreading themselves spaciously out, enjoy their traditional meals. Not only is the manner of their eating far from ceremonially and scrupulously clean, but the aftermath is worse still. For they leave endless litter behind, including the bones of the fish and the chicken they devoured, all of which are strewn around the grave. All do their very best to explain to these simple, superstitious folk the error of their ways. Sad to relate, however, the results are not at all promising; for these members of oriental communities are very loathe to abandon their age-old traditions, outmoded as they may appear to be. They are not inclined to budge from these hoary customs of donating parties to be enjoyed at the tomb of King David. Their ideas of respect and decorum totally differ from ours.
It once happened that Reb Zanwill visited the Mount in the company of a very distinguised Minister of State from another country. The visitor was enraptured with all that greeted his eyes until they came to the Tomb of David when all their delight was transformed into sheer disgust. For there, as large as life, were sprawled out to their fullest extent, an Iraqi family, Ezekiel, with his two wives and numerous children. On the stone floor around them on which they sat, were spread out all kinds of oriental dishes, each with their pungent smell of garlic, onion and other strong, savoury scents. Both the distinguished visitor and Reb Zanwill literally turned all colours at such a profanation of a sacred spot.

Reb Zanwill, in embarrassment and by way of excuse, tried to explain to his surprised guest the significance of this meal to Oriental Jews.

After speeding farewell to his departed guest, Reb Zanwill summoned Ezekiel before him and reprimanded him for his conduct, for thereby he had polluted a spot most holy. The other looked at him with undisguised surprise, protesting his innocence. Wherein had he desecrated the Tomb of David ? On the contrary, his intention was to honour David and to perpetuate a custom as old as the Bible itself. For are we not told in Lev.X.13." And you shall eat thereof in a holy place", namely in the Tent of Meeting before G-D Himself ? Surely, the Tomb of David was not holier than the Tent of Meeting ? Do we not read that in Temple times, families in their hundreds and thousands would ascend in pilgrimage to the Temple Mount and, after offering their sacrifices, would partake of a large and joyous common meal together ? The guests would include all the various sections of Israel, priests and Levites, women and children, all happily gathered together in a united manifestation that all they enjoy on this earth belongs to Him who generously provides for all their wants. So, asked Ezekiel of the Director : "Wherein have I sinned ?".

Reb Zanwill was deeply moved by this sincere explanation, though he could never agree with the logic of the argument. The Tomb of David was not holier than the Temple, yet it was in a totally different category altogether. "Do you mean to tell me", persisted Ezekiel, "that the Tomb of David should be honoured more than the Temple?"

Reb Zanwill was quick in his reply : "Of course, nothing is holier than the Temple; yet the Tomb of David is of a different nature. In its precincts, prayer and hymns are more suitable than food and drink. "To illustrate his remarks, Reb Zanwill narrated to him the following legend :

"When God told David that not he but his son Solomon would build the Temple, he became very dejected. All his life he had planned and prepared for the day when he would see the Temple raised in his own life-time and now his dream had ended in the nightmare of frustration and disillusionment. He would never see it established on

Zion's hills and not his would be the joyous privilege of worshipping within its sacred precincts.

Noticing his abject dismay, God sought to comfort him! "David, my son, it is better so. Let me assure you that one prayer, one psalm of yours is far more precious in My eyes than a thousand oxen sacrificed in my Name by Solomon : The sacrifices of David do not consist of animal offerings "followed by food and drink, but of prayer and song."

But though Reb Zanwill sought to persuade Ezekiel that it was not the right thing to do in eating ceremonial meals before the Tomb of David, yet he did not have the heart to stop those who, like Ezekiel, brought their families up the Mount there to partake in front of the sepulchre of David of the meal they had solemnly offered to provide for their family and guests. In order to satisfy all parties, that is those who felt disgusted at such sights as well as those who fondly and sincerely believed that they were fulfilling an ancient religious cere- mony, Reb Zanwill provided a special room in the proximity of the Tomb where the meal could be enjoyed without causing embarrass- ment to those who hailed from western communities and whose standards of living and social behaviour differed totally from those of their oriental, pious and naive compatriots. In the ways of con- sideration and understanding, as in the ways of the Torah, peace and harmony prevail.

IN THE HOUSE OF THE YEMENITE RABBI

On an other similar occasion Reb. Zanwill almost made up his mind to put a stop, once and for all, to all these "family meals". It happened to be a stormy day when he had been asked to receive a very import- and ambassador and to show him around the Mount. He agreed to do so. After receiving him hospitably in his office, where they held sweet discourse together on the tradition and customs of the Mount, he invited him to take a walk with him outside, where he could explain the various activities they engaged in there.

When they were about to enter the spacious courtyard which flanks the sepulchre of King David, one of the officials whispered into the ears of Reb Zanwill not to take his distinguished guest there. Why not? Because it was then the scene of a very large and most sumptuous "Vow Banquet", in which the participants were Yemenite families of all ages and stages, all bent on having a "good time" while fulfilling the "vows" they had made when they were in distress and which they would fulfill when salvation knocked at their doors once again.

Reb Zanwill asked the ambassador to excuse him for a little while, as he wished to address a few words to those making merry within. So, leaving the distinguished guest in the care of the official, he entered the courtyard and asked the gathering to vacate the place for a short while, as he wished to show the ambassador around. Among the assembled was their spiritual leader, their Rabbi who also hailed from Yemen. The latter adamantly refused to grant the wish of Reb Zanwill on the plea that the tomb of David belonged to him and not to the diplomat whose main purpose is only to gaze and not to pray. When the plea of Reb Zanwill, was directly refused after several repetitions, the latter was aroused to anger. In was then that he resolved in his mind, to proclaim a ban on such festivities from now on.

After the ambassador had gone, Reb Zanwill rebuked the Yemenite Rabbi for being so obstinate and unobliging. He further admonished him, that as a Rabbi, it was his bounden duty to see that more respect be given to the Tomb of David. Eating and drinking, shouting and singing and leaving litter behind, were sights hardly in consonance with the respect demanded by that holy spot.

At first, the Rabbi paid little heed to this rebuke, regarding it even as an impertinence to be "told off" by one who was "a mere official." It was only when he was apprised of the status of the one who rebuked him and what he was doing for the Mount by word and deed, that he apologised profusely to Reb Zanwill and asked him to join him and

51

his family at their Sabbath-eve meal in the Rabbi's house. He would then explain to him why he, as a Rabbi, allowed eating and drinking before David's Sepulchre, going so far as to participate himself in the festivities which ensued.

Reb Zanwill, though surprised at this invitation, did not have the heart to refuse it point-blank.

When the Eve of Shabbat approached, he made his way to the house of the Rabbi in order to hear the explanation offered. It would be instructive as well as interesting, he thought, to hear the views of men simple of faith and the heirs of traditional observances. The night of the visit was also a stormy one and heavy rain converted the way to the house of his host into bogs, quagmires and mudpuddles. Reb Zanwill, clothed in rain-coat and rain-boots, pursued his long and weary way to the Ma'Abarot (Transit-Camps) around Talpiot, where the Yemenite Rabbi had his home.

On entering it, he was received by his host with open arms and a most welcome Shabbat greeting. He made his guest sit down on the bed which also served as a seat around the table. Reb Zanwill threw his glance all around and saw that the contents of the one room consisted of one large bed on which were arranged blankets, sheets and pillows. In the midst of this room, stood a table on which two lights were burning in the two candlesticks and which was decked with plates and cutlery, glasses and loaves of bread, fish, onions and all kinds of fruit.

The room was in a very dirty state and was inhabited by several women and many small children who kept on wandering and crawling about around the table and the large bed. The whole scene shrieked of poverty, yet the Yemenite Rabbi and his entire family seemed to be in a very happy frame of mind. All of them sang, shouted and clapped hands, while the children wandered around the room. hapily, without let or hindrance. The Rabbi made Kiddush over wine and they all proceed to wash their hands, prior to partaking of the traditional Shabbat-meal prepared for them. After every course, the room

was filled with the melodious tunes of the Sabbath "Table-hymns"
Throughout all this, Reb Zanwil felt far from happy. He was not
accustomed to such a Shabbat-meal. Besides, the air in the room was
oppressive and he almost revolted at the sight of so much untidiness
and even dirt. He sat there, as if compelled to do so by some satanic
power. Do what he could, he was not able to concentrate on what
the Rabbi was saying to him. Even the Zmirot possessed no charm for
him. As for the food well it was not his "cup of tea". He had only
one thought in his mind throughout that evening: "When will the
meal end and what will be the nature of the explanation which the
Rabbi promised to give him? Moreover, what was the real intention
of the invitation?"

Just when the "Grace After Meals" was about to be recited, he asked
the Rabbi to explain to him the reason for this invitation. "Do tell
me now", Reb Zanwill asked his host, "why you claimed almost personal ownership of King David's Tomb?"

"What?", retorted his host in surprise, "do you mean to say that after
all this time that you are sitting here, you have not yet learnt my
explanation and heard my answer?"

"No", replied Reb Zanwill.

The rabbi then replied with a smile clothing his face: "Since this
is so, then please listen attentively and you will understand." He
began to sing again the opening song "Shalom Aleichem" in which
the Angels are welcomed to enter each Jewish house on the Eve of
Shabbat, to the accompaniment of his wives and children. After this,
they began to sing the second hymn, written in Aramaic and attributed to the "Holy Ari", which begins with the words "I have arranged a royal meal", and so on.

When they finished re-singing these two hymns, the Rabbi turned
his two luminous eyes on Reb Zanwill and said: "Do you now understand my explanation?" "Not yet", was the reply. "Well, let me try
again", said the Rabbi. "My house consists of a bed, a table and a
kitchen, filled with cooking-utensils and provisions. I invite the Mi-

nistering Angels — and even God Himself — and they come to my home, disregarding the poverty, the dirt and the outward untidiness. Well, if they do not mind, how much less concerned is David — His servant? Then why should I be deprived and ashamed of fulfilling my nows before him? David is used to this and your ambassador must also be used to this .Reb Zanwill understood and smilingly tapped the shoulders of the Rabbi.

Yes, he now more than understood. So much so, that he felt sorry for having asked the Rabbi to leave the courtyard so as to make way for the ambassador. It was the Rabbi who felt hurt at his request more than he had done at the other's refusal.

In order that there be no recurrences of the incident with the ambassador, Reb Zanwill decided to arrange a special corner of the courtyard before David's Tomb, where those hailing from the Orient, could arrange their thanksgiving banquets and "Vow" parties when occasion arose in the future.

THE SHABBAT SHOFAR AND THE HATZOZEROT

Shabbat may be described as the apotheosis and patron of hospitality. A proof ? That when a Yomtov happens to occur on a Shabbat, the latter makes way for the special prayers and Torah-reading of the former. The Shabbat gives pride of place to its colleagues which colour the Jewish year annually, instead of as it does, at the end of every six days. An outstanding example of the self-effacement of Shabbat before Yomtov is the incidence of Yom Kippur on its own special day, when it almost eclipses itself entirely as if it did not exist that day at all. For fasting then takes place, shoes are not worn, washing of the body is not allowed — prohibitions usually forbidden on the joyous Seventh Day. Moreover, the Shabbat has even yielded that the Shofar be not blown when Rosh Hashana falls on its own day; also that the Lulav be not handled on Sukkot nor the benediction recited over the Etrog.

The Halacha gives its own reason for the Shofar being put aside on Rosh Hashanah and the Etrog and Lulav on Sukkot. This is a precaution lest these objects be carried from the home (a private territory) to a scholar who would train them in the specific laws attached to these observances, thus carrying on the Shabbat from private territory to public territory, a thing forbidden on a Shabbat in places where there is no Erub. This is one reason and no doubt the correct one. There is another, however, which appeals more to the popular imagination. The Etrog and Lulav are set aside because they are proud of their fragrance and appearance (the Torah refers to them as "goodly fruit"); the Shofar is brushed aside on the Shabbat, because it "blows its own trumpet", as it were ! Judaism prefers the humble to the proud. God appears in "the still small voice, not in the thunder earthquake and storm". Because of their boastfulness, custodians of Halacha did not allow them to infringe on the lightest demands of the Halacha, such as being permitted to carry the Shofar and Lulav and Etrog more than four cubits from a private to a public domain. Scholars are not in favour of such glib interpretations, though these are replete with ethical meaning. In Temple times, although all the tenets of Judaism were meticulously observed, the Shofar was blown on the Shabbat of Rosh Hashana and the Four Species were used on Sukkot, one of its days being a Shabbat. The fear was then expressed lest these two religious pre-requisites be carried on that day into the public domain for more than four cubits. After the destruction of the Second Temple, Rabbi Johanan b. Zakkai permitted the Shofar to be sounded on the Shabbat of Rosh Ha'Shana in Jabneh, the seat of the Sanhedrin in his day. Other prominent rabbinic authorities extend this permission even to other centres in Eretz-Israel where High Religious Courts were temporarily established. Other prominent Halachic personalities, such as Rabbi Schlesinger, extended this permission even to Jerusalem. Rabbi Yitzhak, that zealous fanatic whom we have met before in these pages, even went so far as to suggest that the Shofar be sounded on the Shabbat of Rosh Ha'Shana on Mount Zion. It was only after much persuasion that his teacher Reb Zanwill, deterred him from doing so, thus avoiding what would, no doubt, have become the source of long and bitter controversy.

After the Six Days' War, when the "Great Beth Din" of Jerusalem was seated near the Western Wall, Rabbi Yitzhak emphasized his claim that the Shofar be blown on the Shabbat of Rosh Ha'Shana. Is not the authority of the Beth Din of our own day as supreme as that of Jabneh in the days of yore, he argued ? The discussion, swinging like a pendulum, *pro* and *con,* continued almost interminably, day and night. With few exceptions, all the Rabbis were of the fixed opinion that the age-old established customs cannot lightly be brushed aside in order to pave the way for new-fangled ones. Hence, it was not consistent with traditional usage to allow the Shofar to be sounded on the Shabbat of Rosh Ha'Shana. Among the Kabbalists, however, opinions were divided. While some agreed with the majority of rabbinic thought, a large number opined that the time had now arrived when the Shofar should, once again, be sounded as it had been in Temple times near the Kotel and in the presence of the members of the august Jerusalem Beth Din.

Reb Zanwill would not give his consent to this, contending that to do so would be tantamount to "a smack in the face" and a Laesa *Majestatis* (blasphemous act) toward the Ruined Temple, of which the sole remining relic was the Kotel. He advised those itching to restore pristine Temple customs to wait until such time when the Temple would once again be rebuilt and house the Divine Presence Then would all the various soundings of the Shofar once again reverberate and echo thunderously throughout the Hills of Judea. When Rabbi Yitzhak heard these views of Reb Zanwill, his emotions burned within him to such a high pitch that he hurriedly left the circle which hung on their leader's words. The mention of the special blasts of the Shofar kindled within him thoughts too painful for mere words.

As is well-known, the Shofar must be made from the horn of a ram, an eloquent and tangible symbol of the ram whose horns were entangled in a thicket and which served as a substitute for Isaac when his father Abraham was fully prepared to offer up the sacrifice of his own son at the altar because God had commanded him so to do. Thus the ram symbolized the salvation of Isaac and its horn, to this day, is an eloquent prayer that God should equally redeem the descendants of Isaac from extermination by a hostile world. Yet for those who know the secrets enshrined in the various sounds (Hatsotserot) of the Shofar when it was sounded in Temple times, it seems a great pity that despite all the meticulous preparations which go to the making of a Shofar, so few understand the cryptic message conveyed by these holy sounds of the Hatsotserot ("Trumpet-blasts"). Rabbi Yitzhak fully grasped that the reasons why Reb Zanwill was against permitting the Shofar to be blown on Shabbat, were primarily due to the fact that we are unaware of the musical instruments used in Temple times and whose sounds accompanied the liturgy in the New Year. What exactly were the "Trumpet Sounds" (Hatsotserot) and the Sound of the Shofar which had to be heard before the Lord, as Scripture has it? How were these sounds produced? In what key and with what precise notes ? How long was each of these separate notes to last, and what exactly differentiated the various notes known as Teruot (Blasts), Yebabot (Howls) and Shebarim (Fragile and tender sounds?)

Rabbi Yitzhak decided to leave alone the question of permission for the sounding of the Shofar on Shabbat and to rivet his attention, instead, on a concentrated study of the plaintive and jubilant, notes of the Shofar. After long months of penetrating and undisturbed study, he had, so he thought, succeeded in plumbing the depths of the secrets of the varying notes of the Shofar, including the esoteric rules governing the Hatsotserot. He had left no source untapped, be it halachic, aggadic, homiletical or mystical, in order to become thoroughly conversant with the exact notes which had to accompany as well as proceed from the Shofar. Now, therefore, he felt that the time had come for his wishes to be fulfilled.

During the month of Elul, when the Shofar is sounded daily to announce the impending arrival of Rosh Ha'Shanah, Rabbi Yitzhak blew the Shofar near the Kotel to the accompaniment of the exact sounds which he had mastered in the course of his painstaking researches. Those who comprised the circle in which he moved stared at him in amazement, wondering at the strange and weird sounds which proceeded from his Shofar. Was the mind of this poor man sane ? Or had a fit of fanatical madness seized him ? The reaction of Rabbi Yitzhak, to their astonishment, was one of detached aloofness, as if he could not care less what people thought of his behaviour. Why should he worry about what people thought of him when his conscience was absolutely at peace and he knew full well the reason of his conduct ? Besides, was he not preparing himself for the "Great Day" when, according to Reb Zanwill, the Temple would again arise in all its pristine splendour on the Temple Mount and when the Shofar would once again issue its challenging, bell-like sounds on Rosh Ha'Shana and even if it occur on a Shabbat? It was the duty of a Jew, especially if he be a priest, ever to be ready for that Day when the Temple would be re-built, so that no hitch or hindrance might occur in the prescribed ceremonial of the Temple Services.

Imagine, therefore, the pained surprise and consternation of all concerned and especially of Rabbi Yitzhak himself, when one day he found that the Shofar he held in his hand adamantly and obstinately refused to emit a sound ! He tried all he could to produce the exact sounds he had learnt through his endless researches; yet his efforts proved of no avail. He mumbled every prayer he knew, chanted all the incantations he had found in mystical works with which to chase away all satanic forces, yet the Shofar remained mute and dumb, silently defying all his efforts to make it proclaim its

58

challenging message. Try as he might, do what he would, he could not find the "Open Sesame", the key which would burst open the locked doors of the Shofar's notes. What had gone wrong ? Wherein had he erred ? These thoughts distracted him by day and robbed him of precious sleep by night.

In his dillemma, he went to consult Reb Zanwill. Perhaps he could tell him wherein he had gone wrong and apprise him of the errors he had committed. After hearing all his protestations with patience and a kind smile, he assured Rabbi Yitzhak that he had not erred in anything; in fact he had meticulously mastered the differing sounds of the Shofar. The only reason for the Shofar's disobedience and its failure to respond to his call, was that the time had not yet arrived for the "Trumpet Sounds" which, in the days of yore, accompanied Reb Zanwill now unfolded :

"When the time came for Moses to be deprived of his glory and the crown of authority was to be removed from his head, he tried to sound the Shofar with the same strong blasts as heretofore when he had enjoyed full command as the Teacher of God's own people, consecrated by the Torah which he had received on Sinai's flaming peak as Heaven's eternal gift to mankind. But the Shofar pressed against the lips of Moses remained mute at that time. Why ? Since his power had gone and his day of authority had waned, the sound of the Shofar had vanished also !"

Then Rabbi Yitzhak and the others who heard this explanations from the lips of Reb Zanwill, understood. They fervently prayed that the Messianic Age would soon dawn...

IN THE SECRET OF THE GARBAGE

In honour of King David and in order to fulfill his request, it was decided to found a Yeshivah on the Mount where the Torah would be studied. This Yeshivah stood near the synagogue "Bet Ha'Edut," the founder thereof being the saintly Rabbi Shlomo David Kahana, of blessed memory, the Rabbi of the Old City, in whose borders Mt. Zion was included.

Rabbi S. D. Kahane was the first to respond to the "call" of the restoration of the Mount to its pristine glory. As the Rabbi of the Old City, he considered it as his solemn duty to take a personal interest in Mt. Zion and to exert an influence over the students of his Yeshivah to ascend to the Mount in order to repair its wastes and redeem them from the hands of strangers and to restore it to its pristine status of one of the most holy and pure foundations.

Ascending the mountain was a hazardous task in those days, but the elderly Rabbi triumphed over all the difficulties he encountered and the pains he felt in his climb and made his way up in the company of his disciples. He was the old Rabbi who laid the first foundation-stone towards the rebuilding of the Mount. His shining example was later followed by others who went under the name of IZI, the first Hebrew letters of the words: Irgun Ziknei Israel (organization of the elders of Israel).

At the head of this group stood R. Israel Tsurva, who interested young priests (Kohanim) in the study of the Temple and its holy institutions and diverse functions.

Twice daily, did these Yeshivah students laboriously trudge up to the summit of the Mount in order to study at the spot nearest to the Old City which overlooks the Temple Mount. The elder of the students, who knew the Rabbi personally, have many a fascinating tale to unfold in his name, in all of which are enshrined deep and wonderful lessons.

These disciples, although they are now aged and men of vast learning, personally see to the sweeping and great cleanliness of their Rabbi's school-house (Bet Ha'midrash), even taking a pride in the fact that they themselves and no other, polish the floor. Was this not one of the first lessons taught them by their great Rabbi when they first came to the Mount? They often recalled how he had stood there, with his students and cleared away the rubbish-heaps from the mountain-top. His former pupils say that their great teacher taught them, as well as others, to clear away the litter and rubbish heaps, so that the sanctity of the Mount stands revealed in all its pristine glory.

This is the story they are fond of repeating: "When the Rabbi, accompanied by his disciples, first came to Mt. Zion, the Mount was covered with heaps of slags and rubbish, which had piled up from the buildings which had been set on fire and the bundles of ashes — and worse — which had been deliberately thrown there by the Arabs. There was no other alternative but to wade through all these mounds of rubbish in order to reach the sepulchre of King David. When the Rabbi saw the miserable plight of the Mount, he asked his students to bring shovels and pickaxes, spades and brooms in order to remove the dirt and ruins of ages.

The disciples were puzzled at this request. Was this the reason for which they were asked to come here? Had they not come here in order to study and not to be dustmen? But when the Rabbi asked them for the tools, they could no longer refuse and went to comply with his request. The Rabbi then told them of the ancient tradition that in order to bring fire for the service of the Creator, one had to search in the ashes. So let us search among the ashes. Perhaps God will help us find the holy fire which once burnt on Zion; as it is written: "For this light is in Zion".

When they had finished their task, the Rabbi was very happy and told them the story of how the Kotel, in the days of Soliman, was dug up from the mounds of dust and rubbish which had covered it for ages. This is the secret of the Kotel, which was left in captivity in the hands of the enemy.

After the Six-Days War, came disciples from all countries of the Diaspora, to continue the holy work of their spiritual Leader and founded there the famous "Yeshivath Hatfuzoth".

THE TALITH OF HEAVEN

One day, Reb Yitzhak, "the Fanatic", had stayed-up all night on Mount Zion. He very often went there and spent hours on end near the Tomb of King David, gazing at the Temple Mount and reciting Psalms. Sometimes, when he was too late, he used to spend the night out on the mountain itself and then he always ensconced himself in some chosen corner which he sought out among the ruins, arranging his bed for the night on the stony ground. Reb Yitzhak, the Fanatic, loved to sleep like this. He even used to go so far as to say that it was the only way to get a perfect night's rest — far superior to that enjoyed by townsfolk and the lazy pampered denizens of the great cities with their soft beds. A good sleep on a heap of stones and especially on the stones of Mount Zion, he said, was just like the sleep of the Patriarch Jacob !

At dawn, he would come down from the Mount with his heart full of the fruitful dreams of the night.

On this particular night, he had stayed in front of the Tomb of King David until a very late hour. As soon as he had finished his Prayers and Psalms, he went off to rest on his stony couch. The officials of the Mount asked him why he had not gone down to take part in the Slichoth, (the penitential prayers which are recited during the month of Elul and on fast-days) in one of the Synagogues of the city. Rabbi Yitzhak smiled and said : "Today, I shall not leave the mountain. You will see, however, that the Slichoth will be recited here on Mount Zion !" How this would come about, he would not tell them; but he already knew in his heart that here, on this sacred spot, the penitential prayers would be said. The officials teased him gently, but went off and left him to his dreams.

It was towards midnight, when he was lying stretched out on his stony couch, that he heard a knocking. Jumping up, he went to investigate the cause of these heavy blows. He found that they proceeded from the grotto of the Tomb of King David. What could be happening ? The door was locked and padlocked on the outside and no one could possibly be on the inside. Putting his eye to a tiny hole in the door, he could only see that the Eternal Flame burned brightly, while all around was in total darkness. Then he heard the knocking for the second time.

"Who's there ?", he cried. No answer ! So he hurried off to tell the officials keeping the nightwatch, sitting comfortably some hundred yards away; but, knowing him, they only laughed at him. Reb Yitzhak returned by himself to the grotto and had hardly got there, when he heard the knocking for the third time. Thinking he had better have just one more look round, he suddenly saw an apparition which froze the very marrow in his bones. On the other side of the entrance, standing in the thick darkness near the Tomb, he clearly saw Reb Leib, the aged beadle with the humped shoulders who hailed from his little native birthplace in Poland. In his right hand, the old man held one of those hammers which Polish beadles use to waken the faithful and call them to prayer. Reb Leib remained standing there, saying nothing but holding up the hammer as if it were a sceptre. "What are you doing here, Reb Leib?", asked Reb Yitzhak, all of a tremble. "Surely, it is years since you gave up your soul to God in a German Concentration Camp ? What are you doing? How do you come here ? Am I dreaming ?" But Reb Leib moved not, but just stood, fixedly looking at Reb Yitzhak, the Fanatic. At last, the latter took his courage in both hands and undid the locks and threw the doors wide open. Quickly, he lighted all the candles he could find and, soon, hundreds of little flames blazed in the room, like a Synagogue on the day of Slihoth...

Everything was now ready for the Prayers. But how find a minyan, that essential quorum of ten adult males ? A sudden, desolate sadness came over Reb Yitzhak, as though he had prepared a grand banquet for all his frends and none of the guests had come. He was overwhelmed with shame.

Then, just as midnight chimed, a sudden wind came blowing from the North and swept across the summit of the Mount. There could be clearly heard the chanting of King David and the music was that of the Slichoth. Panic seized the poor Fanatic, Reb Yiyzhak. Here was the hall flooded with light. King David already chanted the Prayers of the Slichoth, but the vital minyan had not yet been formed ! It was an intolerable situation. Rushing out in a desperate attempt to find witnesses, he had not yet arrived at the Mount when he saw, coming up the road to meet him, the band of Elders of Mount Zion. Seeing his thankfulness mingled with amazement, they explained their timely appearance : "The Song of the Mountain is not only heard upon the Mount itself. Its swelling music flows to the four corners of the earth and fills the hearts of those who will listen for it. The Elders of Mount Zion are always the first to hear its melody !" No sooner had they heard the first words of the Prayers, than they realized that King David has begun to say the Slichoth and they were hurrying up the hill to join him."

In the Hall of the Tomb, they washed their hands ceremoniously; but when they took stock of each other, they discovered that not one of them had brought his Talith (prayer-shawl), as none of them had thought that he would be called upon to officiate before dawn. The eldest among them, however, quoted Rabbi Mendel who had ruled that : "If one has no Talith to wear, then he can wrap himself in the Talith of the Lord of the World which covers the earth from each of the four cardinal points..."

The old man made a sweeping gesture with his hands as if wrapping himself in a voluminous mantle and began the Prayer : Yitgadal Ve-Yitkadash...

THE THIRD GATE

THE HEALING FLOWER

Reb Zanwill has a charming custom of sending a healing flower to his friends when they fall ill or become sick.

This does not mean that he attaches to these flowers any special healing-power from the lofty hights of the holy Mt. Zion. It is an expression of his blessings, nothing more.

The healing flower has this legend.

Long, long ago, during one of the terrible droughts in Jerusalem, a pious man went round from well to well and from cistern to cistern, desperately seeking water for his sick daughter. Peering into a well near Mount Zion which he had not noticed before, he dropped his pitcher into its depths.

He asked some bystanders to hold a rope while he climbed down to retrieve his loss. To his astonishment, he found at the bottom of the well a beautiful garden, but arrested in growth as if in sleep! Its flowers were closed, its birds silent, its trees dry and gray as ashes. Plucking a branch as proof of what he had seen, he ascended the rope. When he showed the branch to his friends, he saw that it had burst forth into the most exquisite blossoms. He hurried back to his sick child. When she had but touched the fragrant branch, her fever vanished and she immediately recovered.

Then all understood that this was the Garden of Eden, dormant underneath Mount Zion. The grateful father planted the seeds from the blossoms on Mount Zion. Even today, some of them still flourish there. Later on, they forgot the place whence the healing flowers had come, but sometimes sick people would look for them.

65

In the village of Mei Neftoah, on the outskirts of Jerusalem, lived a Yemenite widow and her small daughter Mazal. Every morning, the woman went to Jerusalem to do housework and laundry, while Mazal went to the village school.

One evening, the widow returned from Jerusalem shivering with fever. The whole night through she groaned with pain while Mazal sat beside her. The next morning their neighbours came to visit the widow, bringing jam and honey, oranges and raisins and advice in the form of tried and **proved remedies.**

One said: "In Yemen, we rub the patient's eyelashes with a dove's feather and a willow-twig," Another said: "Apply a little horseradish, the skin of an onion and a piece of garlic to her forehead." And a third said: "In Yemen, these remedies might heal, but in Eretz Israel they are useless. The only thing which will help you is to put a flower from Mount Zion under your pillow."

The old widow said: "I shall ask the sage Zecharya which remedy is best." So she called the wise Zecharya, who listened patiently to her story and then answered her with a quotation from the Psalms of David: "You shall take strength from Zion." The widow understood the hint at once. and said to Mazal: "Now go to sleep and to-morrow, at dawn, climb up to Mount Zion and bring me a flower."

That night, Mazal dreamt that she was ascending Mount Zion and came to the tomb of King David. There, she saw a gray-haired man lying on a couch, his eyes closed. Above the bed hung a lyre and a dove hovering in the air and beating its wings above her head.

The beating of the dove's wings aroused Mazal from her sleep. When she opened her eyes, she saw that the sun was rising, and at once she set-off through the streets of Jerusalem for Mount Zion. When she reached the summit of the mountain, she asked one of the workers for a flower, but he replied: "None have come out yet." Mazal ran round the hill, searching desperately for a blossom, until she found a plant with one open flower which she picked together with the root. But the alert watchman of Mount Zion who saw her, ran after her. When he caught her, he asked her why she had taken the flower. She told him about her sick mother. The watchman wanted to punish her, but Reb Zanwill told him to let her go with the flower. She ran to her house and put the flower under her sleeping mother's pillow. Soon afterwards, a doctor sent by Reb Zanwil arrived at the house and gave the window medicine and instructions.

From that moment, the widow began to feel better and soon she completely recovered. Some of the neighbours maintained it was because of the doctor and his medicine, others because of the flower. When the widow could walk again, her first thought was to go to King David's tomb and give thanks for her recovery. When the watchman of Mount Zion saw Mazal and her mother, he said to them : "Come and see why I was so angry with you before — you have left an empty patch in the garden." But when they came to the garden, they saw, to the watchman's great astonishment, a fully- grown rose tree covered with fragrant blooms, standing in place of the plant Mazal had taken. Ever since, the flowers from that tree have been called "The Flowers of Mazal" — which in Hebrew means good fortune — and sick people pick its blossoms in order to be healed.

THE FLOWER THAT REVIVED

Reb Zanwill has also a custom to present his friends with different flowers plucked from the garden of Mount Zion; this, especially before the advent of the Shavuot festival, the "Festival of First-Fruits" seven weeks after Pesah. This withered flower that makes a strange impression on the guest. In fact, he is often not a little surprised at this miserable gift. The purpose of this presentation, however, is in order to tell the visitors the legend clinging to this withered pressed flower. These flowers are also meant to symbolize the Dawn of Salvation, hinted at in the observation of the talmudic Sage Rabbi Abba, who opined that : "There can be no clearer indication of the 'end of days' than this; for we are told (in the Bible) that: 'As for you, Mountains of Israel, you will produce your branches which will be laden with luscious fruit!" To Kabbalists and those who delve in the realm of the mysterious, the Salvation of the future is designated by the name of Perah, a "Flower". The exact phrase they use is : "Reed, Carob and Bloom — these will grow luxuriantly on Mount Zion at the approach of Elijah the Prophet and the Royal Messiah!" There are many splended tales abounding on Mount Zion, of most of which the theme is flowers linked with the coming Redemption of the world.

For many hundreds of years, the City of Jerusalem had been desolate. Constantly a battle-ground, it had been fought over, conquered, taken and re-taken and for centuries it finally drooped under Turkish rule. There was virtually no progress, no cultivation, very little building; certainly, no ardent, pulsating life of commerce or agriculture. Not only was there no going forward but, instead, it persented a sad-sterile scene, lapsing into arid stagnation. There was nothing to refresh the mind and inspire the heart with memories of, and hopes for, Jerusalem the Golden. The soul of the city was waiting, in a patient and uneasy sleep, for that awakening which God promised some day, that magnificent rousing-up to work and toil to a refreshment of mind and spirit from which new and eternal life would spring when the Children of Israel returned to their own Land.

There is a beautiful legend and the allegory it tells is ageless. It is told of two of the most famous periods in the history of the Holy Land. Sometimes, it is recounted of a Knight setting-off for the Crusades; at others, of an officer on the Staff of the British Commander-in-Chief, General Allenby. In either case, the story is about a soldier who honestly believed he was setting out to deliver the City of God from the infidel.

The soldier had a great friend who was a holy Rabbi. Before going off to the Wars, he went to see the Rabbi to ask his blessings and also to ask if there was any little token or treasure he could bring back

68

as a gift from the Holy Land. The Rabbi blessed and embraced the soldier and then spoke with touching hope about the promised gift. "Let it be something," he said, "which will show me that soul of Jerusalem still lives and awaits the homecoming of the people of Israel."

Many months later, after much hard fighting, Jerusalem was taken and the soldier found himself wandering through the desolate city as one of its conquerors. He bethought himself of his old friend, the Rabbi and the gift that he must bring him. In vain he searched all places.The countryside was so barren and sterile.Nowhere could he find anything of beauty and, still less, anything that seemed to bear any hope for a resurgent, fruitful and promising future.

Returning to base and having virtually given up his search, he walked across the summit of Mount Zion. There he saw, among the dusty stones and rocks, a small withered flower, once a lovely little blood-red anemone, symbolic flower of Israel,but now, a poor dried-up and faded stem. The soldier hesitated, shrugged his shoulders and carefully gathered the pathetic scraps. It was the best he could do. When he got back to his quarters, he put the dead flower up to its top in water, hoping that it might still find some tiny pulse of life. There was, however, no sign thereof. Finally, all he could do was carefully to press it and bring it back to his friend as something which had, at least once upon a time, lived and bloomed in Jerusalem on holy Mount Zion.

When he arrived home again, the soldier went to greet his friend the Rabbi and very apologetically handed to him the little withered flower, feeling considerably abashed and ashamed that this was the best he had been able to manage by way of a gift. The Rabbi took the dead flower in his hands with the greatest reverence. With infinite tenderness he held it gently against his heart. Fresh or dead, this flower had come to him from the Holy Mountain and his tears of heartfelt joy trickled down his cheeks and fell upon it.. And there, before the rapturous eyes of the Rabbi (and the startled look of the soldier!) the miracle happened.

As the tears fell on them, slowly the stem plumped out and turned a soft living green. The leaves and fronds became fresh and crisp; the exquisite little head was once more proudly held erect with its blood-red petals... It had become a living vibrant flower again, alive in full perfection.

The Rabbi expounded to the wondering soldier the mystical meaning of this marvellous phenomenons. Though to all intents and purposes barren and dead, Zion was but dormant. It would spring again to renewed and eternal blossoming under the loving toil and self-sacrifice of her sons and daughters when, once more, the Chosen People of God had returned to Eretz-Israel. "When you take this flower, revive it my friend with the warmth of thy heart. The country still possesses many evil places; the earth is dry and wicked, awaiting you to make it spring into life.

THE PRAYING TREES

He who ascends Mt. Zion and enters the forest thereon, is amazed to find that all the trees there seem as if they were kneeling towards the Temple Mount. He cannot help wondering at their posture. When this question was put to Reb Zanwill, he smiled and narrated three legends which he had heard from both old and young people;

I. The leaders suggested that the trees felt that they were in the living presence of their King David who walked about on the Mount. It was for this reason, that they continually prostrated themselves in respect and worship.

II. The young people opined that the trees stood in worshipful attitude, because they faced the Temple Mount, the original site of the Temple.

III. A third hypothesis was that when the trees beheld the destruction of the Temple, they despaired of continuing to grow and thrive and were about to fall down altogether. "What is the use", they argued within themselves, "of growing and providing shade from the

70

blazing sun at a time when the Heavenly Light itself has been extinguished?" As they were about to fall to the ground, Heaven frowned at their decision and rebuked them thus: "Why do you meddle with the mysterious ways of providence? It is your mission in life to continue as you were hitherto since Creation."

On hearing this, while not inclined to remain erect as before and unable to topple down altogether, they remained in this bent attitude until the Temple will be rebuilt.

Reb Zanwill was fond of combining all these legends together in order to weave a story therefrom.

"Happy is the man that hath not walked in the counsel of the wicked..." sang the Psalmist. "...He shall be like a tree planted by streams of water..!" When a son was born to the Kohanim in Jerusalem and to the High Priests, in the days of the Temple, the proud and happy father planted a tree on Mount Zion. The tree was believed to symbolize the life of the child, through youth, manhood and advancing age, growing straight and strong as did the boys. It put out leaves, deep, strong roots ever praying for his soul, but drooping when he was ill and bowing down when he was sorrowful and withering sadly if he committed deeds of sin and shame. Only when he died, did the tree not die but continued to live on, sometimes for hundreds of years, always with its moving branches, murmuring leaves and flowers and fruit as he excelled in the virtues of manhood Upon Mount Zion, there were many groves of trees, all of which had this close and holy connection with the Temple. There is a beautiful legend that when the Temple was destroyed by fire, all the trees turned their horrified heads towards the flames and their trunks writhed and twisted, as though they felt the burning agony in themselves. Some of the Priests died in trying to defend the Holy House of God. Some, in despair, suffered themselves to be burnt with it rather than face the empty desolation of living without that which had been their all-in all to them. Others were driven out and fled with the Jewish outcasts.

The High Priest raised his arms in supplication, his face ravaged with grief and cried out to the Creator in his anguish, imploring succour and guidance. When the flames had done their dread work, the mighty Temple was but a heap of smouldering ruins and all the Jewish People driven out. What would now happen to the soul of Jewry ? With all his heart, he believed that the prayers arising from the Temple kept the Children of Israel the Chosen People, within the favour and protection of God and the predestined Redemption.

With breaking heart, he mourned over and over again : "How will the sublime power of the Temple Prayers be continued ? Surely, the Almighty will not deprive the whole earth of that great force He has created?...

And the answer came ! All the Trees planted by the Priests as symbols of the deathless souls of those born to pray and offer sacrifice, turned their branches towards the holocaust and bowed themselves low in grief and shame. Then, strong and steadfast, did the murmuring of the leaves, the soughing of the branches, the creaking of the roots,grow into a chorus and arose, as though inspired by an angelic choir from Heaven :

"We shall pray ! Ours will be the prayers, the praises, the lamentations lost from the Temple ! Every prayer we offer will be from the heart of every Jewish soul driven forth and cast out from the Land of Israel. Through all the ages yet to come, we shall keep faith with the Jewish People, the Chosen People of God, until their return to their own Land. The greater their suffering, in the far-off places, the deeper their humiliation, the more despairing their heartbreak, ever more surely shall we, the Trees of Mount Zion, keep trust with them... God will eternally hear our prayers and receive them into His Heart !"

Blinded with tears, stunned with horror and confusion, the High Priest found his way to the sacred groves and bowed his head against them.

ISAIAH'S TREE

The song one hears on Mount Zion is that of King David, who was a patron of hospitality as well as a *maestro* of the Harp This song has a melody attached to it which is unique, sui generis. Those who live on Mount Zion seem to hear its reverberation at every step and at whatever point they happen to find themselves. They can easily distinguish its melody from that of any other in the world. Countless are the current legends concerning the music produced by the strings of that royal harp which, according to the Talmud (Ber. 4a) were stirred into melody as the breeze of awakening dawn rippled across the insstrument; and even before that, at the bewitching midnight hour, when it awoke its royal master to pour out his thankful heart to the Giver of all Life. One of these innumerable legends is connected with a tree which bears the name of "The Tree of Isaiah".

It all began on Shabbat Hazon, the Sabbath immediately preceding Tisha B'Ab. Then it was, that the haunting song was first heard on the mountain. Although this song was, at first blush, similar in melody and cadence to the usual song, yet there was something about this tune which made it not *parum inter pares*, "equal among equals", as the old Romans used to say; for it possessed a harmony far more sublime than with which any other song was endowed. Those who had made Mount Zion their home, looked upon each other with amazement when they first heard this strange but bewitching melody. They asked each other : "Is it possible that this is the tune originally produced by the royal, sweet singer of Israel, King David, on his magic harp?" They could not imagine that the music they were hearing on this mountain could be that of any other musician. Their wonder grew apace when they realized how different was this tune to any other heard on land or sea. Moreover, what did those unique and phenomenal tones betoken?

Stranger still was the fact that wherever their wonder led them to seek the source from which the singing seemed to pour forth with such sweetness, their steps usually led them to the Sepulchre wherein the mortal remains of David were laid to rest. At times, however, their trek led them beyond the border to the extreme edge of the mountain. There, they listened most attentively. Were they dreaming, or fired by wild imagination? For on these occasions, the music seemed to proceed from a source concealed in a giant tree which stood at the very brink of the mountain; As they thus concentrated, straining their ears, they thought they heard the chant which usually accompagnied the *Haphtarah* for Shabbat Hazon, taken from the Book of Isaiah (I), and beginning with the exhortation. "Hear ye, O Heavens: and hearken intently, O Earth!" They looked at each other in bewildernment and perplexity, unable to understand this remarkable and uncanny phenomenon. Their confusion grew apace when the same thing happened on the following Shabbat after Tisha B'Ab, known as Shabbat Nahamu. On this second occasion, however, the tune appeared to be a new one. In some ways similar to the song they had heard on the mountain itself before continuing on the gigantic tree, others of its characteristics were totally different. On hearing it, the Elders followed their path of the previous Sabbath and then realized that this new tune was also proceeding from the great, gnarled trunk of the same tree. This time, however, the chanting was that usually heard for the reciting of the Haphtarah for this Shabbat (Nahamu.) It seemed as if they heard the words of the Prophet Isaiah (XL.8) saying to them, "Ascend the Holy Mountain, the High Mountain, thou herald of good tidings for Zion; raise your voice loudly to proclaim the good news for Jerusalem!" Again, they regarded each other with a wonder knowing no bounds. Was it possible that this heartening tune proceeded from the tree? Or was it some figment of the imagination. Was it just their fancy?

After that Shabbat, they no longer heard this unique tune. In the process of time, their strange experience passed into the limbo of things forgotten. The Custodian, however, in accordance with his usual practice when such events occurred on the mountain, recorded everything

74

meticulously in the special Diary which he kept, concerning every happening, especially anything untoward which occurred on Mount Zion. He possessed his soul in patience, with his characteristic confidence that the secret still hidden in the womb of time, would one day be given birth.

On the Eve of the Fifteenth of Shevat, he and his close circle of disciples were celebrating a special Seder which had been arranged by the young "Whelps" (Disciples) of the Ari (the "Lion"; but a word really formed from the first ther initial letters of Alohi Rabbi Yiyzhak Luria), known as the Ari Ha'Kadosh. The table was laden and bedecked with the fruits for which Eretz-Israel is renowned and as was fitting on a day designated in the Talmud (Rosh Ha'Shanah. I.1) as the "New Year for Trees." The table was also furnished with glasses and bottles of wine, a replica of the Pesah Seder Table. As each cup was drunk, the assembled guests regaled each other with legends clinging to the Land and to Tu B'Shvat. When the company was about to partake of the Fourth Cup, they opened the door of the room, just as is the procedure during the Pesah Seder, praying that dew should descend on the trees which adorned Mount Zion and on the burgeoning flowers and growing plants which, after their long slumber in the soil during the cold and rainy months of winter, were now showing signs of awakening life. A fragrant scent entered, as the door was opened and a perfumed atmosphere filled the room. Everyone inhaled deeply and enjoyed with great satisfaction this most pleasant odour. When the Seder Service came to an end, they proceeded to the forest on the mountain to begin planting fresh seedlings, as was the custom on the Eve of the New Year for Trees. It was regarded as specially meritorious to plant at the bewitching hour of midnight, at the time when the Heavenly Gates opened and the dew came down in abundance. All took a special pride and pleasure in this planting ceremony, for it cemented their links with the soil of the Holy Land and helped them to implement, in a practical way, the divine commandment to establish anew their ancestral Homeland.

When they were about to begin to plant, one of the oldest among them encouraged his colleagues in their agricultural pursuit, by telling them the story of Honi Ha'Me'Agel (The Circle-Drawer, told in tractate Ta'anit). He also refreshed their memories of the prophecy of Isaiah. "No longer will it be said of Thee (Zion) that thou art abandoned; neither shall Thy land be designated as wasted and destroyed!"

While thus engaged in their horticultural labours, their ears were suddenly once more filled with that haunting, subtle melody which had previously resounded so mysteriously through every nook and cranny of the mountain and which had since just as inexplicably ceased to reverberate or to make itself heard. Needless to say, the planters stopped their work to regale their ears and rejoice their hearts with this enchanting and haunting music. Their faces were illumined with celestical joy and dazzling brightness. But this state of elation did not last long. Sad to say, their faces once again took on a very puzzled expression and bewilderment looked out of their eyes. For this melody was not the usual one, heard throughout the mountain at all times. No, it was that eerie music which they had heard on those two former Sabbaths — the one which preceded the Ninth of Ab and the other which immediately followed it; namely, on Shabbat Hazon and Shabbat Nahamu.

Once again, they decided to follow the Voice of Song which, as before, led them to the edge of the mountain. Yes, as before, the Voice of Song appeared to proceed directly from the huge tree which stood there, all by itself, alone and seemingly forlorn. As they looked intently at the tree, they noticed a ceaseless stirring and rustling among its thick foliage and abundant branches. They stood rooted to the spot, spellbound by what they saw and heard. The old man, who had encouraged the others to proceed in their planting and who was one of the oldest dwellers on Mount Zion and was intimately acquainted with all the legends and customs clinging to this holy spot, endeavoured to explain to the Elders round him the import of this haunting melody which now filled their ears. He unfolded before them the incident which happened

76

in the days of King Manasseh, a scion of the Royal House of David, between Manasseh and his grandfather Isaiah, the Prophet. "Generally", the old man explained to them, "a man is buried in ground four cubits in area. The contract which the Creator made with Mother Earth — from whose dust the first man (Adam) was shaped in the image of God — was that this same Mother Earth should receive back into her bosom every living soul whose time on earth had reached its end. Earth has kept this condition, for it has always opened its heart ready to receive each returning child of God. This, in accordance with the Scriptural text. *"For from the earth was he taken and unto it shall he return!"*

"Very different, however, was the case of the Prophet, Isaiah, the son of Amoz; for he lies buried yonder under a tree. Thereby, hangs a tale recorded by Ben Azai, which he discovered in an old, genealogical Book of Records. The story is as follows:

"When King Manasseh introduced a graven image — an idol — into the Temple for purposes of worship, Isaiah began to foretell the doom impending both over Zion and the Temple with the forthcoming invasion by Nebuchadnezzar. Menasseh boiled with rage when he heard of these gloomy prophecies and issued a command to his servants to seize hold of Isaiah who, however, had managed to escape to the forest where he was swallowed up by a giant cedar-tree. Only the fringes of his four-cornered garment remained revealed to view. When the servants returned to the palace, they reported to the furious despot the strange thing which had happened to the Prophet. Whereupon, King Manasseh issued another command: "Go and fell this great tree. When it is cut down, slice up the trunk with a saw." As the servants of the King were engaged in the process of sawing the tree into sections, blood began to flow from the hidden body of the Prophet whom the tree had concealed, in order to protect him from his persecutors. When the edge of the saw was about to touch the mouth of Isaiah, his soul departed heavenwards. This was as a punishment on account of the Prophet's declaration. "I dwell among a people of unclean lips!"

77

(Isaiah VI. 5). Even a Prophet must not malign his people whom he should try to show lovingly the error of their ways.

"As is well known, Manasseh was not buried on Mount Zion in the cemetery allotted to the Kings of Israel. Instead, he was interred in Gan-Azza. The grave which had been originally reserved for him was given to Isaiah, who was also descended from the Davidic dynasty- Because of the fact that the Prophet had been embosomed by a tree for his protection, this tree was, as a reward, re-planted on Mount Zion. It is for this reason, that the words of Isaiah, set to music, are occasionally heard on Mount Zion, together with the Songs of the other Kings of Davidic descent. Especially is this so on Shabbat Hazon and Shabbat Nahamu, the two Shabbatot which are dedicated to the memory of the Prophet Isaiah.

"Each recurring Tu B'Shvat, when trees are planted on the mountain, restitution is made for the diabolical orders of the wicked King Manasseh to saw up the tree which was sheltering the Prophet. By the planting of fresh trees, the wounded heart of Isaiah is thus healed.. His song floats from this chosen tree, so that its lovely music enters the ears of the Kings of the House of David — Jotham, Ahaz, Hezekiah — who are interred on the Mount and in whose times, Isaiah had thundered forth his Prophecies.

UPROOTED TREE

"When a fruit-bearing tree is uprooted, the sound of its destruction pervades the world".
At the foot of Mt. Zion, close by the road leading to David's tomb, there once stood a very old tree, withered and fruitless. Both in summer and winter, (it was) bare of any leaf or flower, possessing no apparent sign of life. People who chanced to pass by this old tree were sure that the time was not distant either when it would be cut down, or a wind would cause it to topple down altogether.

78

An old Jew chose this tree, of all others, which to sit beneath. He was one of the poor who had become one of the "residents" on the Mount, preferring this as his venue for asking alms. At first it was his custom to lean against its trunk, as he stood up to attract the generosity of the passersby. With one hand he held a Book of the Psalms, from which he never ceased reciting, while his other hand remained outstretched and in which he hoped to receive the offerings of those who passed by. When he found that the alms he collected were not sufficient for his barest needs, he tried his luck by engaging in some little "business". He began to sell religious requisites, such as candles for Shabbat and Yom-tov lights for Havdalah, Books of Psalms, small bags of earth from Eretz Israel (for burial purposes), and so on and so forth. From the tree, however, he did not budge even for one day.

It seemed that the old man and the tree were inextricably connected. Verily as the Bible has it; "For man is as the tree of the field". Both were endowed in years, both were now lacking in vitality, both of their lives seemed to be bound up with the impending darkness.

As the days passed by on their endless cycle, the old man often bethought himself of the fate awaiting his faithful companion — the tree. When he noticed how it seemed to shrivel, day by day, he began to busy himself with it, in order to restore it to life. Each morning, he would hoe with a small shovel the clods of hard earth that clung around its stem. He also watered it frequently. When the official gardener on the Mount saw the old man's care for the tree, he taught him how to prune the withered branches that were drooping down lifelessly and how to remove the rot from the projecting joints and vertebrae of the roots sunk into the soil.

It was not so long before the apparently lifeless tree began to respond to the gentle affection given to it daily by the old man. It would seem that it gradually began to bestir itself from its long spell of lethargic sleep and arise to a new lease of burgeoning life. Slowly but surely, green leaves began to sprout and flourish thereon. Its bare branches were transformed into loving tendrils and twigs, which blossomed

79

forth into verdant foliage. The branches clothed themselves with twigs and soon, lovely flowers began to appear. All those who had seen the tree in its former dismal state, now gazed at it with breathless surprise and admiration.

Reb Zanwill had a special consideration and displayed tender feelings toward this old man, not only by aiding him financially from his own pocket, but also defending him against those who did not suffer 'schnorrers" (beggars) gladly on Mt. Zion and other holy places. Many were those who bitterly complained to Reb Zanwill that it was not in keeping with the sanctity and decorum of he Mount to allow these "miserable creatures," clothed in rags, parading the mount as a kind of "Order" and frequenting every place likely to be visited by the tourist or pilgrim. Reb Zanwill always did his best to appease their indignation by d lating upon the great virtues of dispensing charity to the needy, especially in holy places. It was just this feeling of proximity which then existed between these poor people and those upon whom fortune has smiled that made the world kin and would serve as an aid in the granting of their prayers. Despite this Niagara of persuasion, appeasement of the ruffled feelings was not always possible, and more than once were the police summoned to the scene in order forcibly to remove these persi'tent beggars which proved to be "a thorn in the flesh" to those "refined and noble spirits."

This old man, who had made his "port of call" beneath the tree, was a cause of much concern to Reb Zanwill. The reason? Because this position happened to be across the narrow path leading to the ascent to the Mount. All passers-by could not help brushing against the old beggar and his tree in their climb upwards. They would sternly rebuke the old man for blocking their path, even demanding at times for him to clear away from their path. The old man listened to these rebukes without uttering a word of protest; with the result that frequent rows occurred between the pilgrims and the custodians and more than once resort was had to Reb Zanwill to settle the dispute.

Though the latter often defended the old man, yet it was not always that he succeeded in soothing tempers.

It happened one day, when Reb Zanwill was not on the Mount, that a group of distinguished tourists ascended the Mount accompanied by their guide. As they were about to pass by the stand of the old man, the guide rebuked him and asked him to clear out of the way. This, the other refused to do; so the guide began to use insulting language to repeat his demand. The old man, silently but admirably "stuck to his guns," a stance which only caused the rage of the guide to burn even more fiercely. The police were called and the old man was forcibly removed by them far away from his regular spot. Weeping, he told his aggressors that he would place his case before the Creator and Judge of the Universe.

From that day onward, the old man was no longer seen on the Mount. When Reb Zanwill was apprised of what had happened, he was plunged in great sorrow. He sent out men to search high and low for the old man, but all attempts at discovering his whereabouts proved of no avail. He had vanished into thin air. To make matters worse, nobody knew his name, where his house was, or whether he was still in the land of the living.

The disappearance of the old man began to be noticed in the Mount itself, for from the day of his disappearance the tree felt deprived of its faithful companion. It began to wither and shrivel up and its leaves began to fall and its branches to wither, fade and shrink. Its flowers closed, its blossoms no longer fourished. After a little time, the entire appearance of the tree began to become thinner and thinner and to assume its previous lifeless aspect. The gardener was summoned to attempt to revive the tree, but all his laborious efforts proved without success. Reb Zanwill had no other alternative but to record this strange and remarkable phenomenon in his Diary.

Three whole months had passed since the disappearance of the old man, when a violent storm broke out one winter's night. The storm was accompanied by a deluge of rain which was floodlike in its violence. The streets were deserted, for no man dared venture from the threshold of his house; the Mount, too, was absolutely bare of any living thing.

People gazed from the windows at this abnormal storm and flood raging in the empty streets, but the elders in the Mount were assembled together as was their practice in the silent hours of each night, in order to catch strains of the "song of the mount" which could usually be heard by them during these bewitching hours of darkness. All they heard, however, that night, was a sound of wailing that even pierced the violent storm and thunder which raged at that time. They heard that the sighing and sobbing proceeded from the Mount and this fact terrified them. For they at once grasped that something terrible had occur. d in the depths of the heart of the Mount. They decided to go up to the Mount despite the inclemency of the weather which prevailed without, in order to find out the mystery of this wailing. The heavy rains and the tempestuous storm, however, blocked all their atetmpts at sailing forth into the street. It was just beyond the bounds of possibility to carry out their intention and ascend the Mount.

Reb Zanwill's heart also pounded disquietingly within him, as he listened to the sound of the wailing. The sighing certainly came from the Mount and, what was even more passing strange, the wailing voice sounded very familiar. But for the life of him, he was unable to identify it. He realized that the only alternative he possessed was to ascend to the summit of the Mount, despite the fact that such an attempt would prove, to say the least, a most hazardous expedititon. He was the only one that had chosen to brave the mighty gusts of wind and to wrestle with them, but they forced him to proceed with difficult steps. He struggled on, being drawn on his way by that mysterious sound of wailing. After much effort, he finally reached the end of the wood at the foot of the mountain. The hour was now very late, almost midnight. The water which flowed down from the mountain. along its slopes and declivities, flowed in large pools which coursed their way all along the area, filling the foot of the Mount like one vast pool.

It was with the greatest difficulty that Reb Zanwill managed to cling on tightly to the rope along the slope and to climb gradually upwards. Throughout his adventure, the sound of wailing ceased not to drum into his ears. He was drawn by that sighing and endeavoured hard to identify the sound of him who moaned and which seemed so familiar to him. He clung firmly to the rope, climbing up step by step until he reached the place where the tree stood. There he was amazed to see how this tree was bravely, yet despairingly, almost locked in a struggle with the titanic force which was causing the tree to be rocked around and around on all sides, doing its utmost to uproot it stem and branch and all.

In the midst of its struggle, the tree, though being battered about by the storm, emitted a wailing sound such as to terrify all hearts. He now realized that this was the moaning and groaning which had pierced the empty space of the world, resembling the death-rattle of a man gasping for his final breath of life. When he looked at the tree, it seemed to him as if he beheld the likeness of a man standing near him.

He stepped backwards, startled at the apparition. In a voice tinged with fear, he asked: "Who goes here?" But the wind drowned his voice, and for this reason, he could hardly expect an answer. Finally, he conquered his fear and approached the place of the howling. Fear and trembling then seized him as he encountered "the man who had sought the second half of the night;" that is, the man who used to visit the Mount during the night at frequent intervals and pose as if he were the attendant of King David. For the most part, he would appear at midnight to move, metaphorically speaking, the second half of midnight forward. This, in order to hasten the dawn and to transform the beginnings of salvation into complete Redemption.

Reb Zanwill used to relate often concerning his frequent confrontations with this man, notably on the Festival of Independence (Iyar 5). This time, he again came across him as he was lying prostrate and in a worshipping position on the ground around the tree, shivering with cold and soaked on account of the rain, his teeth chattering with the effects of exposure on such a wild night.

Reb Zanwill fixed his eyes upon him for a few moments as he examined his face, while holding on to the tree to support him against the stormy winds. After a brief interval, the man turned to him as if he had fully realized the meaning of the searching looks of the other, and said: "Dear Reb Zanwill, I know you are most eager to know what I am doing here now in the very thick of this whirlwind. Well, let me tell you why I am here now. I am absorbing within me the whirlwind which has broken forth from the bowels of the earth and wishes to uproot the tree."

When he saw that his words did not seem at all clear to his companion, he added: "I would have you know that this storm does not come either from heaven or from the inner space of the world. It surges forth from this spot of the earth in which we are both standing now. Just bend down on the ground and incline your ear to the soil: if you will hearken intently, you will see that I have spoken correctly".

"You are absolutely correct," Reb Zanwill agreed after he had obeyed the other's directions. Yes, it was from here that the storm had broken loose and it was from this very spot that the wailing proceeded.

Both remained lying on the ground, wet and storm-tossed, listening most intently to the moaning and wailing of the ground beneath. After some time, Reb Zanwill plucked up sufficient courage to ask: "Perhaps you will be good enough to explain to me both the nature of this wail which breaks through the whirlwind and whence is its source?".

To the question, the stranger retorted: "The sound emanates from the groans of the man who is bound up within this tree. Come, brother, and I will show you its ultimate source." Filled with trepidation and curiosity at these words, there was no alternative for Reb Zanwill than to accompany him. Both arose from the ground and walked on together, struggling against the stormy gusts of tempestuous winds and tormented

84

and drenched by that wailing sound which seemed to proceed before them the entire way.

On they went, right into the thick of that wailing storm, until they reached a small house where they beheld a light burning in one of the rooms. This was the light of a soul that was burning, casting around it thousands of legions of shadows, seemingly countless in number.

When they reached the room, they could discern that someone was lying here on a bed of sickness.

It was obvious that the man had reached "journey's end" of his march through the labyrinthine roads and pathways of life, and that he was now experiencing the twitching breath-rattle which precedes death.

Reb Zanwill could no longer restrain his wonderment: "Who is this dying man? Whence all these shadows?", he blurted out in quick succession and uncontrolled amazement. The answer he received was:

"When a great soul is about to depart this life, it is immediately surrounded by the shadows of all the people with whom he had contact during his lifetime. Gaze at this dying old man and behold the thousands of shadows that have assembled to bid him farewell and that now crowd his room." The strange man added: "It is better that we hasten to step inside that we might be able to save him from his plight even at the twelfth hour".

At first, Reb Zanwill hesitated to comply with this suggestion, but his companion laughed his apprehension to scorn. "Why this procrastination? Is it because you are of priestly descent? Well, let me assure you that you will be in good time to emerge from the room before death takes place. For a great soul does not depart so hurriedly; perhaps, it does not become uprooted at all."

Moreover, here you will find a totally different world, a world where all is symbolism, and a priest does not become ritually unclean when he comes into contact with symbols and hints."

Reb Zanwill entered and found the room chokingly cramped and filled with a smell of incense. Tens of thousands of shadows pressed around the walls of the house, while on the bed there lay a man who

85

was moaning without stop in a frightening howl. Reb Zanwill was startled to recognize in the dying man the old man who had been under the tree and for whose whereabouts all attempts to discover had proved in vain. It seemed only right that events should turn out so, for he, too, was bound up with the dying man as if he had been transformed into one of the shadows that had come to part from this great soul.

Meanwhile, the sharp aroma of incense and the stifling atmosphere of the room had caused Reb Zanwill to sink into a deep slumber. When he awoke from his slumber, trembling seized every fibre and tissue of his body. The cry of the dying man symbolized the departure of the soul. Then did Reb Zanwill realize that he was a Cohen and he hurriedly left the room to be followed by his companion. It seemed as if his companion had now become transformed into the one who had stood at the crossroads to the Mount, rattling his charity-box and appealing for alms, crying: "Charity, Jews, give me the means of a day's livelihood and help a man about to die." He continued to do so until he fainted from sheer fatigue. Then it was that the dying man breathed his last. The light was extinguished and the stranger and he, went each his own way. Reb Zanwill returned to the Mt., and found the tree uprooted and dead. It was then that the storm stopped.

THE FOURTH GATE

THE CELLAR OF THE HOLOCAUST

Mount Zion also harbours the "Cellar of the Holocaust", in which are tangible symbols and monuments erected in sacred and painful memory of communities which have been destroyed. Here are deposited the charred ashes which remained of the six million Jews who were martyred for no other reason than that they were Israelites.

Near the grave of King David, where he lies fettered until his chains will be broken open by the blast of the Shofar announcing Redemption, can be found the "Cave of the Holocaust." Gathered therein are the Ashes which have been brought from the Nazi Crematoria and hellish Concentration Camps. This Cave serves as a kind of "Unknown Grave" of six million Jewish souls. Near it, the traditional everlasting remembrance of these martyrs has been arranged. This consists of the Kindling of Candles, the learning of Mishnayot (the Hebrew word "Mishnah" shares the same four letters as the word Neshamah — "Soul") the saying of Kaddish and other such activities. The sole purpose of all of which is to perpetuate the memory of vital communities and dynamic spiritual leaders who have outsoared the Valley of Despair of this world and entered into the ethereal, azure realms above.

When you visit the Chamber of Destruction on Mount Zion, you go down from the bright sunlight into the darkness of the low, vaulted smoke-blackened rooms leading from one to another and which have been crouching there since the Crusaders built them nearly a thousand years ago. You pass through the first chamber, with its walls covered with memorial tablets.

Within it, are more than two thousand commemorative tablets of communities which have been devastated. Each of these tablets, written with letters of tears and fire, tells not only a silent chapter of suffering without end, but also one of heroism and sanctity. These tablets cover the entire walls of the Cellar, each in close proximity to the other. Silent as are those letters on each tablet, they wring the very heart and nerves in their bitter tragedy. Indeed, the Prophet was right: "The Stone shall cry forth from the Wall." Even at night, the Cellar is never without, at least, one bereaved soul shedding tears for a departed, loved one. In the urns, in which the Ashes are kept, there is a perpetual ferment and unrest which fills the hearts of those nearly with fear and shuddering.

Around the deposited Ashes, there are many "Witness Chambers" which appear to be guards of honour before the Unknown Grave.

In these chambers are stored multifarious objects which recall the heroism of the mighty Fallen. Judging by the torn Prayer-books and Sifre Tirah, Tephillin and Prayer-Shawls, and so on, it is apparent that the Nazis waged war not only against the Jews themselves but also against their God and their religious observances. For the rooms are crowded with broken Decalogue Tablets; torn Ark curtains stained with blood, soles of shoes, bloody relics of holy objects all brought to Eretz-Israel by those lucky enough to escape from the jaws of death, to be deposited in the specially designed rooms surrounding the Cellar. In accordance with the Halacha, objects once used for religious purposes, retain their sanctity even when no longer so in use. Placed here in earthenware vessels, are torn Sifre-Torah too far gone for repairs to be undertaken; Tephillin and Mezuzot, disqualified for further use and other sacred religious requisites.

Next to the room of the Ashes, you will enter the room of the Eternal Flame, forever burning in honoured memory of those lost in the infernos and on which the names are written on the brooding black slab — Dachau, Buchenwald, Auschwitz... On, into the heart-rending place of the Ovens, and the Urns of the Ashes of those who were burnt therein, ashes from thirty different Concentration Camps.

The Cellar also possesses an upright Menorah, which was constructed by the inmates of a Nazi Camp and which is fashioned like a Magen David. This very badge (Magen David), which was regarded as badge of shame, was transformed into a token of heroism and Kiddush Ha-Shem by the valiant defenders of the Ghettoes.

The pillar of the Star of David, its dim, upper light gleaming through the wreath of barbed wire encircling it, is in the centre of the small room through which your way lies, to the outer courtyard and the fountain of Tears created by Dr. Frauenglass where the water drops slowly with the pathetic music of the mourners' ceaseless weeping. Down a few steps, at the end of a quiet cloister and perhaps most moving of all, is the Room of the Children — countless little plaques, each with its tiny perpetual candle.

There is still one more chamber, that of the Torah Scrolls, which have been deliberately and fiendishly violated by Nazi mental perversion. The Holy Writings have been wrenched from their rollers, torn in pieces and then used to fashion a multitude of secular objects — purses, lamp-shades, parcel-wrappings, shopping-bags and dress-patterns. In one instance, the exquisitely written parchment was profaned in a particularly diabolical way and sewn together with great skill.

There is a pulpit covered with a most skillfully-stitched jacket, the work of a Nazi tailor who was expert in making the most fantastic garments out of Torah parchment. Of course, he carried out this nefarious work in mockery of objects held by Jews as sacrocanct and inviolable. Little did that wicked tailor realize that there is a Nemesis which punishes evil, in the final analysis. With this cloak, there is connected the following story.

It happened in the terrible setting of Buchenwald, when the Nazi guards made hideous sport with an elderly Rabbi. Throwing at him the torn pieces of a Sefer Torah, they ordered him to put on the Torah-jacket. He recoiled in horror at the idea of such sacrilege and refused with all his being, but his brutal tormentors beat him and tortured him, jerking him back to consciousness when he fainted and could endure no more. Each time, they stopped short of his death. At last, they forced him to do that from which his whole soul revolted.Then a light began to shine in his mind. Carefully and meticulously, he sorted out the Holy Writings and sewed the coat so that all the Ritual Curses were on the outside and all the Blessings formed the lining. When it was finished and the Rabbi was ordered to put on the coat, the Nazi devilry went further. He was commanded to dance for the amusement of the drunken guards.

Grimly, resolutely, the old Rabbi danced until his frail strength gave out and he could no longer stand. His merciless captors then called in fifty other Jews whom they knew to be devout and pious. These were shown their venerated Rabbi in abject prostration on the ground and then bidden to watch while the commander whipped him to his feet again and bade him dance again. The fifty Jews, forced to witness such sacrilege, could not bear to look on the degradation of their beloved and revered leader; but taunted and buffeted, they had no choice save to watch, helpless and terror stricken. Then, suddenly, the old Rabbi, with what seemed an accession of almost superhuman strength, began to dance frantically. Leaping towards the soldiers, he turned and twisted, shaking the coat nearer and nearer before their eyes. And then the tormented onlookers understood ! They could read the outer parts of the ravished Scrolls and recognized their Rabbi's skill. He was flourishing Anathemas at the soldiers in a dance which seemed to have become almost a Ritual Cursing.

"Cursed be the man that maketh a graven image... that dishonoureth his father and mother... that maketh the blind to go astray.. that perverteth the justice due to the stranger, the fatherless, the widow... Cursed shalt thou be in he city... and in the field... the fruit of thy body and of thy land... when thou comest in and when thou goest out... in all that thou puttest thy hand unto..."

The Jews who watched began to smile, not at the bawdy ribaldry of the soldiers but with profound appreciation of how their Rabbi had turned the tables upon his tormentors. Though they did not know it, the soldiers were receiving the omnipotent curses of the

Almighty, whom they mocked in the persons of His Rabbi and His Chosen People. Humiliation and desolation had become a powerful spiritual victory.

One Rosh Ha'Shanah, just when the Shofar brought from Bergen-Belsen was about to be sounded in accordance with the custom on the Mount, it occurred to a pious man among the worshippers there that it would be only right and proper for him, to sound the Shofar, to put on his Tallit and Kittel (a white gown worn on Yamim Noraim) and the embroidered jacket brought from the Camps. When the congregation heard of this bold suggestion, fright seized hold of them Reb Zanwill also thrust the proposition summarily aside; for it was his firm conviction that no man in our generation was qualified to don this holy cloak even for a sacred purpose. To quell the argument, it was decided to deposit the Cloak on this very day of the Festival within the Cellar, there to be kept and to be donned only by one who was prepared to give up his life "Al Kiddush Ha'Shem". When the cloak was lowered into the cellar, three people silently wept : Reb Zanwill, the Ba'al Tkiah, and the proposer of the suggestion which was not accepted. He who ascends the Mount sighs continually, for he is convinced that had the man about to blow the Shofar donned this cloak, something very momentous would have occurred on the mountain.

Near the cloak, lies the Drum. Thereby, hangs another tale. When they crowned the King of Kings, the people went out in procession, accompanied by the sound of drums and timbrels, as it is written in the Psalms : "Praise Him with drum and dance". This music ceased with the Destruction of the Temple, as a symbol of mourning. On Mount Zion, the sound of the Drum was once renewed. This was the drum made by the Nazis out of the torn parchment of the Sefer Torah which a Warsaw Jew brought with him to Israel, in memory of the hell through which he had passed. He told the Keeper of the Cellar that the human devils had made this drum in order to beat it on the day when the Warsaw Ghetto Rising was quelled and countless num-

bers liquidated in order to commemorate this "victory". When, however, they suffered an ignominious defeat and fled from the Warsaw
Ghetto to save their own life and limb, they hurled the drum into the
midst of the valiant defenders. When this drum was carried to Mount
Zion, it was discovered that it was made from that portion of the
parchment on which the Decalogue was inscribed. Most strange to
relate, the words which stood out boldly on the drum were; "Lo
Tirzah" — Thou shalt not murder!"

The Book of Blood. The Cellar is the repositary of a Torah, totally
saturated with blood. This is the blood of an unknown Jew of Preshkov
who was trying to save it when he was stabbed with a sword. His
blood soaked into the Sefer Torah which he had clutched to his heart.
The Synagogue, where it was kept, was set on fire in a wild Nazi orgy.
The scorched parchment, stained with blood, has now been encased
in a glass-cupboard. Of the words, which are almost entirely obliterated,
the three forming the exhortation in Hebrew may still be discerned;
Ve'Havta L'Reacha Kammocha("Thou shalt love thy friend as thyself)
Near the Cellar, there has also been established a Diaspora Yeshivah
for young people who have strayed, hitherto, from the pleasant paths
of Judaism but who now wish to retrace their steps to Torah and
Mitzvot. The students find their way here from all parts of the world
throughout the five Continents.

Near the Cellar, stood a tottering furnace, threatening to fall to
pieces at any moment. This furnace is a closely kept secret on the
Mount. After a year had passed since the Ashes were deposited
here, a body of experts resolved to erect on this spot a stone Memorial in the shape of a furnace, to symbolize the tradition of casting
into a Furnace of Fire, from the days of our Patriarch Abraham,
right down to our own days. This man's bold suggestion was warmly
received. On each Tenth of Tevet, a fire is kindled in this
trumbled-down memorial furnace from which thick smoke belches
forth. When those who passed through the Camps, such as Birknau,
observe these flames and smoke, terror seizes them almost to the point

of fainting. At first, those in authority on the Mount wished to dispose of this furnace; but when they were about to do so, frightening sobs broke out from all the others there present. They seemed to hear once more those mocking murderous voices, calling out to their victims in German: "One! Two! Three!" These sounds ringing in the ears of those who now wished to dismantle the furnace in front of the Cellar, stayed their hands from completing their intention. The furnace remained in a half-broken state as a nerve-shattering memorial of a long and terrible nightmare. When it collapsed, they erected the memorial Tear-Foutain of Dr. M. Frauenglas in memory of 1,200,000 children that had been put to a cruel death.

Nearby, Jerahmiel and Cipora Wolfsohn erected a special corner, in memory of the Jewish Child and a synagogue. A special Yeshivah for Elderly Rabbis, named the Yeshivah of Rabbi Kahana is attached to the Cellar. Regular memorial services are held there.

Every Thursday night, a Memorial Service is held in the Cave. It begins with the singing of Ani Ma'amin, their marching-song to the Crematoria. This is followed by the Yiddish song. "Mein Shtetele Brennt" (My little village township is in flames"). During the celebration of Hanukkah, the ten Hanukkah Lamps which have been saved from the destroyed communities, are kindled therein to the accompaniment of the songs hummed in these villages during the celebration of this Maccabean Anniversary. During the year, eight such Services are regularly held in the Cave, according to a definite programme: Tenth of Tebet, which commemorates the general Day of Mourning; Shabbat Zachor (before Purim) and Shabbat Va'Yikra (when the Book of Leviticus is begun). This marks the mourning over the million and a quarter children who were massacred. (It was the custom, in olden days, for the child to begin his study of the Torah with the Book of Leviticus which deals with sacrifices which had to be without blemish, before they were offered up at the Temple Altar). A Service was also held in the Cave each Erev Pesah, to perpetuate in loving and tearful memory, the Uprising of the Warsaw Ghetto which began on that day. Another of these Services was arranged for the Twentieth of Siwan in memory of the massacres perpetuated by the Crusaders in the Middle Ages, as well as the pogrom of Chmelinitzki (1688 C.E.) and the destruction of Hungarian Jewry. On Erev Shabbat Hukkat (Numbers XIX-XXI), the Service painfully commemorates the burning of the Holy Scrolls of the Torah (the Sidra deals with the Burning of the Ashes of the Red Heifer). The eighth Service is held on Tisha B'Av, a day which, apart from all the other national tragedies which occurred thereon, sparked-off the liquidation of the Ghettos in Central Europe. In addition to these statutory services, hardly a day passes without such a service being held there in perpetual remembrance of an individual or community that perished in those hellish flames which burnt not only in the Crematoria, but also in the bestial Nazi hearts — if they had any...

Obviously, such services are many. They are not meant to be national observances, for the Cellar simply could not accommodate the thousands who would wish to throng there. They are primarily intended for those in charge of the Cellar and who supervise the safe custody of the Ashes and the other relics deposited there and which feed undying memories. It is impossible to visit the Cellar at any time without being enslaved by the bitter thoughts which spring to life before our mental gaze of that terrible tragedy in all its vivid, stark reality. For this reason, permission has been given to each visitor to inscribe the names and dates of those of his family who perished. These details are commemorated by those who officiate on the Mount, with the Kindling of the Yahrzeit Light, the saying of the Kaddish, the learning of Mishnayot and other traditional practices observed in remembrance of such mournful occasions.

The Holocaust Cellar fulfils a national duty, one that is obligatory on our generation which has been fortunate enough to witness the first rays of Redemption, towards the past generations who faced with matchless courage hellish tortures and fiery deaths, but who never despaired of the ultimate Salvation that will come to our harassed nation one day. It is their Kiddush Ha'Shem (Martyrdom) which planted the seeds of our present Tehillat Ha'Shem (Praise to God).

When the Ashes were first brought to be deposited near the Sepulchre of King David, the original intention was to regard the Holocaust as a link in the long chain stretching right-up to the point of Salvation; just as the road to the Messiah is paved with thick clouds and blinding darkness. The Holocaust was looked upon as the darkness preceding the light, as a force which forged ahead and made possible the advance with which the State was established. Was it not Rabbi Yohanan who observed : "When you behold a generation laden with sorrow flowing endlessly as a stream, then expect something to happen!"

THE STORY OF THE MAGGID

Many are the legends and tales inscribed in the archives kept on Mount Zion which give expression to the spiritual ties between the Holocaust and the Commencement of the Redemption. One of these tells of the Jews of Anapol who petitioned at the grave of their revered preacher that he should beseech God on their behalf to save them from the devilish machinations of the Nazis. Their erstwhile Rabbi, however, did not heed their request. It would seem as if he were unwilling to hasten the end and interfere with the Divine Plan. Prior to his death, he requested his disciples to bind him hand and foot, so that he would be unable to emerge from his grave and cry to God with them. When even this precaution proved of little avail and he appeared before them from his tomb, he was completely petrified and became a living monument of marble. When even this proved powerless to restrain him, his heart burst open, his spirit became broken and all his body floated in tears.

But he was afraid to help, not to stop the paamei hamashiach "the steps of Geulah."

THE STORY OF REB PINHAS

A similar story is that of Rabbi Pinhas, of Koritz, who is said to have emerged from his grave and revealed himself to the long-suffering Jews who petitioned him to be their intercessor before the Heavenly Throne.

He explained to them the Secret of Creation, which was the phrase used in mystic circles as "Shevirat Ha'Kelim" (the Breaking of the Vessels); namely, that all created things start from nothing, just as the young chicken must first break the egg which its mother had laid before it can enter life on earth. Similarly, the planted seed must first become decomposed in the slumbering sod before it crumbles and then triumphantly emerges into burgeoning existence. This is how the Rabbi of Koritz explained the Talmudic dictum; "There is no Mazzal (belief in constellations) in Israel", taking the word Ain (not) to mean in this phrase; "It is just this word "No", which ultimately turns out to be Israel's good luck!" (Sabb. 156a).

Of the spiritual healer of Pshisha, the story is told that when the needy and hungry, who sat begging for alms at street corners, came appealingly to him for sustenance, he raised his eyes to them in amazement, saying : "Patience my friends! We are on our way, day by day, towards the Great Heavenly Banquet, one fit for Kings — and you speak of plates of potatoes and noodles ! Please, brethren, a little more patience on your part..."

The Song of the Cellar is taken from the Song of the Sea (Ex. XV) : "The Lord is my song and might; He (Va'Yehi) has become my salvation." It is the Va'Yehi which, according to the Talmud, always betokens trouble ahead, that has become for me a source of salvation (Va'Yehi — Li Li'Yeshuah).

The depositing of the Ashes on Mount Zion is linked with a plethora of legendary tales which emphasize the inner, spiritual connection between the cataclysmic catastrophes showered upon Israel by the Nazis and the rest of a hostile world and the pangs of labour attending the birth of the Messianic Age. The jubilant tune of the Hallel in praise of the salvation witnessed, mingles harmoniously with the lugubrious notes of the Ani Ma'Amin ("I believe in perfect faith") which were sung by those who were marched to their premature deaths in the Crematoria of the Concentration Camps. The aim of the Cave is not so much to recite sorrows, but rather to tell of the astounding

96

heroism of men and women who so bravely withstood their terrible ordeal and hallowed the Name of their Heavenly Father. The Cave depicts an accurate image of the life and customs, joys and sorrows, of the communities which have vanished in the flames kindled by devils in human shape.

There are two chief memorials on the mountain : that of King David, which symbolizes its Messianic destiny as well as the hope of the re-birth of the City, and that of the Holocaust, which foretells the dissolution of the Diaspora and the end of slavery and subjection to hostile nations. Both are interrelated and possessed by the longing to unite the first generation to witness the beginnings of the Redemption with all the preceding generations who carried within their hearts the vision and the hope of future Redemption. The "Holocaust Cellar" is no innovation, nor is it simply an annexe of David's Tomb. It is, actual-ly part of it. David is identified with the People and his Tomb symobli-zes the tribulations of his People — the poverty, sorrows, the crematoria and destruction. Together with their faithful King, whose remains are believed to be deposited in this grave, the nation awaits Redemption and Resurrection. The Crowns which have been placed on the Tomb have been gathered from the Synagogues destroyed during the Holo-caust. They are the Crowns borne aloft, whilst wading through rivers of blood and tears, grief and tribulation.

On Yom Ha'Atzmaut, the programme of celebrations begins at the Tomb and concludes at the "Holocaust Cellar". On the Day of Mourning over the Destruction of Jewish Communities, mostly in Central Europe, the programme is reversed : beginning at the Cellar and terminating at the Tomb. At first, opposition was expressed by different sections to the idea of depositing the Ashes of the Martyrs in the "Cellar of the Holocaust", on the grounds that since doubt exists as to whether David actually lies buried on the Mount, there should be no new addition to this dubious sanctuary. This opposition was countered by the arguments of Reb Zanwill who explained the con-nection which exists between the Tomb and the Cellar (see above).

97

Israel's Redemption will succeed the dissolution of a large section of the Diaspora, just as the Destruction of Eretz-Israel in 70 C.E. subsequently gave birth to the Golah and its vicissitudes and tribulations. Hence, when we celebrate on the Mountain the miracle which is the upbuilding of our national Homeland, it is only fitting to honour, at the same time, the heroism displayed by the victims of the Nazi Holocaust. It is only right to encourage those who emerge from the Cellar of the Holocaust, to proceed immediately to David's Tomb — the symbol of the revival of the State. Since this discussion took place during the week when the section of Hayye Sarah (Gen. XXIII-XXV. 19.) is read on the Shabbat, those arguing in favour of placing the Ashes on the Mount found ready support in one of the opening verses; "And Abraham arose from his Dead (Sarah)"; implying that we are to rise from the Unknown Grave of the Six Million Dead and march with uplifted heads and hearts towards the Tomb, the symbol of a new, national birth.

He who walks through the labyrinthine paths of the Mountain and the arched gateways and doors of its buildings, imagines at first that he can hear two separate sounds : that of exultation from the Tomb of David, linked in popular tradition with the Messianic era with King David and the "Book of Uprightness" which lies in his cave. As well as a weaker sound, that of the heavy sighing which emerges muffled and muted from the chamber of the deposited Ashes near the memorial tablets of those communities which have been liquidated, as well as from those religious institutions which were once the pride of the Old City of Jerusalem but were so brutally razed to the ground by the Arab Legion. These may appear at first as two separate "Voices"; in reality, however, they are but one. One mighty Voice —- that of awakening Youth, whose cry resembles the roaring of a lion aroused from its den. Yea, it is like unto the rising crescendo of a stirring chorus of song.

The men of the Mountain are fond of the story of the two Cantors who both wished to sing on Kol Nidre, as they stood before the reading-desk in the Synagogue on Mount Zion. One of them hailed from the Old City, a scion of the sixth generation of dwellers in Jerusalem; while the other had just immigrated to Israel from a Nazi Concentration Camp in Poland. Each of them staked his claim to be the Cantor fit on that solemn evening which is the most impressive in all the. colourful Jewish year. Since it was extremely difficult to decide as to whose qualifications outweighed that of the other, it was resolved that they should both sing together before the Ark. To this, they both agreed. As they sang, each voice and each melody seemed totally different from the other. They sounded as distinct from each other as the two differing Songs of the Mount. Despite this, however, the congregation heard only one blended harmony, for the two voices and their separate tunes, instead of being raucous and cacophanos, rose as one melodious voice — the melody of Mount Zion, which is the Voice of the most ancient of peoples, now about to renew their youth as an eagle.

THE SHIELD OF DAVID

After having been arrested by the Nazis and made to do the most menial work for a whole week, from morn to night, a work which reduced his strength and wasted him away, he rarely ventured out of his home. So ill was he on account of the blows he received and the insults heaped upon him, that he was compelled to be confined to his bed for weeks on end.

R. Pinhas , for that was his name, who happened also to be a man of character and culture, used to say: "No punishment can break man's spirit as can shame and degradation." As proof, he would cite the case of Moses, who asked God : "What will the Egyptians say?". Another proof he cited was that of the wife of Pinhas, the son of Eli, the High Priest. More than her grief at the death of her husband and father-in-law, she was troubled over the departure of glory from Israel.

You will recall, he would add, that Saul, when his Kingdom was torn away from him, only made this request: "Please give me, at least, honour in the presence of the elders of my people."

So R. Pinhas'l stayed at home. Did not our talmudic sages advise: "When the Angel of Death stalks about the city, gather in thy legs (stay at home)?".

When the Jews were made to wear the blue Magen David as a rag on their arm, the intention was to humiliate them. Not content with the most devilish of modern insults, the Nazis also dragged out the degradation imposed upon Jews in the Middle Ages. When R. Pinhas'l heard of this new degradation, he was not at all troubled but accepted it calmly. It had been used for holy purposes, such as mantles for the Torah, or bags for Tallit and Tephillin. He found a piece which had once belonged to the Tephillin-bag which his mother had herself sewn for him on his Bar-Mitzvah.

This remnant, he cut up into several pieces, sufficient to make Magen David badges for him and his entire family. Many hours of day and night did he sit stitching these badges, consecrating each one with the recital of this verse: "The thread of blue at the corner shall be to you for fringes". After working at them the whole of the night, he placed them under his pillow and went to bed.

When dawn broke, R. Pinhas'l arose from his bed, "like a lion to do God's work", washed his hands, and dressed himself with the blue badge and recited the biblical verse: "And it shall come to pass that instead of being said to them: "You are not my people, it shall be said unto them: "You are the children of a living God". Proud and erect of mien, he went out to pace the highways and byeways of the city. With the badge on him, he paced with dignity all public places, engaging in business and communal duties, with none to say him nay. The badge seemed to guard his legs at all times from falling into an evil trap. It was to him what the Ephod was to the High Priest. When his friends expressed anxiety for his safety, he would point to his badge and say: "I am not afraid. My shield is my badge".

When he was taken to Auschwitz, he descended from the wagon, as if he had come to a hotel. He brushed his clothes, displayed proudly his badge and walked upright in front of the chief Gestapo officer. The latter, seeing his dignified approach, deemed him to be a very important man, smacked his lips at the thought of extra insults and indignities he would heap upon him. So he ordered him to be placed on the side of those singled out for hard labour, before their turn came to die. That day, the guards were changed, and so R. Pinhas'l was saved from the gas-chambers. The new guards took no notice of him, and so he emerged from serfdom. When he came to Israel, he entered into great light.

Even in Israel, he walked about with the badge, until he was told that those who saw it were pained, because it brought back such sad memories. So he removed it forever. But he brought it to Mt. Zion, to be deposited there among the treasures of King David, the Faithful Shield of Israel. The disciples of the Diaspora Yeshivah on Mt. Zion wear from time to time the badge of Magen David in his memory.

KING DAVID'S ROBE

There is a pious and beautiful Jewish belief that one day, in the triumphant future of Israel, the great and noble King David will return and usher in the Messianic Age. For such world-shaking splendour, the King must wear his most royal Robe. This Robe is being endlessly woven for him throughout the ages and covering all the Universe. This eternal material is made on Earth from all the good deeds, selfless renunciations, heroic martyrdoms. and long silent patient endurance by which all the good people of the world, in every age, have kept faith with their Creator, ever offering Him the best they possessed. These are the very warp and woof of the priceless fabric of the Robe. No matter that the offerings be from be poor and ignorant, unlearned and primitive; no matter what be the race and country of those who tender them, but so long as they be the best that the light of the lives of these faithful ones has shown to them — they will all become precious threads in this great tapestry.

"What is the colour of my Robe?" asked King David. "The colour is green, O King! The colour of all the verdant life on earth by which mankind is nourished and can live." For legend tells us that wherever the steps of King David trod; wherever, in fact, even the sound of his feet was heard, the whole land brought forth its most glorious verdure; on the hillsides, in the valleys, in the forests and almost up to the mountain-tops. Pasture-lands, great wide-spreading plains, all burst into the vernal beauty of Spring-time, a rich, fresh, vibrant green. So green was chosen for this most regal of all Robes.

But the Firmament also must join in its contribution to that of Earth; and so the Robe was richly sewn with stars which shone and radiated light like the fairest jewels. There is, however, a strange thing about these jewels: they are of two colours only, a deep ruby-red and that of the purest silver.

Then the King asked: "What is the meaning of the stars which adorn my Robe? Why are there so many of the ruby jewels, that they almost hide the pure beauty of the green?" The sombre answer was: "O King, those stars are gems formed by the countless drops of blood so cruelly shed, of all the victims of bloodthirsty men throughout the ages. Those inhuman monsters who have massacred the innocent, old and young, men and women, even infants torn from their mothers' arms. All who have been the helpless sufferers of sin and evil, of lust and selfishness, of the hunger for power and of the hatred born to fear..."

The King asked his third question: "How came the silver stars to adorn my Robe? They are so bright, so glorious — and yet they are so few." The answer, born of eternal hope, was: "O King! These are the spirits of all the benefactors of mankind; of all who have striven for mercy and justice, compassion and fair-dealing, freedom and human rights for all their fellow men, of all the wise and incorruptible

102

governors and kings and men in authority throughout the world and the generations."

Then the King asked his fourth question: "When will my Robe be ready for me to wear and for me to come and herald the approach of the Messiah?" And he was answered: "Alas, O King! That time cannot come until the stars of silver have outnumbered those of ruby-red; that is, until the Divine Plan of the Creator has triumphed over the wickedness and cruelty of men. But yet, O King, be of good heart! For slowly but surely, the stars of silver are appearing in ever greater numbers and will do so until, at last, they mark the Ultimate Victory. On that day, O King, your Robe will be complete, lovely, fragrant and holy for you to put it on..."

Legend tells us that King David had one more question to ask. Every night does he come to see his Robe and to find out if he may now put it on and set forth on his glorious way to announce the Coming of the Messiah, but every night the answer is: "O King! Thine hour has not yet struck. Thy Robe is still far, so very far from completion."

And every night, Kind David must still go away grief-stricken.

The disciples of the Mt. Zion Diasporah Yeshivah hear his sigh.

THE BALLAD OF KING DAVID'S CLOAK

During the impressive celebration of the Yom Ha'atzmaut Independence Day, (Iyyar 5th) on Mount Zion, it has become the custom to deposit a crown on the tomb of King David — who, tradition asserts, lies buried there. This act was meant to symbolize the placing of a crown on the head of the rejuvenated Jewish Nation. While this act is being performed, Reb Zanwill bids all present to stand up with raised head and proud mien — thus asserting that they must now regard themselves as free men, emancipated from the servile attitude thrust upon them by life in the Diaspora. At the same time, the royal tomb is draped in flags, with the Magen David in the centre. The

103

latter is intended to symbolize that King David is looked upon as our shield and protector.

When this impressive ceremony was being performed several years ago, there happened to be present among the eye-witnesses one of the gallant defenders who actively participated in the War of Liberation in 5708. At the end of this moving service, he made the stirring suggestion to Reb Zanwill — the Master of Ceremonies on Mount Zion — that, on future occasions of this nature, it would be fitting to place among the other flags, the torn, blood-bespattered flag which was carried by the gallant defenders of the Warsaw Ghetto, which was stored in the Chamber in the vaults of Mount Zion among the other sad relics stored therein, sad reminders of the bloody Nazi Holocaust. The suggestion did not find favour in the eyes of Reb Zanwill. True, he himself associated the tragedy of the Warsaw Ghetto and the haunting memories of the concentration camps and blazing crematoria with the grave of David. But he preferred to view the Holocaust as the Gateway of the Redemption and the paving of the Way of the Messiah. Of this approach, the first steps were the establishment of the Jewish State.

The twenty-seventh of Nisan, the anniversary commemorating the Nazi Holocaust, should be regarded as the precursor of the Hag Ha'-atmaut. Reb Zanwill sees a strong connection between both these dates, Despite this belief, however, he could not favour the suggestion made by the valiant fighter in the Battle for Independence. It was only after the obstinate refusal of the latter not to accept "No", for in answer to his suggestion, that Reb Zanwill reluctantly agreed to comply with the proposal. The Warsaw Ghetto flag was removed from the "Holocaust Chamber" and handed to the proposer of the idea who, reverently and with deep emotion, placed it on the grave of King David.

As he did so, he explained to the onlookers why he was so insistent that his proposal be accepted. He unfolded into their listening ears, some of the experiences he had lived through during the War of Liberation. They concerned the officer of his brigade who — although he would not name him — all his hearers knew was none other than he himself. It is much easier to tell a story in the third person, so as not to appear too egocentric.

The actual event, he told his eager audience, took place thirteen days after the Proclamation of the State, that is on LAG B'OMER (the 18th of Iyar) 5708. "We, Jewish soldiers", he continued, "had just retreated from the Old City and had withdrawn to Mount Zion. The situation was most intense and precarious. The Old City had been taken by the Arabs and none knew what dread events the morrow might bring forth. One disaster usually follows another. We were all plunged in the most abject despair, dread of what might happen next haunting our very being.

"It was then that our Commander, with eyes glazed by his tears, turned our steps towards Mount Zion. Like shadows, did we creep among ruins that paved our way towards our destination. From the distance, we could clearly hear the deafening sounds of heavy shooting and thunderous mine-explosions. At this moment, our Commander gathered us at the grave of King David where we all poured out our bitter hearts in long and fervent supplication, praying with all our souls for the safety of Jerusalem and the Jewish State. Our orisons ended, the Commander remained rooted to King David's grave, muttering quietly some further prayers to him to whom tradition has assigned the rôle of the Messiah.

"We could just make out what he was muttering as if to himself: "David, Our King and Messiah! Arise, we pray thee, arise, to help thy people and their Land! Be a Saviour to your afflicted children, the Tribe of the Wandering Foot, despised and rejected by a hostile world, hated and baited by so-called "civilized" nations. Our mothers, when we were young, and from whom we learnt the first rudiments of our faith and history on their knees, were fond of telling us that when the Cup of Tears — in which our Heavenly Father deposits the tears of all the afflicted Jews — would be full, then thou wouldst emerge

105

from the grave, and usher in our Salvation. O King! is not the Cup already filled to overflowing? See, it is already spilling over the top, tears that can fill a vast sea. So why are you still so slow in coming-out to bring us Salvation from our sorrow? Our plight is so bitter and almost unbearable! Do thou rise and bring us help forthwith!"

"As he uttered these invocations and heartfelt sobs with thumping heart-beats, King David trembled in his grave, rose therefrom and said to the Commander: "Bring me my cloak!" "But where is your cloak?", retorted the Commander, both full of fear and exalted with joyous expectation; "What does the cloak look like, so that I may know what to search for and so be able to bring it to you without undue loss of time?"

"The reply he heard from the tomb was: "What! Have not the mothers of Israel told their children about my purple cloak which is woven from the souls of the saints and martyred heroes who died for Kiddush Ha'Shem in the Cause of their God and their People of the House of Israel? Has my cloak already been totally worn-out and cast away?"

"It was then that the Commander quickly bethought himself of the idea of bringing to King David the flag under which the gallant defenders of the Warsaw Ghetto had battled so heroically against the overwhelming hordes of the devilish Nazis and their satellites. The flag was almost torn to shreds and bespattered with the blood of the martyrs; yet these dark-red stains glistened as brightly as the dazzling stars in the dark canopy of Heaven.

"This is thy cloak, O King and Messiah!" our Commander called out into the grave. Thereupon, King David wrapped himself up in the torn, blood besmirched flag as the pious Jew enfolds himself in his Tallit (Praying-Shawl). Thus enfolded, he emerged from the Tomb in which his bodily remains had been encased, ready to help his People as he had been implored to do by the Commander.

"What happened then you all know: Triumph over our enemies was

106

miraculously won and we were witnesses to behold, as we now say in our prayers "the beginning of Salvation, the first seeds of our Redemption !"

The narrator then finished this extraordinary account of his experience with the following words : "To this day, we still wait patiently and prayerfully for the advent of the Messiah. The "Cup of Tears" is more overflowing than ever and the Cloak of the souls of our martyrs and saints is bigger than ever it was in the time of King David. So let us now place this Cloak, the flag of the Warsaw Ghetto heroes, on his grave."

Thus it was that the torn-to-shreds, blood-bespattered and tear-besmirched flag of the Warsaw Ghetto heroes and martyrs, is placed on the Tomb of King David annually on the festival of Shavuot, the anniversary of his death, as well as the day which commemorates the giving of the Torah, on Mount Sinai during the Revelation.

THE POWER OF A TEAR

"Tears", said Reb. Zanwill, "harbour many hidden powers".There are are many Jews who ascend Mt. Zion and pour out their broken hearts with no spectator amazed at the scene. Why not? For the simple reason that everybody is aware of the experience that, from time to time, one feels that he simply must give vent to his pent-up emotions to somebody. There are occasions, however, when one observes people praying on the Mount whose very appearance there occasions the greatest of surprises.

From time to time, Reb Zanwill would come across there the aged Reb Yehezkiel, a man lame and ailing, who despite these bodily defects, persisted in dragging up his weary and aching body almost daily, step by step,to the top of the 150 of these steps. This number is equated to the chapters comprising the Psalms composed by King David, whose bodily remains lie intered in a special vault on the crest of the Mount

107

When he arrived at the Sepulchre, he would rest a while, then take up the Book of Psalms (Tehillim) and begin to recite these heavenly compositions which reflect the emotions of man, sad or gay,and which every mortal has himself experienced during his eventful pilgrimage from birth to death, from the womb to the tomb.

Reb Zanwill could not help being full of wonder at this man's determination to scale the heights almost daily in order to pray at David's Tomb, where he would kindle a flickering-light and commence his supplications. When the man had finished his prayers, he would make his solitary and painful way up the tortuous, dangerous steps leading from the Tomb to the very crest of the Mount, called the Mitzpeh-Ha'Bayit (The Watch-Tower of the Temple). It was from there that the worshipper could see the Western Wall below, to which all approach by Jews was forbidden from 1948 till 1967 — the year of the breath-taking miracle of the Six-Day War.

When Reb.Zanwill observed all this effort on the part of the old, lame and ailing man, he could no longer contain his curiosity and astonishment. Approaching the man, he asked: "What makes you climb up this ascent perilous for a man of your age and state of health ? And then, not satisfied with this feat, you even climb up to King David's Sepulchre and from there, even higher — to the very summit of Mitzpeh-Ha'Bayit ? Whence do you derive these inner resources of physical powers and duress? Moreover, why is it at all necessary for you to come all this way to pray ?"

The other replied : "You are absolutely correct in asking me all this Actually, I lack nothing and I have enjoyed all the things I wanted throughout my life, thank Heaven.

"But there is far too much suffering, for my liking, in the world at large; suffering which my heart cannot easily endure. Hence, when I encounter the pain and need of those around me, I feel compelled to ascend the Mount and pray to God for Him to remove these tribulations from an afflicted world. After all, a man must not live his life for self alone."

"You are absolutely right", Reb Zanwill assented. "Man should not live for self alone and should do his utmost to render less the sum of human wretchedness. But my question is : "What inner power enables you to mount these 150 steps which lead to the Mitzpeh-Ha'bayit?"

By way of reply, Reb. Yehezkiel pointed to the taxi. "This drives on for thousands of miles, all because of the small amount of benzine spirit which had been poured into its tank."

"Is this not equated to what enables a man to drive through the hills and rugged places of life?? His benzine, however, are the tears he sheds or those he observes streaming from the eyes of his close friends in their tribulation. It is these tears that gird him with lion's strength to scale the rugged heights, in order to summon relief for those who suffer."

To implement his parable of the taxi, he unfolded before Reb Zanwill the pain suffered by his neighbour.

She was a poor widow whose only little daughter was dangerously ill. With hands clasped as an expression of grief, she sits weeping beside the bed of her child. "It is those tears," Reb Yehezkiel assured Reb Zanwill, "that gird me with superhuman strength to ascend all those 150 steps to the Tomb of David" and even higher to the Mitzpeh Ha'-Bayit overlooking the Kotel Ha'Maaravi. To clinch this, he then related the story of his grandfather.

His grandfather was a grandson of the famous Hasidic teacher, R.Mendele Rumanover. Such piety and learning were his, that many flocked to him for advice and miraculous cures, as well as to pour out before him the things which gave them no peace of mind and also wrought havoc to their physical health. He himself, however, did not believe that he possessed those extraordinary powers that were attributed to him

When people flocked to him with sorrows too full for tears, he would plead with them : "Who and what am I?" At first, he would strongly discourage people coming to him with their burdens of sorrows which they wished him to shuffle off. As old age crept on, he would receive

109

his tearful supplicants and patiently hearken to their endless tales of woe and despair. As an expression of sympathy, he would clasp their hands in the manner of a doctor when listening to his patient's pulse and raise his eyes heavenwards as if in prayer. He would then tell his supplicant, in most sympathetic terms : "I myself cannot do anything to bring you relief, but while I am praying for divine help in your grief, I scale the lofty heavens where my grandfather Reb Mendele now resides, and I entreat him to pray on your behalf before the Heavenly Throne."

When he was asked : "What gives you, an old broken man, the inner torce to scale the lofty, azure heights where your grandfather resides in the eternal bliss reserved for the holy and righteous ?", his reply was : "The inner force which enables me to do so, originates from the tears I see streaming from the eyes of those who suffer. On the wings of a tear, one can soar aloft to the azure heights. With the propelling force of one tear", Reb Yehezkiel assured Reb Zanwill, "my grandfather soared aloft the seven heavens to his grandfather Reb Mendele. With the same tear, he pinioned along on his wings of mercy to the Throne of Glory itself — and all this by the force of one sincere tear." He concluded : "When I stand a little while near King David's Tomb, I can behold the colossal, mystical powers of human tears."

THE GATE OF TEARS

The Tomb of King David, on Mount Zion, has been called symbolically the Gate of Tears, because it is there that so many pilgrims and mourners pour out their weeping and sorrows, strong in the belief that the King will hear their grief and bear it tenderly before their Heavenly Father. They know that none will ever call in vain for King David's aid, or remain unheard and sent away rejected. One of the most beautiful characteristics of the King was his sympathy, understanding and tender heartedness towards all the poor and lonely and desolate among

110

his people. Filled with a great spirit of Justice as well as Mercy, he strove endlessly for the welfare of his people throughout all his kingdom. He appointed ministers for the different offices of his government, with the intention of maintaining the highest standards for the health and wealth, security and progress of all those over whom he ruled, especially of those in humble position.

The administration by those in power, however, was by no means always as fair and as unimpeacable as it should have been. In integrity, it fell far short of the royal example. It was well-known that everyone, even the most ignorant and illiterate, had the right to petition the King and plead for the redression of what they felt to be their wrongs and difficulties. As time passed, however, more and more complaints were heard; either the petitions never reached the King, or else he had hardened his heart against them.

In due course, these resentful mutterings came to the ears of David himself. Having made full enquiry into the substance of such reports and finding that they were, in essence, true, he issued a proclamation that, in future, a new office would be set up which would ensure that every petition should indeed reach the King and would be properly investigated and dealt with. The people were directed to bring their petitions to a certain door at the palace and pass them through a special opening. In order that they might bring them without fear, let or hindrance, they would not see the official who received them but only feel his hand as he took the purchment from them.

Soon, instead of murmuring dissension, cheerful and favourable comments were heard. For now, in actual fact, the petitions were reaching the King and were being answered with speedy justice and with such simplicity, that even the most ignorant could undersand. It happened that on one occasion, a widow from the country, near Gilgal, brought her request, that an anxious problem might be solved for her, to the special door of the palace. As she had never been in Jerusalem before and had told no one of her intention, she did not know what she ought to do. So she pushed the door open and went inside with her plea.

111

She could not clearly see the face of the official, for the light was dim. Confused and humble, she hardly dared to raise her eyes but she knew that he smiled at her and told her very kindly that the King would see that justice was done for her cause. When she got home, her neighbours questioned her with eager curiosity when she told them her tale. She could speak of little more than the impression of a kind smile and the assurance of a gentle voice.

Many months later, at the Feast of Tabernacles, the widow again we it up to Jerusalem, all agog with excitement to celebrate her first Sukk t in the great City. She went with special happiness, because her petitic n had been favourably answered and she was now free from all anxious care. In her great gratitude, she longed to offer praise and thanksgivii g in that earthly Jerusalem, whence they would rise up to the Heavenly City just above, straight to the Throne of the Almighty Creator Himself. All around her, as far as she could see, were the huge crowds, bringing their harvest-offerings of every kind. All along the great procession were those bearing the fruitful symbols of Etrog and Palm-Brench. Everyone was singing songs of praise and joy for the abundant fruits of the earth, the reward of all their hard toil and labour :

"Thou hast remembered the earth and watered her, greatly enriching her... Thou preparest them corn... Thou blesseth the growth thereof... Thou crownest the year with goodness... The meadows are clothed with flocks. The valleys are covered over with corn. They shout for joy. Yea ! They sing !"

As she went along her way, happy and excited, she saw at the head of the procession, a great, fine, tall, handsome figure of a man, leading and commanding all around him with the radiance of his smile and the melody of his voice. Suddenly, the widow cried out as loudly as she could : "There is the man ! That is the man !" Her neighbours in the throng tried to hush her. Such shouting was not seemly, for that vibrant figure leading them all in the dance was none other than the King himself ! But she would not be silenced and proclaimed more stridently than ever that this was, indeed, the man who had received her petition and who had been sitting at the special door of the Palace, taking in the papers with the requests of all who came to him! Her petition had been granted... ! Those around her grew angry when she would not stop her clamour; when, suddenly, the leader turned and gestured that he wished to speak and be heard. Then did he proclaim that, indeed, this poor woman was right ! It was he, the King, who had himself received and answered all the countless complaints and sorrows pleaded by the poor and the down-trodden of his people... What an acclamation there arose from the vast crowd! What shouts resounded from David's Friends : "Long live the King! Long live the King !"

Legend tells us that many years later, when this great and noble King was called to the Heavenly Realms above, he was met by the angels and archangels. Gabriel asked him : "What is now your greatest wish? What will you choose as your reward in Heaven? Will you continue to sing the glory of your Psalms? Or will you lead, with your harp, the Heavenly Choir ?"

King David answered : "When I was on earth, it was my duty and my greatest privilege to receive the entreaties of my people at the Gate of Tears. Now, I will still stand at the place where I may receive all the pleadings of their breaking hearts, all those beseeching in their humiliation and despair, all those weeping and lamentation, so that I may bring them for ever to the foot of the Throne of their Creator and All-Merciful Heavenly Father. Then, most surely, will He allow me to bear back to them. His tender consolations, His healing of their poor wounds, His Peace for their minds, souls, and bodies..."

Thus the Jewish People know that their great King David waits on Mount Zion to receive their prayers and supplications, as of old at the Gate of Tears. There will he bear them straight into the Divine Presence, bringing back to them thereform the balsam of Mercy and Peace.

DEW OF TEARS

The Psalmist sings of the dew which falls on Mount Zion and comes from the North, from Mt. Hermon. Why should this be so and what is the meaning of this song? Some say that it is because of the wind which blows from the North, that same wind which rises at midnight, stirring the strings of King David's violin into heavenly music. It plays a sentimental tune which rends the heart. It is that wind which brings the dew of the Mountain where he lies buried. Reb Zanwill confirms this theory and says that it is based on the ancient legends of the nation. It is related to the story of the Mount Hermon in the north, white with its perpetual snow. This mountain is the original source of the dew, as it is said: "As the dew of Hermon falls on Mount Zion."

Rabbi Zanwill tells the story of the white Hermon, which rises high above the borders of our Land. This mountain has many names : Shanir, or Shiryon, are the ancient names. Today it is called Mount Hermon, or the White Hermon because of its snow-capped summit. In Aramaic, it is called Tor Talga — the Mountain of Snow. This meaning is also apparent from the name Shanir. Children call it the "Mountain with the White Dunce-Cap". They say it stands at the gates of the Land of Israel because it is too ashamed to enter the Land itself.

The mountian conceals many a secret under its white cap, one of which is awe-inspiring. This story reveals the secret of the whiteness of the mountain. It is said that it all began on the day when God told Abraham that his sons would be slaves in Egypt. At this time, Abraham was standing at the foot of Mount Hermon and was so sad that his hair became white with grief. Accordingly, the peak of the mountain turned white in sympathy with the Patriarch.

That night, a terrible darkness descended upon earth. There had been no such darkness since the Creation and there was nothing like it again until the threatening blackness which descended over Egypt, hundreds of years later. Only the Hermon was witness to God telling Abraham

114

that his sons would be exiled to a strange land where they would know toil and tragedy for four hundred years.

"Know then, that your Seed shall be sojourners in a land not their own !"

On hearing this declaration of exile, Mount Hermon groaned and lowered its head, for it knew what exile meant. More than once, exiles had stolen away to rest a few hours at its foot to cry out against the bitterness of their fate. Mount Hermon knew what exile meant and its heart shrank when it heard the decree.

When the Lord continued: "They shall be slaves, and they shall be afflicted, for four hundred years," the mountain groaned even more deeply and its hair began to turn white. It knew what slavery meant and also the meaning of torture. When it heard the length of time during which the generations would suffer, it turned completely white. Four hundred years! What nation could withstand four hundred years of exile and hardship ? The mountain began to weep and the tears froze into snowflakes; hence, did its peak become eternally white.

Since that time, Hermon has stood, with its white peak overlooking the countryside, till the awaited day will come. After which, there will be no more exiles or afflictions.

The sufferings of Mount Hermon are the sufferings of the People. Its tears are as dew for Mount Zion whence, through suffering to Redemption, King David will announce the Messiah's advent.

THE HEAVY HEART

The vale made the ascent difficult. There was no doubt that the bridge would facilitate the climb. Others even suggested the construction of an electric-lift or train, to make it even easier for pilgrims. To both these suggestions, Reb Zanwill and his colleagues objected. Their objection was based on the supposition that such modernization would transform the mountain into a kind of amusement park. The only

115

thing on which agreement was arrived at was to pave the road leading to the Mount, so that walking be made less tiresome.

On the whole, ascent today is not unusally difficult, although there are still about a hundred steps to mount, of which many complain. Those responsible for the custodianship of the Mount do not heed these murmurings, prefering that the ascent be accompanied with difficulty rather than with upholstered ease. Reb Zanwill assures them that all things which are sacrosanct are acquired as a result of hardship Although the ascent seems to be at the expense of much physical endurance, yet it actually affords much spiritual relief and satisfaction. He is fond of unfolding the following story in this connection. It once happened that a visitor to the Mount complained bitterly and with resentment, of the difficulties he had encountered in reaching the top. He approached Reb Zanwill and poured forth a pitcherful of complaints on those who made such ascents so difficult as to almost be back-breaking.

Reb Zanwill saw that his complainant was neither an invalid nor inferior in any way, but simply one who was cradled in luxury and spoke with arrogance. So he retorted quietly, without any show of displeasure, that as he was only one of the countless throngs who constantly climb up, he saw no reason why he should complain above all others.

Not being satisfied with this reasoned reply, he continued his complaint, even with added arrogance. "What others do, does not concern me at all. They may be used to hardship, whereas I am not. The only place where I walk is in my own house, and a car is ever waiting for me outside to travel elsewhere. Whereas here, I had to make my way, climbing wearily on foot, a burden too heavy for my body."

Laughingly, Reb Zanwil replied: "It is not your body that weighs heavily on you, for all bodies are about equal in every respect. It is your heart that is too heavy for you and which weighs you down like a heavy stone. My advice to you is to break it into smithereens, so that your ascent will become an easy matter." The man looked upon Reb Zanwill with eyes of wonder that sought for an explanation. It was

116

then that the latter related to him the story of the stone.

The entire area of the Temple was once strewn with large stones. When King David wished to clear the site for the erection thereon of the Temple, he hired laborers to do so. This work proved too difficult for them, so they, were forced sighingly, to give it up. Then David addressed them thus: "First break up the massive stones into smaller blocks, and then their removal will present no difficulty." They did so, with the result that they successfully cleared away the entire area.

THE YOM KIPPUR LIGHT OF THE MARTYRS

The old-established Jewish custom of kindling a Yahrzeit light on the eve of Yom Kippur in memory of the martyrs — each household commemorating its own personal tragedy — has assumed a deep legendary significance in our own day. Especially widespread is this custom among those who luckily escaped the fatal effects of the Nazi holocaust.

Reb Zanwill, who is responsible for the setting-up of the "Holocaust Chamber", on Mount Zion, has done his best to propagate this kindling of the Yahrzeit light on Yom Kippur, supplying it with the additional meaning of a mystic nuance. This is the belief which is current in Mount Zion circles that the holy martyrs descend from on High on Yom Kippur, in order to participate in the prayers of the worshippers and especially in those of their near and dear ones praying in the Synagogue. Accordingly, each Yahrzeit light serves as a beacon to the departed martyrs, to illumine their way earthwards. Many are those who piously believe that their own dear departed parents and relatives in whose memory the lights are kindled, participate with them as a result of their action, in their petitions on the most solemn Jewish day of the year.

The records kept in the "Holocaust Chamber" tell the sad story of Flora who could not restrain her tears on the night of Yom Kippur, as she thought of her mother who had entered eternal life through the hellish flames of the Auschwitz Crematoria. During her first year in Israel, where she had come to settle, Flora came to worship in the Synagogue attached to the "Holocaust Chamber on Mount Zion; for the Kotel Ha'Ma'ravi was still in Jordanian hands. She could not understand why the "Horror Chamber" was ablaze with so many flickering candles on this holy night. So, turning to the friends who had brought her hither, she asked them to explain the reason. Her grief was intensified when they told her of the current belief that these candles illumine the way of the martyrs who descend from Heaven in order to pray with their dear ones on earth on the Day of Atonement. How she longed, once again, though in a dream, to behold the face of her dear mother to whom she had been dedicated body and soul during her lifetime and from whose pious memory even the Angel of Death could not sever her ! She was especially grieved to feel that whereas the departed mothers of all those who had kindled lights in advance of their coming would join their children, her mother would be absent from her and all because she had, though totally ignorant and unaware, failed to light the commemorative, guiding candle. Even if her mother should descend earthwards, the absence of this pilot-light would cause her to go astray and wander off in the darkness, far away from the place where her daughter was pouring out her soul to her Heavenly Father.

Having been estranged from the Jewish way of life for many years, Flora was not aware of the fact that a Jew is forbidden to kindle a light on Yom Kippur, as he also is on Shabbat. Her first instinct was to light a candle there and then, on Yom Kippur. When she was about to turn her thought into action, she was deterred from doing so by the concerted loud cries of those around her: "Yom Kippur! Yom Kippur! One is forbidden to kindle lights on this Holy Day!" At this, Flora burst out crying and left the small crowded Synagogue adjoining the "Horror Chamber", piteously sobbing her heart out.

When she arrived home, she fell on her bed, tearfully beseeching her

118

departed mother to come to her despite her ignorance and innocence in not having kindled a light in her memory. As she was thus sobbing and praying, she felt sure of her mother's forgiveness. Had she not always readily forgiven her when she had mistakenly erred and pleaded for pardon? Yet fear gripped her heart, lest her mother should not find her way to her because of the unlit path which led to her daughter's presence. At this thought, her tears fell more heavily than ever, bedewing everything she wore with her weeping.

Flora's mother, however, did answer her prayers; for she visited her in a vision that night, with a beaming face. Flora's joy at the sight of her dear mother was indescribable. Leaping out of bed in her dream, she clung to her mother and embraced her, as if nothing could ever separate them again one from the other.

Addressing her mother, she said: "I knew you would come! But how did you find where I was, since I had not illumined your path for you?" Her mother replied: "You need not have entertained any fears, my dear one, of my losing my way in the darkness; for your tears kindled a legion of lights to show me my path to your whereabouts. See how your tear-bedewed clothes and bed, wet with your weeping, have been converted into myriads of blazing stars, all beckoning me on down a trail of light to you! Who could lose their way with so many sparkling and shining lights leading them on?"

THE MISSING WILLOW

The halacha prescribes that the Mitzvah of Lulav and Ethrog can only be fulfilled with the presence of not less, and not more, than the four species of Ethrog, Lulav, myrtles and willows. To diminish or to add from that number is to violate the biblical law which prescribes "You shall not add, nor diminish thereof". The story I am about to narrate happened in the concentration Camp of Birknau during the Sukkot festival of 1943, when R. Ezekiel permitted, as a temporary measure only, the use of only three of the species. This is what happened.

With the approach of Ellul, the pious inmates of the camp began to be anxious about acquiring the Arba Minim. Despite the tortures and cares attending camp-life, they sought meticulously to observe even those precepts occasioned by time. They did not rest and spared no cost to obtain secretly an Ethrog and Lulav, and even the myrtles, but not the willow. But they did not worry about this, as willows grew in abundance around the camp.

Erev Sukkot, the three other kinds reached them. The myrtles were not of the best kind, as was demanded in the Torah. In ordinary years, they would not have regarded them as legally valid, but in their plight they rejoiced with them as those who light upon unexpected treasures. After all, with no possibility of a Sukkah, they had, at least, the Arba Minim.

Imagine their grief the next morning, when they discovered that the willow was missing from the Lulav. What happened was that R. Moses, whose task it was to obtain the willows locally, was arrested that very morning and sent to the furnace of the camp to be burnt. None knew exactly what had happened. The fact remained that there was no willow. All the money and effort they had self-sacrificingly spent in obtaining the Four Species, were in vain. The Mitzvah had practically been snatched from their hand.

While they were sunk in a painful dilemma as to what to do in such a contingency, R. Ezekiel comforted them : "Why are you so perplexed? Why you do not take the Lulav and recite the blessing?". They showed him the missing willow. He then raised his voice loudly, saying :

"Is it only the willow that is missing to you ? Have you then a Sukkah? Have you "the joy of the festival" which is prescribed ? Have you wine and hallot for Kiddush ? Why, then, make such a lament over a missing willow ? Take the three species you have and fulfill the command but minus a blessing. The Almighty will accept this as if you had fulfilled the precept in every detail. You cannot be expected to

120

achieve the impossible. Besides, God exempts from punishment those who are compelled not to fulfil a command. Are we then not doing our best to do everything humanly possible?"

Acting on his decision, he set the example and took the Lulav and the Two Species in his hand and performed the ceremony of shaking them to all the four sides around him, all the time assuring them of the talmudic principle that "he who comes to do a pious act, is helped from Heaven towards its fulfillment". Yet, the pious in the camp still had doubts whether it was right so to do.

Whereupon R. Ezekiel tried again to appease their doubts. "I will explain to you the reason of my decision. There are some rabbinic teachers who seek to explain the precepts with the reason for doing them.

Actually, their fulfilment does not rest on reasons. We mortals will never be able to fathom reasons for all the duties which the Torah commands us to do. Actually, what matters it *why* we do it? Is not the important thing that we *do* it? Take the Four Species which the Rabbis say reflect the four kinds of Jew. The Ethrog, which has taste and fragrance, resembles those who combine a knowledge of Torah with pious deeds. The Lulav which has taste (in its fruit) but no fragrance, reflects those who practice kindness but do not study Torah. The myrtles which have fragrance but no taste, correspond to those who study but do not perform kind deeds, and the willows which have neither taste nor fruit, reflect those Jews who neither study nor perform good deeds. Now tell me, why do we need willows here ? To reflect the thousands who neither study nor act kindly?

At this reasoning, all doubts, even those of the ultra-pious, were appeased and peace came to their troubled conscience.

THE RING OF THE KING

Many are those who stood before the Tomb, praying with eyes wet with tears. Tears are good in the efficacy of prayers. It once happened that Reb Zanwill was praying with his disciples and noticed them weeping. At first, they seemed abashed when discovered crying, so in order to reassure them that they were doing the right thing, he related to them he story of the Ring.

"Once upon a time, there was a powerful monarch who possessed a son that was most precious to him. He removed the ring from his hand and gave it to his son, telling him that : "This ring is a key with which you will be able to open all closed gates and, before it, all bolts will be kept open. The heavy locks and chains which guard treasures as well as prisons and warehouses will all open their gates before your Open Sesame — the ring."

His son took the ring and hid it in his safe keeping. Days passed, and the prince committed a crime for which he was placed in prison. There he suffered very much and constantly appealed for an amnesty. So grievous was his crime, however, that the judges who had sentenced him to a long term of imprisonment, remained impervious to his pleas for release from prison.

He kept on sending messages to his royal father, appealing for mercy. The answer the King gave to the messenger was: "What does he want of me? Have I not placed in his possession a miraculous ring just for this purpose ? Let him try it at the prison gates and he will succeed in ecaping from the prison."

When the prince heard this reply, the memory of the ring flashed upon him. He took it out of the place where it was hidden and where it had accumulated much dust and rust after all these years of safe concealment. Taking the key excitedly in his hand, he essayed again and again to open with it the doors of his cell but alas, with no success. His heart broke within him and he began to weep, the tears falling without stop on the ring. The result of this soaking which the

122

ring now received was miraculous; for it washed it thoroughly and cleansed if of all the dust and rust it had accumulated.

The royal prisoner took the ring in his hand a second time to try his luck again — and then the miracle happened : The Gates of the prison stood open. It was the Tears which brought about this miracle. The moral ? The Psalms are the royal Ring. It is also the Book most extensively used on the Mount. There, it is to be found in every corner and recourse to it is had at every given opportunity, both in moments sad or gay. This Book is their food ration, metaphorically speaking, and is the pearl of the royal scriptures. It is a pearl fashioned out of the pure and warm tears of the messianic King David. All those who are connected with this Mount, however tenuous this link may be, whether as active workers thereon, or just "friends" who assist its activities from without, consider it as their primary duty to recite several Psalms daily. Those who pray at the Tomb and recite the Psalms, of which he was the inspired author, wholeheartedly believe that this chanting of the Psalms will remove from them all tribulations and harsh decrees. They sincerely believe that David has only to decree, and God will have no other option than to confirm They implicity believe that it is within the power of David to "sweeten harsh judgments, to avert evil decrees, and to convert for good the prayers of those who stand before his sepulchre chanting his Psalms. The elders of the Mount foster this belief and bind crowns around its power, dedicating a special night, which they designate by the name of "The Night of the Seal." This night is the night of Hoshana Rabba.

Lest you ask : "Wherein does David differ from all other saints and patriarchs of our nation?", then let me explain.

On the night of Hoshana Rabba, the men of the Mount usually assembled in the Sukkah on the Mount, where they twice concluded the Book of Psalms, starting from the first Psalm. As there are 150 in the Book, this twofold repetition totalled up to 300 — the numerical value of the Hebrew word for a village (Kfar). Having read the Psalms twice, their night vigil in the Sukkah is entwined with the specially-prescribed order of service arranged for this night. When the whole Order was completed, sleep began to make them drowsy.

Among the company was an old man. When he saw one of the assembly drop his head and his eyes to close, he gave him a flick with his middle-finger in order to avert him from falling asleep. He would accompany this action by addressing those present: "Have you seen a man who was being tried in a court and falling asleep during the procedure? Of course not. How could he do so, seeing that fear is tugging at his heart, his hand trembling, his joints stricken at the course his trial would eventually take? Instead of falling asleep, he would be conducting an intense search of creed and deed, and would tirelessly hunt for qualified and persuasive defendants to plead his cause favorably before the judges, so that he might emerge from the Court free and innocent. So what place can be found for sleep and diversion at a time like this?

When the company felt that this old man was in a mood to reason with them, they surrounded him with questions in tone with the mood "What is the meaning of a "Slip of Paper" (Petek) used in connection with Hoshana Rabba ? What is the association of this day with the trial said to be held thereon, seeing that the judgments of life or death of every child on earth have already been sealed on Yom Kippur?"

To these questions, the old man replied: "Do not ply me with questions which are in the realm of the mysterious. Why seek to enter the secret domains of heaven? Besides, I know as much, or as little, about these things as any other man on earth; but I know a story that I once heard from a wise man when I was but a raw youth."

When they heard that he had a story to unfold, all became wide awake : they turned themselves in the direction of the old man and gave their ear to what he was about to tell them. The old man began

124

his omission and commission. Determine that you will not repeat, in the Temple still stood, those who came to Jerusalem from the Golah immediately directed their gaze towards the courtyard of the Temple and began to utter praises, saying : "I rejoiced when they said : "Let us go to the House of the Lord, to Jerusalem, the rebuilt, as a city all connected together ?" When they reached Mt. Zion, they found the place strewn with thrones. Why thrones? As they were still wondering at the presence of so many thrones, the Judges that comprised the Court of David emerged from their rooms and ensconced themselves on these thrones, all set to pass in judgment those arraigned before them. When they beheld this scene, all the festival pilgrims assembled there, burst forth into song : "For these were placed the thrones for the seats of judgment, thrones for the House of David".

Those songs also told that it once happened that among the festival pilgrims there was a young man who joined the procession wending their way to Mt. Zion. When he came to the top, an old man approached him and, fixing him with sad eyes, said : "My son, I am rather worried about you, for I noticed as you climbed up that your sadow was missing. We have a tradition that one who is bereft of his shadow on the night of Hoshana Rabba has cause to be worried. You ask why? So let me tell you.

"You will remember it being written in the Torah that when our ancestors in the wilderness were under the impression that they were impregnable against attack by enemies, they said : "Their shadow is removed." Hearing this explanation, the young man cast a backward glance and found that the old man was correct. His shadow seemed obliterated, shrunk in size almost to less than half of its usual proportions and certainly unlike the shadows of the others.

When the old man noticed that the youth began to fret, he tried to calm him. "Listen to me," he said. "Instead of being so worried, make your resolution at once to return to God in perfect remorse and manifest, in a practical shape, your regret at having been guilty of sins of

125

omission and commission. Determine that you will not repeat, in the future, your sins in the past."

The young man turned to him pleadingly: "I wholeheartedly promise to abide by your advice." Having said this, he was asked by the old man to follow him to a corner of the Mount. When they reached the spot the old man said: "Let us now pour out our supplications before our Father in Heaven by reciting together some of the Psalms composed by King David."

When they had finished reciting the Psalms, the old man led his young companion to one of the judges of the Court of King David. There his elder guide declared before the Judge: "This man has determined to make complete repentance." On hearing this statement, the Judge immediately handed him a slip of paper on which was inscribed in Hebrew block letters the words of the Psalmist: "Let there be peace in your rampart and prosperity in your palaces."

The old man then gladly turned to his young companion and assured him: "My son, happy and lucky are you that you have emerged from the trial innocent and that the decrees originally issued against you have now been totally rescinded and reworked."

The young man could hardly believe his ears. He urged the other to tell him how does he know all this. The reply he received was: "This has been handed down to those faithful in their minute and meticulous observance of Jewish precepts and who are afforded glimpses into the realm hidden from most human pilgrims on earth. But this judge is one of those select few who can pierce the veil screening the future from the present. When a Jew comes to this place, full of remorse and wishing sincerely to repent, imploring the assistance and patronage of King David, his sins are immediately forgiven him; even if his judgment and punishment have already been sealed on Yom Kippur. His evil decree is rescinded and torn up and he emerges an innocent man with a clean slate in his hands. This slip in your hand is a certificate of the King of David and bears the authority and validity of royalty. "Lest you ask: 'Why was David vested with the power of converting

guilt to innocence and obtaining pardon for those who seek his aid?"
Well, let me try to explain : "This is in order to teach mankind how
great the power of genuine repentance is; that even if a man has already been sentenced to death, good deeds and repentance have the
power to render this sentence null and void. It also teaches that "he
who says: 'David himself sinned, is only uttering an error. For the
real fact is, as we see in the Bible, that as soon as David said to Nathan
the prophet "I have sinned unto the Lord," he was immediately forgiven.

It is also told that when the son of Bat-Sheva, David's child, died,
Satan came to David and provoked him to anger by taunting him
thus : "Is it possible for one who is held in the greatest reverence as
King and Messiah to plead mercy for his child to be spared from death
— and not to be answered"?

David remained silent at this attempt to put him to shame. It was then
that the Heavenly Angels took up his cause above. They pleaded before God : "Can this despicable creature be allowed to bring the blush
of shame on to the face of God's annointed, while we remain silent?"
They pleaded before God and He told them to allay their anger. "I
will appease the mind of people not to express anxiety over the fate
of My annointed. All will then acknowledge that "My servant rules
over them as King".

God assured David that he will be King on earth just as God is King
in Heaven; just as He is judge in Heaven, so will David be judge on
earth and given the authority to be judge and defense consel of those
pleading before him for mercy. All who repent will have their judgment passed on Yom Kippur, if it be for evil it will be transformed into
good. This belief gave rise to the name allotted to Hoshana Rabba as
the day of "Slips" given to those who repent. So when one observes that
his shadow is curtailed on the night of Hoshana Rabba, he shall imme-
diatelly repair to the Mount and there he will receive forgiveness. And
not only is this on Hoshana Rabba, but every day are repentance and
the Psalms operative. They are the royal ring which can burst open

all locks and break all bars. Happy is the man who possesses this lucky Ring.

THE BEATEN HOSHANNA

One of the main purposes of Rabbi Zanwill's vigilance of the Horror Vault on Mount Zion, in which are preserved relics of the Nazi Holocaust which cost six million innocent Jewish lives, is to keep alive in the heart of the Jew the dangers involved in living amidst alien, hostile surroundings and the necessity to be identified with the sorrow as well as with the joy of others. In his many public and written utterances, he has emphasized this lesson adding in his own mystical way, that he who performs a Mitzvah (a good and pious deed) must himself become the incarnation af the deed which he performs. Thus, the Hassid who could not pray, was himself transformed into prayer.

Thus, Rabbi Joelish, who was unable to fulfil the Mitzvah of Mishlo'ah Manot (Gifts) on Purim while in the Nazi concentration camp, regarded his imprisonment in the crematoria of the infamous Auschwitz concentration-camp as his Mishlo'ah Manot to the Almighty. Similarly, when Rabbi Jacob was doomed to the hellish fires of the camp, at the advent of Hanukkah, he regarded himself as the Hanukkah Candle prescribed to be kindled during that "Festival of Lights". This was the theme of Rabbi Zanwill whenever he spoke or wrote about the Holocaust. A similar theme did he observe in the story of the beaten Hoshana used on the seventh day of Sukkot, to symbolize the shedding of our sins by a merciful, heavenly Father. The beaten Hoshana, he identified with the pitiful, maimed survivors, who were rescued from the hellish and infamous Birkenau Concentration Camp and from the Barrack numbered 231.

Sukkot, 5703, found the inmates of Birkenau in a most desperate position. With the exception of an isolated few, the others were not

128

even aware of the procession and pageant of the colourful Jewish year, which paraded in the free Jewish world without. Even the few who did realize the advent of Sukkot, were not able to observe it even in the slightest degree. It was their sadistic Nazi tormentors who knew full well that Jews the world over observed their Sukkot at this season and who decided to impose upon their victims, throughout the eight days of the festival, extra menial and degrading duties. They were made to run around the camp, while being chased by wild, madly-barking dogs only too ready to spring at them at the bidding of their cruel task-masters. In addition, they were constantly lashed with whips which lacerated and bruised their bodies mercilessly. The result was that many fainted after such inhuman treatment. On Hoshana Rabba and Simhat Torah, when seven circuits are made around the Bimah with the Willow-twigs and the Scrolls of the Torah, respectively, they were ordered by their sadistic overlords to run round the camp seven times, the target of maddened dogs and beasts in human from. One of the Gestapo leaders happened to be familiar with Jewish traditional customs and knew all about the seven Hakkafot on the last two days of the Sukkot festival. It was he who organized these devilish manoeuvres. Addressing the tortured inmates on the eve of the Sukkot festival, he sarcastically told them : "I have made all arrangements that you observe the seven Hakkafot both on your Hoshana Rabba and Simhat Torah."

Seven times were they ordered to run around the camp, at the mercy of the wild dogs and human beasts. When they fell in a dead faint as a result, the Gestapo Commander ordered that ice-cold water be showered upon them, to arouse them. When they opened their eyes, they were greeted with the sarcastic, sardonic tones of this Gestapo Commander who addressed them thus : "You can be happy now, for you have observed your traditional Hakkafot".

How they managed to force a smile to appear on their bleeding faces above their bruised bodies, will always remain a puzzle. One of them, Rabbi Ezekiel by name, was in a special, joyful mood. Bleeding and bruised from head to foot, all his teeth knocked out, his fingers cut off, with not a sound limb in his entire body, he even began to sing and dance for joy when he was aroused from his faint by the showers of water. Those around him could hardly believe what he was chanting : "Thank God for having enabled us to celebrate Hoshana Rabba! At least, we were able to fulfill one Mitzvah connected with Sukkot!"

His fellow-inmates gazed at him with merciful looks, thinking to themselves that Ezekiel, poor soul, had lost his senses as a result of his tortures. Were they not themselves almost losing their wits as a result of the indescribable tortures to which they were subjected ? But Ezekiel had preceded them in succumbing to the inhuman treatment before they did, it appeared. They turned to him sympathetically, saying in bitter tones : "Yes ! We have fulfilled the Mitzvah of Hak-kafot. A curse on the heads of our persecutors !"

Actually, Rabbi Ezekiel was far from having lost his senses ! On the contrary, he was perfectly aware of the implications of his assurances to the room in which he sat, surrounded by his relatives, all sad on account of the bruises he had suffered. He explained to them exactly what he meant to convey.

He had been aware during the entire ordeal they had been forced to undergo that it was Sukkot and he thought to himself. "If only I could observe one of the many Mitzvot which adorn Sukkot ! Oh, for the possession of an Etrog and Lulav ! Oh, for the erection of a Sukkah ! But our cruel torturers have well seen to it that we are debarred from observing any of the tenets or fragrant customs of our Faith." He continued : "Early this morning, Hoshana Rabba, I searched for a twig of the willow in order to fulfil at least one of the Mitzvot of Sukkot :"As if in answer to my despair and prayers,this wicked Gestapo leader burst in upon me, hurling me round seven times and beating me sevenfold, as we do on Hoshana Rabban with our willow-twigs. As he was torturing me, my lips mumbled the seven poems (Piyutim) we recite at each of the seven circuits with the Lulav and Etrog on Sukkot. But fortune was against me even in this quest. I was plunged

130

in sorrow all the seven days of the festival as a result," he added.
Continuing, he then spoke to his admiring but amazed fellow
sufferers: "When he finished throwing me around and beating me
mercilessly, he left me lying on the ground, as you see me now, a
beaten Hoshana!"

"I am filled with joy, despite the fact that no part of my body remains
whole. I have been transformed into the incarnation of a Mitzvah
of the Torah. And how much greater is the achievement itself!
What greater achievement is there possible for the Jew than to
be himself embodied into one of the six hundred and thirteen Mitzwot?
"Cannot you see in me a symbol?" he concluded, "of the beatings
that take place in one of the hellish death-chambers of the beastly
concentration camp?"

Those who heard this story from Rabbi Ezekiel's dying lips will never
forget its implications as long as the breath of life within then lasts.

THE FLASK

It is the custom on Mount Zion, on the tenth of the month of Teveth,
to place before the Vases containing the Human Ashes in the Chamber
of the Holocaust, a flask of water wrapped in a white cloth, embroidered with a Magen David, as a sign of mourning. This custom,
which is found in one of the little directives of the Talmud relating
to the dead and to mourners, was introduced to Mount Zion by Rabbi
Mendel on the tenth of the month of Teveth. The Director permitting
this after he had heard the story of Yitzhak, the Gravedigger, from
the lips of Rabbi-Mendel himsel,

Yitzhak worked in the "Hevrah Kadisha" of his birth-place, the town
of Kresnig, assisting in the funeral ceremonies of the Jewish community
there. He looked on his work as a sacred mission, one of the most
holy vocations which a Jew could have.

The time came when the death-trains brought him to Auschwitz and

131

the uniformed murderers before whom he stood. He was told that he must pass before the "Selection Committee". He was brutally questioned about his profession; and when, in all simplicity, he answered. "Grave-digger", he caused roars of ribald laughter among them? Am I not, myself a beaten willow-twig, cast away after we have made the prescribed ritual use of it? It is for this reason, that I was assigned to a party of gravediggers who were inclined to congratulate themselves as privileged, because they would surely come very far down on the list of candidates for extermination ! At first, Reb Yitzhak was truly happy to feel that even here, in the hell of the Auschwitz camp, it would still be possible for him to go on with his mission of giving a reverent burial to the dead... But on the first day of his "work", when he was taken into the forest to bury in a vast common trench, thousands of men, women and children still alive, he was taken in by these Jews who had been mobilized by the Nazis for sobbing and moaning. An utterly simple, pious and unsophisticated Jew, what had been demanded of him was totally beyond his comprehension. It was with pathetic naivete that he went and reported to the Camp Commandant that he had "made a mistake". "I registered myself yesterday, as a Grave-digger", he said to the Commandant, "but I am afraid you have misunderstood me. I bury the Dead — not the Living... I cannot do such work. It is beyond me to manage such a thing..."

The brute shot at him a furious glance, rapped out a hideous oath and ordered the guards to thrash him with a hundred lashes, "to teach him how to get on with burying people alive !"

The guards laid hold of poor Yitzhak, and flogged him until he lost consciousness. Usually a man in that condition was thrown without more ado into the ovens of the crematorium, but with a fiendish refinement of cruelty they brought him back to life with several pails of cold water thrown over him. and then sent him back to his work-party of which they now put him in charge.

The unfortunate grave digger, feeling that the horror of it all would drive him mad, tried to throw himself against the live-wire of the electric fence which surrounded the camp, but the Germans knew how to beat him off. Then he went to ask help and counsel from Rabbi Shlomo, a most wise and pious Jew, who was with us in the camp. Reb Shlomo reminded Yitzhak, as he did all who sought his advice, that his first duty, above all others, was to keep alive.

To Live ! was the supreme commandment — to keep alive, in spite of everything, holding on against the monstrous Nazi evil...

So Reb Yitzhak went back to his place among the other gravediggers; but doing everything that was humanly possible to come to the aid of those who might still be spared. He buried the living in such a manner, that many of them were among those who succeeded in freeing themselves in the darkness of night, and fleeing into the neighbouring forests. It was thus that countless Jews were saved and owed their lives to Yitzhak, the gravedigger.

But for those other unfortunates whom he could not save, Reb Yitzhak performed a nostalgic little ceremony. As he could not light candles, he placed in the death-trenches a little flask of water, wrapped in a fragment of white cloth, as used to be the custom among gravediggers, to call forth men's mercy — pure water being a symbol of mercy. The Camp Guards wanted to know what these little bottles were all about, but when they had satisfied themselves that they only held water, they left Yitzhak alone.

When Reb Shlomo learnt about these things, he was filled with admiration at this resourcefulness of the gravedigger and called to mind that this custom was already common at the time of the Second Temple under the reign of the tyrant Antiochus, who had banned from the Jewish people their ceremony of the Marriage Canopy, hoping thus to mark the difference between the candles of the marriage lights and those of mourning which the Jews still lit in secret. And as this custom of the tiny flasks of water had come into being during a period of persecution, to outwit the oppressors, it was right, indeed, that it should now be restored to thwart the German Amaleks. It was

133

in this way that Reb Shlomo encouraged Yitzhak, the gravedigger, to persevere in his compassionate practice which took the place of lighting the candles of remembrance...

And ever since, on the initiative of Reb Mendel, a little flask filled with pure water and wrapped in a white cloth, embroidered with a Magen David, is placed before the Vases of Human Ashes in the Chamber of the Holocaust, on the tenth of the month of Tebeth, which is the day of Kaddish for the Martyrs the Special Prayers for the Righteous Dead.

THE FIRST REVOLT

The twenty-seventh day of Nisan has been proclaimed by the Knesset as the day of the Holocaust. Previous to this, the Chief Rabbinate had ordained that the Tenth of Tevet, one of the fast-days in the Jewish Year, should be the day of memorial. A compromise was reached between these two dates as follows : The Tenth of Tevet should be the day on which Kaddish should be said by the relatives of the martyrs who are unaware of the exact Yahrzeit of their death, whereas Nisan 27th should be kept as an anniversary on which to recall their heroism. As a further reason for choosing the latter date to commemorate their heroes, is the fact that it was in Nisan 5703 that the denizens of the Warsaw Ghetto made their remarkable stand against the murderous Nazis, a revolt as heroic as it is almost legendary. On Mt. Zion, which contains the burnt ashes of many victims of the camp, and gathered together in one grave to symbolize the six million victims, the commemoration on this day takes on a distinct form.

On Erev Pesah, the day when the Warsaw Ghetto began its revolt in 5703, the scholars of the Yeshivah on Mt. Zion, named after the beloved and sainly Rabbi of Warsaw at that time, Rabbi Shmuel David Kahana, begin to study the tractate Ta'anit. This was the decree made by the Warsaw Rabbi on the day of the revolt itself, though it was Erev Pesah when fasting and sadness are brushed aside. In the "Cellar of the Holocaust" on Mt. Zion, the torn, patched blue and white flag brought from Warsaw to Israel is spread over the grave of ashes. In the Warsaw Ghetto, this flag was the symbol that the revolt is to be regarded as of a national character, not just the whim and obstinacy of a few doughty spirits.

The torn-flag drapes the "Cellar" from Erev Pesah till Nisan 27th; that is during the duration of the Revolt in the ghetto in Warsaw. Reb Zanwill surrounds this draping of the flag with the air of a solemn occasion, when special Memorial Prayers are recited, Kinnot chanted and stories recounted of the outstanding heroism and matchless self-sacrifice displayed by those who waged this grim battle against overwhelming odds. The object of this ceremony, besides honouring the dead, is also intended to be the means of implanting the same Maccabean spirit into the youth of Israel, as it moved the stalwart Warsaw Ghetto Champions for freedom and liberty.

Where and when the first stand was made against the Nazis is unknown. It is difficult to ascertain precise details from the material of dates and facts extant in the archives of Mt. Zion. One opinion is that it all began in the townlet of Gablin, at the head of which was the leader of the community, R. Isaac.

It was during the first days of the gruesome deportations. Even then people knew already what these labour deportations meant, although they were called by grandiose names. One morning, the Gestappo of Gablin sent for R. Isaac, commanding him to place a few hundred Jews at their disposal the very next morning for forced labour. On hearing this, the Jewish leader's face turned all colours· for although he knew that this really meant, he was in a dillemma how to act. Shall he draw up a list himself of the victims and hand them into these bloody hands ? Or shall he risk the safety of the entire Jewish population of the townlet and simply refuse to grant them their request ? The thought of what to do in this predicament tortured him. Not knowing whither to turn first, he went into the Beth-Ha-midrash. Perhaps his friends there would be able to advise him; for his torment of mind did not give him any peace and his heart thumped with anxiety.

So sunk in perplexity, his eyes suddenly lighted upon R. Nathan, the ninety-year old Shammash of the old Rabbi. Yes, he would ask him how to solve his burning problem. Though his hearing and his speech were both very weak indeed, the old man narrated what he had heard sixty years ago from his Rabbi.

"In the story of the "Binding of Isaac" (Akedah), it is God Himself who commanded Abraham: "Take thy only son, Isaac"; whereas, when He stopped the actual sacrifice from taking place, the command was given through the agency of an angel. The moral ? When it comes to the sacrificing of even one individual, its implementation can only take place at the direct behest of God, even when the sacrifice is to be made for the glory of God Himself.

R. Isaac understood the implication. Placing himself before the open Ark, he put his problem before God. What shall he do? A whole night he waited silently and patiently before the open Ark, his face bathed in tears and his tongue speechless. It was said that Heaven had mercy on him and he was stricken with insanity, so that he should no longer be possessed of the faculty of reasoning and the torment of not knowing how to act in this case.

Next morning, the Nazis waited in the market-place for the labour deportation. The blood-hounds were all ready and so were the police. The carriage-doors of the long train were all opened wide to receive the victims. All was ready, except the victims themselves. The hour was late, and the labour deportation was long past its schedule.

The Gestapoo fumed and cursed. Their leader was mad with fury. It was the first time that these "cursed Jews" had failed to obey his command. What impudence ! Let them find R. Isaac ! They will teach him a lesson for being so intransigent. After a thorough search in all likely and unlikely places, they found him standing in an insane trance, a monolithic figure of a broken man in front of the open Ark where Scrolls of the Law stood arrayed in their majestic dignity.

136

"Cursed Jew", shouted the Gestapo leader, beside himself with fury. But R. Isaac remained dumb, as if he did not understand that he was being cursed and shouted at. He continued staring open-eyed inside the Ark with a vacant, distant smile on his blank face.

"He is dead", exclaimed the adjutant and began to point his revolver at R. Isaac. But his leader stopped him. "No, let him rather be hung", he advised. "But he is dead", the other demurred. The leader was adamant: "He must be hung".

Whereupon, two soldiers seized him and dragged him in *coram publico*, (in the sight of all the Jews) to the gallows. R. Isaac, though dead, was dragged, step by step, to his execution on the tree.

The Nazis wished to give the impression that they were hanging a normal man in full possession of his senses as a punishment for disobeying their command. He was suspended high above the gallows, a warning to all those who also thought of disobeying the Nazis.

IN MEMORY OF THE BURNT BOOKS

A few years ago, on an Erev Shabbat, Reb Zanwill arranged a Memorial Service in honour of the holy Scrolls of the Torah, and copies of the Talmud and Midrashim which, according to the dictate of Hitler, of cursed memory, were burnt wherever they were found. His out-to-out determination to destroy everything Jewish was of a bi-partite nature; that is, not only to destroy the Jewish body but also the Jewish soul and the sources from which it derived its sustenance. Accordingly, all books written by Jews, or that had Jewish substance, were commited to the flames.

After that service on the eve of Shabbat Hukkat, the Director regaled the worshippers with stories woven around those literary auto-da-fe's, which began 2,000 years ago when Epistomos first burnt Scrolls of the Law on the Seventeenth of Tammuz. Because such burnings have continued intermittently till our own days, and because the Director

137

equates the burning of a Sepher Torah with that of a human soul, he ruled that they also deserve Memoral Prayers to be recited at the anniversary of the day when they were committed to the devouring flames, and that they also merited the tearing of garments at the news of their destruction (Keriah). Moreover, the Sepher Torah is tantamount to the whole of the Jewish people because, in the 600,000 letters which it comprises, there is bound up the soul of each Jew. (The number of Jews who received the Torah at the Revelation on Mt. Sinai was also 600,000).

Explaining why he had chosen the eve of Shabbat when the parshah (section) Hukkat is read, as this sad anniversary, he told the following story: "The Magen Abraham (a famous commentator on Karo's Code) reports that pious men of olden times used to observe that day as one on which the Talmud and other books holy to Jews were confiscated to the flames which danced around wildly the large Parisian squares.

It was decided by the Rabbis of that time, R. Jehiel of Paris and R. Moses of Coucy not to observe the anniversary on the day of the month, as is usually the custom, but that it should pair with the parshah of the week during during which the catastrophe occurred. This decision was arrived at owing to the current tradition at that time that these Rabbis sent a messenger to heaven to ascertain whether anything could be done to abolish this outrageous decree of burning these holy books. The messenger came back with the sad news that the decree was categorical. He also reported that when he reached heaven, he heard the Torah being chanted in Hebrew, together with its corresponding (Targum) translation. The portion they happened to be reading was Hukkat and the translation of the first three Hebrew words (Ve'zot Hukkat Ha'Torah) in Aramaic was "Da gzerat Oraita". When he heard these words, the messenger at once realized that it was decreed in heaven (gzerah means "a decree") that the books should be burnt and that nothing could now be done to halt it. Hence it was decided that, for all times, the anniversary of these burnings should be kept during that week when the turn arrives for Hukkat to be read.

R. Zanwill stopped in his tale at this point, in order to remark : "A ve-ry strange story, indeed. Since when have our sages made it their custom to send up messengers to heaven in order to ask heaven whether decrees can be rescinded ? Jewish history is replete with decrees aimed at their extermination and yet, perhaps with the sole exception of the Ten Martyrs after the Bar Cochba revolt, no messengers were dispatched to heaven to revoke the evil decrees. So, in which way was the burning of the holy books in Paris different to all other Jewish sufferings ?"

Those who heard these questions agreed with him. Tears streamed from their eyes as they repeated these questions, one to another. When he saw that their appetite was whetted, he told then the tale he had heard from the lips of his father, the Rabbi of Warsaw. On that evening when the Nazis broke into his father's home and commanded that all the books in his extensive library be assigned to the roaring flames in the courtyard, the flames into which the books were hurled leaped skywards and illumined a large area around. In their mind's eye, they almost beheld the letters jumping from their context and flying about in the air around them.

Pained were the hearts of all those who beheld this tragic sight and all eyes were dim with tears. Those whose sufferings were well nigh un-bearable, were those whom the Nazis had marshalled and dragooned to carry out the most painful task of carrying down the thousands of books from their shelves and hurling them into the flames. They came afterwards to their beloved Rabbi and asked him to ask heaven to grant them pardon for having executed such a terrible decree. Should they have rather suffered death at the hands of those satanic beasts, rather than be the agents of committing sacred books to the fire ? It was then that the Rabbi of Warsaw told them the story of the messenger who was sent to heaven in the time of R. Jehiel of Paris to ascertain whether the decree could be rescinded.

After the decree that the Talmud should be burnt on account of its harbouring offensive statements against the dominant Christian faith, the King of France decreed that all the Jews in his domain should bring all the sacred Hebrew books in their possession to the priests in their vicinity. These would see to it that they were destroyed. Not to fulfill this decree, spelt certain death. One can imagine the grief and dismay which filled all Jewish hearts when this brutal order was published. What should they do ? Obey the order, or rather commit themselves to death ?

The Rabbis who were faced with this most difficult She'elah (problem), found it very hard to give a decisive answer; for they, also, did not know what was the right course of action to adopt in such circumstances. If the intention of the decree was to make Jews change their belief for the dominant one, then it was surely a question of "let me rather be put to death than transgress a cardinal biblical command-ment." But should the intention only be to cause untold suffering and even the death sentence, then it was a clear case of "saving a life" (pikkuah nephesh); and the books could be burnt, rather than their lives be endangered. But who could fathom for certain what exactly their intentions were? So it was not at all easy to make a categorical decision, or give a definite reply.

On the eve of the final day for the implementation of the decree, a large assembly of Rabbis and representative Jews met in the great synagogue, in order to arrive at some definite course of action. Should they be martyred for the faith, or should they hand over the books ? Grief was on every face and anxiety tugged at every heart-string. The Rabbis themselves were perplexed and helpless to arrive at the correct solution. In the midst of their perplexity, R. Jehiel advised that they should stop their discussion for a brief while in order to hold the Ma'ariv Service. Perhaps a solution might be vouchsafed them from heaven during that service ! He asked an old friend of his, R. Meshul-lam, a man of mystic bent, to act as the Hazzan. Of R. Meshullam, it was rumoured, that his prayers burst open the locked gates of heaven. None could have fulfilled this task that solemn evening more, than did R. Meshullam. He prayed with "trembling love", while the sobs burst

140

from his broken heart and the tears streamed from his aching eyes. He swayed the whole congregation with his heartfelt devotion. The prayers of the assembly were transported heavenwards and flapped against the closed doors of prayer in the celestial regions. When R. Meshullam came to the verse : "Who is like unto Thee among the gods (elim), O Lord", he changed the word elim to ilmim (the dumb) "Who is like unto Thee, O G-D, among those who remain silent ?" Hearing this change of word, the congregation raised a cry in correction — elim, not ilmim; but he did not heed their correction. He fell in a dead swoon which lasted for some time. When he recovered, all he could do was to mumble the rest of the service, pronouncing the words in a most incoherent manner.

After the service, he went into the private room of Rabbi Jehiel and told him what had happened during the service. His soul had left his body during the service and had soared into the heavenly realms. The united prayers of that emotional congregation had transported his soul and had brought it direct before the Throne of Glory. He then begged Heaven to rescind the decree awaiting its fulfilment on the morrow, but he maintained a solemn silence. The cries which winged their way from earth did not seem to move them to any definite action. His question: "What shall we do?", remained unanswered. All he met with on the part of the angelic host was a blank stare and a studied silence.

It was then that he burst forth "Who is like unto Thee, among the silent (ilmim) ones, O Lord ?" As soon as he burst forth with this protest, his soul was hurtled down earthwards and it was the impact of his fall to earth that had caused him to swoon. "But as I was being hurtled down to earth", continued R. Meshullam, "I heard them reciting the Torah, twice in Hebrew and once in the Targum (Aramaic) and the portion read was Hukkat. The Torah suffers with Israel and echoes all its trials and tribulations; thus if one is burnt, the other suffers a similar fate. This is the unalterable, irrevocable decree of the Torah." When he had finished his tale, R. Jehiel said to him, with a trembling

141

heart: "My friend, since you have heard heaven's decree, it will be your sad task to carry these books to the flames". R. Meshullam gladly undertook this solemn assignment and R. Jechiel told the people to bring all their books to R. Meshullam, at whose hands the cruel decree would be implemented.

From door to door, did he go to collect all the holy books and place them on the large waggons which the ruling powers had assembled for that purpose. They were taken to a forest outside Paris, as he did not wish to hand them over directly into the hands of the persecutors. On his way, however, he was caught and he and the wagon-loads were dragged to the hellish fires that were roaring away in the Paris square and cast into the flames. From the flames, both a remarkable sight could be seen and a miraculous melody could be heard. The sight was that the letters left their context and flew about in the air. And the melody ? The tuneful voice of R. Meshullam, cheerfully reciting the words of the Ma'ariv prayer "Who is like unto Thee, among the silent ones (ilmim) ᴜ, Lord ?

THE LONG LIST

Among the ashes of the burnt martyrs that are deposited in the Holocaust Chamber on Mt. Zion, is also to be found the burnt remains of "the Long List" which went up in fire at the termination, of Shabbat Nahamu (after Tisha B'Av). The burning, interwined taper used in the Havdalah ceremony, performed after three stars in the sky have proclaimed that the Shabbat has gone and a new working-week has begun, was applied to it and it went up in flames. What is meant here by "The Long List"? The answer was given to Reb. Zanwill by R. Mendel who brought his this "Long List". It all happened in the month of Tammuz in the year 5703, in one of the cells of the Auschwitz concentration camp. In this cell, one of its hapless inmates was R. Jeruham, a grandson of the

142

renowned Rimanov Hasidic dynasty. It was he who used to arrange clandestinely the service for Shabbat, unnoticed by the vigilant eyes of their Nazi task-masters.

On the Shabbat on which the section of the Torah Balak is read, and of which the Haftarah is from the Book of Micah (V. 6. — VI. 8) in which the latter asks: "My people, what have I done unto you and wherein have I wearied you ? Do testify against Me."

R. Jeruham stopped the Reader, as he chanted these words, saying : "Since God asks us to tell Him why we have alienated ourselves from Him, then let us, by all means, tell Him. Does He not implore us so to do?" Having said this, R. Jeruham extracted "a long list" of complaints indited on a scrap of paper and began to read it.

"Here is what you have done, Blessed be Thy· Name; for nothing occurs in this world of ours without your consent and fiat. Take the case of Abraham — the first Jew and founder of our monotheistic faith. Soon after his mother gave birth to him and whilst still a child, he was cast into a dark cellar where he was compelled to be hidden for ten years in order to escape the clutches of Nimrod's Gestappo. When he was finally caught, he was ordered to be cast into a fiery furnace from which he miraculously escaped by a hair's breadth, after having undergone acute suffering entailed in being incarcerated there.

"History repeated itself in the case of his only son Isaac, the pinion of love which dropped into the lap of parenthood when Abraham was a hundred and Sarah ninety years old. As a mere youth, he was at Your command O God, bound on the altar ready to be sacrificed. Jacob, his son and his children, You exiled into Egypt, where they remained subjected to a cruel bondage for 400 years, as it is recorded in our Bible : "And they enslaved them and afflicted them for 400 years". True, you released us from Egyptian tyranny to the accompaniment of plagues on the taskmasters and miracles for the released, for which relief we thank You to this day, O Heavenly Father, but let us not be oblivious of the truth. Only a fifth of

143

their numbers managed to escape (a play on the Hebrew word Va'Hamushim which, instead of its usual rendering "armed", is here meant to convey "a fifth", by a play on the double meaning of the word). The other four-fifths spent their earthly existence in the land of serfdom.

"Then came Moses — the agent of Divine redemption and the one who scaled Sinai's fire-capped heights in order to bring down to the world Heaven's Magna Carta to civilization, who is known as Israel's greatest prophet. When he came with a cry into this world, his mother Jochebed was compelled to conceal the babe's whereabouts for three whole months in a dark cellar of the house, so that his cries be not heard by Pharaoh's Gestappo. When his hiding-place became suspected, his mother had no other alternative in an attempt to save him than by letting him float in some haphazard, fragile, wicker-work cradle in the Nile, there to be buffeted about by the waves, until he would he picked-up by some merciful Egyptian passer-by.

"But why continue the list? Are not the names therein legion? Here are just a few more : Nebuzaradon, Antiochus, Hannah and her seven children, Titus, Nebuchadnezzar, Haman, the Spanish inquisition, the Crusades, the Chmelinitzki Pogroms, Petlura, and so on and so forth. The list is endless, stretching from the dim past to our own day and age, from Pharaoh to Hitler, from Nasser to Gadafi and Amin.   —

"To come down to earth. Please do not suspect me, O God, of lodging a protest against Your direction of history. As a devout Jew, I affirm that all You do is for the best, in the final analysis. This may be true of what happened to our ancestors in past generations. But can Your judgment be honestly stated to be righteous now, in view of the sufferings borne by millions of Your "chosen people" in the hellish concentrations camps? Look down from heaven on the concentration camps and their barbarous machinations, at our forced labour and endless route-marches, the devilish gas-chambers, and

144

so on and so forth. Look at what You are forcing us to endure now. You have asked through the mouth of Micah, Thy prophet, for us to "Testify" against you as to the reason why we have estranged ourselves from Your service. Well, I am now heeding your request and telling you some of our complaints".

Having finished this indictment against Heaven, he raised his "long list" of complaints skywards and enumerated the endless plagues, tortures and persecutions that had been mercilessly inflicted on the Jewish people since mankind was still in its swaddling-clothes. Moereover, since the Holy One is the High Priest over all the High Priests on earth, is it not His paramount duty to examine all the various ailments brought for His inspection ? R. Jeruham's list came to be known as "the List of Plagues".

R. Yeruham raised his "Long List" high and asked the Prophet Micah to deliver its contents to the Lord of the Universe in answer of His challenge — "Testify against Me !" Whether he acted wisely by this response to the Divine challenge, no one can declare with any assurance. Neither are they prepared to declare categorically that Micah delivered his message to the appropriate address. Pious people, however, are convinced that the Prophet complied with R. Yeruham's request. Why ? Because not long after this impressive incident, the blood-bath instituted by the diabolical Nazis, beasts in human form, began to run dry. But from the burnt ashes of the six million in the crematoria, Medinat Israel arose, Phoenix-like, an event which won the concensus of opinion that it marked" the beginning of Israel's long-awaited Messianic Age."

R. Mendel brought this "Long List" to the Holocaust Chamber on Mt. Zion, wherein are deposited the ashes of the six million martyrs and which has become the rallying-point of thousands of worshippers, all tearfully recalling, recollecting. and sobbingly recounting the tales of self-sacrifice and heroic endurance of those who suffered hell on earth.

When Reb. Mendel brought this long indictment list to Reb Zanwill, with the request that he display it in everlasting memory and abiding respect of our people's suffering, the latter became pale and fear seized him at the very thought of so doing. He reasoned within his own heart: "Is is right to display such an indictment of "God's sins" against His people? Would it not constitute a sort of sacrilege, a blasphemy against the Holy Name?"

After much consultation with many distinguished Rabbis and celebrated leaders in the realm of education, he was advised to bury the list, just as pages from Holy Books are buried in graves and to deposit it together with the ashes of the martyrs. He was about to do so, but then he thought otherwise. No, he would send the list back to R. Yeruham and tell him that God had taken note of its contents and had decided to atone for the sufferings He had heaped upon His people. As compensation, He would hasten the approach of the age of Redemption. Is it not a fact that we, of this generation, have already been privileged to detect the first rays of salvation? This was the plan of action that Rebi Zanwill had in mind. R. Yitzhak, his disciple, thought otherwise. Instead of depositing the "List" with the urns of ashes kept in perpetual memory in the Holocaust Chamber, he took the paper on which the list of accusations against Heaven was incribed and set it on fire with the Holocaust candle that had been used at the termination of Shabbat Nahamu a little while earlier. The burnt relics of this "Long List" he threw among the heaps of ashes of the victims of man's inhumanity to man. When Reb Zanwill saw what he had done, fear and terror seized him from head to foot.

Those permanent residents of the Mount are convinced that when R. Yitzhak held the burning "List" in his hand, the letters of the words inscribed thereon soared up heavenwards. They piously believe that when these letters arrived at the Gates of Heaven, they were formed into different words which spelt terms of comfort, joy, hope and implict belief that complete salvation for the Jewish people would now no longer be delayed in coming.

146

Moreover, the name of the "List" would now be changed in its word formation. For instead of the three letters Nun, Gimmel, 'Ayin, which, when combined, spell the Hebrew word Nega ("plague"), the same letters would be transposed in a different order; thus: 'Ayn, Nun, Gimmel, forming the word for pleasure (Oneg), comfort and deep faith.

THE MEAL IN THE ROOM OF THE HOLOCAUST CELLAR

A sad atmosphere always prevails in the Holocaust cellar. All around we seem to hear sighing and weeping. Even the candles flicker, as it they were shaking off tears. No joyous event is ever held there, it being assigned only to Memorial gatherings and special evenings to mark the solidarity of those who hailed from those communities which had been rocked and destroyed by the Nazi beasts in human shape.

The only exception to this rule is on Lag B'Omer, when a meal is arranged in the cellar, near the ashes of the martyrs of the hellish concentration camps. This meal has no connection with the festivities (Hillula) of Lag B'Omer in pious memory of R. Shimon b. Johai. R. Zanwil arranges the Lag B'Omer festivities near the sepulchre of King David. On that occasion, a bonfire is erected in the courtyard facing the royal tomb, and four gigantic, flaming torches are kindled at the following places: Safed, Acco, Miron and in front of the cave at the foot of Mt. Carmel, and near the shore of Sitrin, where it is believed to be the cave of the Bnei Haneviim of Eliahu Bnei Ha'neviim. For these are the few places that bear some connection with Lag B'Omer. R. Zanwill also arranges the ceremonious first cutting of the young child's hair (Halaka), an event performed in the forecourt of the royal sepulchre in a festive spirit of merriment and prayer.

The joyous ceremonies are arranged near David's tomb, for ne is the only one who is able to arrange any kind of festivities for a long-suf fering people. For David alone has left his nation, as a golden legacy. his 150 Psalms that can sweeten life's bitterness, that can help to

147

forget pain and sorrow, and which, above all, are empowered to give each broken-hearted individual a vision of hope and salvation yet to come. Yes, it is King David alone, whose mortal remains have been entombed in Mt. Zion, that possesses the keys which will unlock the barred gates through which the Messiah will emerge, bringing peace and healing to a war-ridden, sick, and stricken world. Only he will usher in an era when Peace will no longer be a fleeting glimpse between one war and another, but an abiding vision of earth being raised to heaven. Bizarre, indeed, is the feast held on Lag B'Omer in the Holocaust Cellar, near the rooms in which the burnt ashes of the martyrs have been deposited. At first blush, it would appear that arrangements have been made for a colossal party, for food, drink and delicacies of all sorts to make the tables groan with plenty. Yet very few are those, apparently, who have assembled here to participate in this banquet. Generally, there are just three to comprise the ritual quorum in order to recite the Grace after Meals with a Mezuman. Only seldom does an anonymous stray visitor appear who participates both in the Se'udah (festive meal) and in the Grace. Despite this fact, however, R. Zanwili considers this Se'udah to be one of outstanding importance, one to which he attributes values of the highest and rarest kind.

Those who participate in this Se'udah first wend their way direct to David's Tomb, proceeding with dignified steps, as if they were being actually accompanied by King David himself. When they gather around the tables, they sit with that respect and decorum which bespeaks of being in the presence of royalty.

Among all the company, a solemn stillness and respect hold. Then one of the anonymous diners arises amidst the silence prevalent, and begins to play upon a broken harp, devoid of strings. This ruin of a harp, the player thereof calls "the harp of David". More remarkable and odd still, is the fact that the Grace after Meals is recited in perfect silence, not a word being heard either from him who begins the Grace or from those who participate in the blessings. What happens is this: the player on the harp invites King David to recite the Grace, seeing

148

that he is, in all reality, both the host of the meal and the owner of the room, as it were.

The diners at this meal are the dead themselves, those holy and pure martyrs. The memorial service held in their respected memory being equated to the solemnity which speaks of Yom Kippur itself. The festive meal is held on Lag B'Omer, because it was on that day that the great miracle occurred when the infamous tyrant, may his name be blotted out forever, decided to commit suicide. In this act, those who had eyes to see beheld the salvation of the Lord and witnessed the realization of their wishes and the implementation of their daily prayer: "O Lord of vengeance, appear and avenge Thyself on account of the sufferings of Thy people."

The holy martyrs of the concentration-camps hungered throughout the Holocaust, not eating even a tenth of the amount necessary for a human being to keep body and soul together. The food left uneaten was added up in order to arrange the gargantuan feast in the Time to Come, when David will appear as the host and the one who blesses the meal. On each successive Lag B'Omer, do these departed spirits asemble, metaphorically speaking, around the royal tomb to appease their ravenous hunger of long standing. Eating and drinking, they sing the Psalms of King David, from whose bounty they now derive much happiness, nursing their fond belief that this Banquet, sumptuous as it appears, is only a sixtieth part of the sumptuous "spread" awaiting them in the Messianic Age.

The following story is told, on this Lag B'Omer Se'udah, by R. Zanwill.

WHEN THE CLOUDS WILL DISPERSE

Towards the end of the Second World War, in the year 5705, on the day preceding Lag B'Omer, R. Zanwill, who was then still living in the house of his renowned father, the late Rabbi of Warsaw, went to the Hadlakah in Meron, accompanied by a group from Jerusalem consisting of elders at home in Halacha and Kabbala. The ascent to Meron was not at all free from risk and hazard, but they eventually reached Meron in good time, ensconced themselves in suitable apartments, studied extracts from the Zohar (the author of which is believed to be R. Shimon Bar Johai, the hero of Lag B'Omer), and prayed the Ma'ariv service with extraordinary devotion.

All was set to participate in the mammoth bonfires which cast their sparkling flashes across the hills and dales which surrounded Meron, and which house the sepulchres of R. Shimon and his son R. Elazar. When the time had actually arrived for the Hadlakah to commence, they climbed up to the roof of their house, together with the Rabbi of Safed, singing as they ascended and prepared for the kindling. The day had been overclouded throughout, with the result that the moon and the stars were not visible in the heavens.

One of the elders, renowned for his expertise in mystic lore, wished to postpone the Hadlakah on account of the inclement and unfavourable weather. The reason he gave for his suggestion was this: "We kindle our bonfires at night, in compensation for the light supplied to us by the sun during the day — a case of "light for light," "measure for measure." "We kindle," he went on, "light here below, in gratitude for the light which came to us from above. Seeing, however, that heaven did not light our path during the day, why should we kindle a light tonight? May I suggest that we wait for the clouds to disperse first, so that the light we kindle on earth may unite with the light sparked off from heaven."

We had to wait a very long time before the clouds eventually dispersed. Meanwhile, the throngs kept on pushing and pounding their way to the roof without let or hindrance. At first, the crowd possessed themselves with patience but after some time, the reserves of their endurance were exhausted and resignation was usurped by resentful impatience. They were all agog to witness the Hadlakah to begin, the time for which was now long overdue. In fact, the Rabbi of Safed had begun to bestir himself and had already taken a bottle of paraffin with which to start the gigantic blaze, whose flaming tongues would kindle all the surrounding, misty mountain tops. The old Cabbalist, however, was still adamant in his objections, and pleaded with the impatient throngs to hold back and to wait for the clouds to disperse first.

Having no alternative but to heed the plea of the old man, out of deep respect for his vast knowledge in the realm of the unknown, they decided to wait. They did so, however, not without tension and disappointment. After some time had elapsed, a spontaneous outburst of joy came from the lips of the assembly, when they espied a messenger hailing from Tel Aviv, bubbling over with the exciting news which had just been flooded across from the wireless : "Hitler is dead; he has just committed suicide."

It was then the time for the old mystic to push his way to the head of the crowd, that was at first impatient but was now bursting with joyous expectations.The mystic raised his voice for all to hear : The clouds have now dispersed. Accordingly, we can now light a fire here below, in gratitude for the dazzling brightness which has come to us from above". Words cannot describe the joyous exhilaration and the frenzied intuition of these narratives which make these visits instinctive as well as interesting and also the make familiar the ideas and lessons connected with these holy and historic sites.

THE KING'S CUP

Popular legend tells of a cup of tears that stands at the head of the couch of David, into which is poured his tears over the sufferings of his people. At every pain felt by his people, his tears flow. When the cup is full to overflowing, the King will awake from his sleep. Then will he take the cup in his hand, recite a benediction thereon and it will be transformed into a cup of salvation. As we are told :

151

"Great and sumptuous will be that Banquet, when all will be assembled around it as its guests and everything will be fully prepared. At the head of the table, will sit the patriarchs, elders, prophets, "men of the Great Assembly," Scribes, Tannaim and Amoraim, Gaonim, Rabbis and pious men, together with their disciples their successors. Seated before them all, will be the holy martyrs, basking in the splendour of the Divine Presence. Abraham will be given the honour to recite Grace after Meals. They will begin to search for the Cup of Blessing, in 'order to give it to Abraham but will not be able to find it.

Abraham will then arise and confess that he has not been given the Cup. They will then invite Jacob, Moses, Aaron and Samuel; but they, also, will not be able to recite the blessing. Then will come the turn of David to recite the blessing. He it will be who will be able to do so. For all he will have to do will be to raise the Cup which has stood for so long at his bed-post and will display to all how full its contents are.

He will then recite loudly the blessing and call upon the Name of God. "I will raise the cup of salvation, and I will call upon the Name of the Lord."

May the name of the Lord be blessed!" David will recite the blessing and his harp will pour forth melodies of its own accord. All will then break forth in to praise and song, proclaiming a poem of praise for the Redemption and the Salvation. May this be His will, AMEN.

THE FIFTH GATE

THE HARP OF DAVID

The Spiritual Guide and Custodian of Mount Zion, Rabbi Zanwill dedicates special days on which he sits with his devoted followers regaling them with wondrous legends of the "Song of the Mount". In these talks, he harmoniously blends the tragic tales of the past which have clustered round Mount Zion, together with the beliefs of future joys to come, the setting of which will be none other than Mount Zion, bathed in beauty and steeped in legend.

"Sing us one of the Songs of Zion...!" One of the Songs of David the Psalmist, David the Poet, David the Harpist! "Thus cried the Babylonians, tormenting their Jewish captives. But how could they sing the Lord's songs in a strange land? Where were their harps to set the melodies and strike the chords? Where, above all, was the harp of King David itself?

Once, long ago, many years after the Captivity, when the Jews had returned home again and set about rebuilding Jerusalem, an old man took it into his head that he must go to Babylon and find there the harps which were hung upon the willows near the rivers. He must bring them back. Wonderful music would then again be played on them as the old songs were sung. So Shabbatai laid his plans and made his preparations, nothing daunted by the amazement of his wife and family nor the jeers of his friends and not even by the amazement and sober conviction of the Elders and City Fathers that he had, indeed, taken leave of his senses. He was an old man and far from robust, but nothing could shake his purpose that he must go in order to find the harps. So he set off one day with his waterbottle, his pouch full of dates, and his staff in his hand.

Long and arduous was his journey. Over mountains, across rivers, through arid deserts, with scorching heat by day and icy cold by night,

153

often assailed by hunger and thirst. Still he bravely pressed on. All these hardships took heavy toll of him. He was a very worn and fragile old man when, at last, he reached ihe outskirts of what had once been Babylon. Sitting down by the wayside, he looked at the passers-by. When he saw a sympathetic face, he would tell his tale and ask if anyone could tell him where he might find the harps, so sadly hung on the willows, many years ago. He asked ever more timidly, because it soon became clear that they all thought him demented. He was shown kindness and hospitality, given food and drink, water with which to bathe his dusty feet and his rags were replaced. Yet no one took him seriously. He slipped away from these good folk and bethought him where he could continue his search.

If human heads and hearts could give him no help, perhaps the Spirits could guide him from their other world. Weary and worn-out, but still full of hope, Shabbatai turned to the old burial-ground. There, with supplications and pleadings, he called on the Righteous Dead to assist him. Surely, among them there must be souls who had loved the tombs; there seemed however, to come only gusty sighs of emptiness, ghostly whisperings, giving him no answer.

Then despair possessed him. Sick at heart, poor Shabbatai gave up hope, doubting if he had, indeed, ever really heard a call to seek the long-lost harps. Aimlessly he wandered, finding himself at last on the banks of the river, with thick clumps of willows growing all around him as they had grown so many centuries ago. Suddenly, a shadow fell across him. Raising his eyes, he saw before him the figure of a man so old, so decrepit, so devoid of almost any living attribute, that it appeared to be that of an apparition.

In a sepulchral voice, he asked Shabbatai what ailed him that he looked so woe-begone ? Shabbatai, grateful for even such sympathy as this, poured out his sorry tale, from its beginning so full of hope to the empty frustration of its ending.

Most astonishingly, this ancient sage looked on the quest in quite a different light. What made Shabbatai so strongly convinced that it was upon willows in Babylon that the Harps had been hung ? When Shabbatai showed him the beautiful Psalm, "By the wa'ers of Babylon, there we sat down, yea, we wept, when we remembered Zion. Upon the willows in the midst thereof we hanged up our Harps..." the Sage said : "You have interpreted its meaning completely in error. When the mourning Jews sat by these willows and lamented, they did not hang up their harps here, for they had not got their harps ! Their grief was caused by the memory of Zion. It was on the willows of Zion that they had hung them, knowing they could never take them and dishonour them by singing to them in captivity! The harps here left behind in Zion; ony there, could you ever find them!"

Slowly and painfully, old Shabbatai dragged himself back on the heart-breaking return journey, until at last he reached Jerusalem. There, for the rest of his life, he sought — but never found — the harps of the departing captives. Until one day, he rested on Mount Zion where the groves of trees were thick and the wind blew through them moaning and plaintive, until it seemed that a loving melody arose, now louder, now softly whispering, rising and falling. At last Shabbatai understood : it was the vibrant strength of their loving remembrance of Zion and its glory, that still kept alive the music of their harps and that of the Harp of David playing its Songs there for ever.

THE SONG CONDUCTOR

The world is full of song, sung by the children of earth as well as by the celestial angels above. They chant paeans of praise to God. In fact, the angels do not commence their melodies before those on earth have begun, as it is said : "The morning-stars sing in unison with the children of God!" The source of song springs from below. It is the heart of man which struggles between life and death, joy and pain, love and hate. Hence he has all the more need for song to lend him encouragement, and to endow him with comfort. It is song which stills the forebodings of his heart, and appeases his qualms of conscience.

It was King David, "The sweet Singer of Israel" who conducted the

155

"Song of the Morning-Star", which began the day with the music of the spheres. The harp, which was suspended above his couch, began to ripple melodiously in the midnight hours, so as to be prepared to hail the Dawn with rapturous song. Following his example, all creatures on earth and all the angels above, likewise, began to sing pervading and surcharging all the ends of the earth with paeans and Hallelujah's to the Creator of all which exists, and flourishes here below. With the death of David song ceased, for there was none to lead the singing; with the result that the world was hushed, so far as melody was concerned. The Ministering Angels kept daily vigil over their allotted tasks, listening intently to catch any strains of song which might rise from below. They yearned to hear the melody from earth so that they, too, could burst forth into rapturous praise of their Creator; but all was silent. Song itself seemed to have died on man's lips and the angelic waiting proved in vain. Through the fast-disappearing hours of the night, did they wait. The first rays of the sun had already begun to paint the skies with a riot of colour, awakening birds had begun their twittering, but the voice of song had not yet begun. "What had happened", wondered the angels? "Fancy", they observed one to another in surprise : "No song from below and no song on high ! Is it right not to thank God for the birth of a new day and without the accompaniment of song? Is not song the very basic foundation and quintessential element of all existence, without which no creation is possible? What plan, or reason, can existence have without song? Is there not ground for fear that as a result of this silence, the world will return to its former state of being "waste and void"? Fear and trembling seized the Ministering Angels as they flew down to earth in order to solve this mystery of the death of song. What had happened to the world which God had created in the form of a Garden of Eden in which harmony should reign supreme and the sound of music fill hill and dale? It was then and there that they learnt that he who had heard and conducted the songs on earth, King David, the Sweet Singer of Israel, the possessor of that magic and legendary harp which never left his hand except

156

in the still hours of night, had been swallowed up by the jaws of death. His passing had introduced on earth a silence as that of the grave. Song had become silent; joyous rapture had frozen into the coldness and stillness of the cemetery.

So the angels went to search for a successor to David to whom they could hand over the harp and thus begin again the daily harmony of earth below with the spheres above. For a long time was their quest not crowned with success, with the result that existence withered and all Creation seemed to wilt and languish, for it was Song that breathed life into all things living.

The anxiety of the Angels increased daily and terror seized them lest Creation should come to naught. What plan could they devise so that Song should be born again and save the world from extinction ?

At last, their patience and long searching were rewarded. They quickly flew down to David's grave, and transported his mortal remains to the abode of Celestial Song, so that he could ever be there in the forefront of the ranks of Heaven to conduct the music which should daily reverberate from one end of the world to the other.

Hence, the Psalmist sang (**XXXIX**,1.) "A Psalm of David. Ascribe unto the Lord, O ye Sons of Might, Ascribe unto the Lord, Glory and Strength !"

THE SYMBOLISM OF DANCE

Dancing takes pride of place, especially in the religious life of Mount Zion. The entire mountain re-echoes with the sound of song and reverberates with the rhythmic movement of dancing feet. No religious celebration is allowed to pass without being honoured by dancing, during which a circle is formed, composed of inter linked hands.

The dance begins, at first, at a slow, measured pace, with the body poised on "a light fantastic toe". Gradually, however, it increases in fervour and intensity, casting almost a spell of enchantment and ecstasy

157

over the hearts of all participants. The raising high of the feet seems to keep pace with the elation of the emotions. Mystics on the Mount argue; "Was not the origin of the Mount itself thus ? Beginning first with a few clods of earth, it reached, in the course of time, its present grandeur and majesty. Is it not so with him who dances ? At first, his feet are raised on tip-toe until, at the end of the dance, his head almost touches the Heavens above." The main thing, they exhort the dancers, is to raise ourselves high above this petty, sordid earth with all its foibles and follies. One thing, however, must be borne in mind : To attain this, co-operative efforts on the part of the entire group of dancers must take place. For it must be borne in mind that the dance does unite all, just as the pilgrimage to Zion's Mount links all shades of opinion and diverse beliefs into one united band of joyous worshippers !"

Hearing this self-confession, the old man invited his interlocutor to go with him to a quiet corner of the Mount where both perched on two large adjoining stones. He then revealed to him further the secret attached to the symbolic dancing on Mount Zion. This is what the old man said :

"Dancing unites all those who participate therein, because the pace and rhythm of the dance is sparked-off by its Leader and Director. One day, a celebrated musician happened to visit the Mount and he gazed in rapturous admiration at the jubilation, ecstasy and almost hilarious abandonment which characterized the dance. Even more remarkable was the harmonious rhythm with which the dance was accompanied. It was as if a large orchestra played solo. The celebrated musician was spell-bound, almost breathless with admiration, searching in vain for the conductor of this remarkable orchestra of ballet dances. With a raised voice, he appealed to those around him to introduce him to this Maestro of song and dance, for never had he come across one who wielded a more successful baton — one that was able to transform cacophanous sound into mellifluous harmony."

When the musician was led to Rabbi Zanwill — perhaps the one most qualified to answer his question and thus set his mind at rest the Director replied : "I cannot introduce you to the Conductor, for he is not the individual who can alone achieve this elation of body. For this the community is necessary. Symbolic of this achievement, is the raising of ourselves on tip-toes when the word "Kadosh" is thrice repeated in the Kedushah.

The dance on Mount Zion is contagious, enveloping in its magic circle all its pilgrims and spectators. Its participants are indeed a "mixed bag"; comprising aged Jews, attired in their traditional gabai Jines and fur-hats (Streimlech), as well as the younger generation, clad in khaki shorts. All are linked together in a joyous dance, beaming at each other as if long years of friendship had cemented them together in harmonious co-operation.

When one of the oldest and most scholarly participants in the dance, was asked why he so cast away all his dignity and the respect due to him to the winds, tip-toeing hilariously with all and sundry, his reply was : "Firstly, I do not regard myself as a great scholar; secondly, since each dance takes the form of a circle, one cannot tell who is first or last, in the middle of the periphery of that circle !" He continued; "You see, the dancing-circle equates young and old, boor and scholar, the haughty and the humble, into one equal group, none being different in rank and prestige from the other. Distinctions are made only by those who pace Life's daily round with their feet touching *terra firma* all the time. As soon, however, as they raise themselves a little above the earth, this snobbery and class-distinction vanishes. It is for this reason that dancing on Mount Zion is known as the "Mahnaim (Camps) Dance", for it unites all congregated there into one large integrated camp, in which all hearts beat as one."

As he finished his discourse, the old man caught hold of the hand of him who had occasioned this long reply by his question and dragged him into the middle of the circle. When, in the height of paroxysms of intensified enthusiasm and deep ecstasy, the dance had come to an end, the questioner turned to the aged scholar, saying : "Rabbi, He

159

not confined to one place! He is Omnipresent and visible; although He fills the whole earth, no living mortal can see Him and remain alive ! It is He, my friend, who is the conductor of all song and dance. Does not David "the sweet singer of Israel", exhort the earth to 'dance before Him in joy'? He alone is the source of all harmony and true joy !"

The famous musician took the hint. Henceforth, he would pray to the Almighty for Divine guidance. With this determination in his heart and the blessing of Rabbi Zanwill in his ears, the musician soon became world-famous in his profession.

The old man concluded his heart-to-heart talk with his questioner: "Now you surely realize why the dance levels us all; since we all dance in His direction, we are all hence equal in His eyes". He finished with a saying of the Director, that the Psalmist's outburst. "I have placed (Shiviti) God before my eyes at all times," is wrongly interpreted; for Shiviti, besides meaning, "I have placed...", also has the meaning, "I consider as equal all those with whom I come into contact !"

Judaism has no more valuable lesson than the equality of all in God's eyes !

THE SONG OF THE VIOLIN

The world of the Almighty is full of song.

When Adam was created and went out into the world, he burst forth into Song. That day was Friday eve and it was twilight. In the dusk of day, Adam began to sing "A Psalm for the Sabbath Day." His voice rose, vibrant and melodious, as pure as the flowing streams of the Garden of Eden that so attracted his soul before he sinned.

But after he sinned, his spirit was troubled and his world became dark. It lost its attractiveness and interest. The song was stilled.

However, once Song came into being, it was never to cease. Removed from the earth, it grew wings and soared heavenward where the angels

160

awaited it and were envious of man who had originally merited it.

From that time forth, song was to be divided between man on Earth and the angels on high. On Shabbat it rose from below, but during the week it was Heaven's possession.

Man was jealous of the angels who shared his precious gift. He came before God and complained: "O Heavenly Father, on what grounds are the angels allowed to use Song ? They have given nothing for this privilege. They do not wrestle with human problems, nor suffer from the incompleteness that marks man. Without human failings, Song dies as soon as it is uttered; without human emotion, it is toneless. Only a mother's heart can hum a lulably and only a Hassid can hum a song of love to his Creator. Only he who tastes pain can appreciate the melodious cry of the Hazan who beseeches God's favour for his people Israel. Hence do I ask", concluded Adam," why do the perfect angels need song ?"

All his life, Adam remained unsatisfied, unappeased. Yet, interestingly enough, legend records that Adam died seventy years before his time and these final years were added to those of King David, "the sweet singer of Israel". At that time, the flowing well of Eden was reopened and the world was filled anew with Song. The beauty and purity of the melody is like nothing else, except the Song of Adam before he sinned. From that time on, Israel was more beloved to God than were the angels.

King David saw with prophetic insight, that a day would come when the Temple would lay in ruin, the service of the priests ended and the song of the Levites stilled. He wondered what would become of that Song

At that moment, the birds came and said to him : "David, we who dwell in the sky where the enemy's hand cannot reach, shall carry Song on our wings. Even if the Temple be destroyed, Song shall not be silenced. We shall guard it until your children are redeemed from Exile and return home." David's heart was filled with gratitude.

When the Temple was destroyed, the birds of the sky fulfilled their

161

promise. One bird cried unceasingly at the Wailing Wall. Her feathered friends called her the "Levi bird", because she always sang Levitical tunes and prayed for the restoration of the Temple. For centuries, the faithful bird and her descendants treasured the music of the Wailing Wall. However, when the War for Independence broke out in 1948 in Israel, the gallant army of Israel, stretched so thin, was unable to conquer the Old City of Jerusalem from the Arabs. Rather than remain in captivity, the "Levi bird" retreated with the Israeli troops, sad and dejected. Suddenly, in an instant, a bullet whistled through the air and struck down the bird; but her soul rose to heaven.

Nevertheless, the Song did not die. On that very day, Mt. Zion was captured by the Israeli forces. The violin that hung over King David's bed began to play once again.

THE SINGING STONES

It was around dawn and the faint glow of the coming sunrise was lighting the eastern sky, when the early pilgrims, the first of the day, came winding their way up Mount Zion. As they neared the summit, the rough track ended in a flight of shallow stone steps, hollowed out by the footsteps of thousands of past climbers. As one by one, their feet touched the first stones, each pilgrim began to sing, softly at first and then in a swelling chorus, their voices rose pure and clear with a loving fervour which would have delighted the Psalmist as he touched his harp :

"O Lord, our God ! low glorious is Thy Name in all the earth..."
"I will give thanks unto the Lord with my whole heart. I will tell of all Thy marvellous works..."
"I love Thee, O Lord, my Strength ! The Lord is my Rock, and my fortress and my Redeemer..."
"The Lord is my Light and my Salvation ! Whom shall I fear..."

"They that trust in the Lord are as Mount Zion, which cannot be moved..."

What was it that urged these loving souls to sing, each one a different song according to the step on which he trod? Rabbi Zanwill, the Custodian, tells us that, in the beginning, each of these stone steps — which number exactly one hundred and fifty — had a Psalm inscribed on it. Later on, it was felt that it was not fitting for even the most reverent feet to tread on these sacred poems. They were erased from the steps and are now written on stone-tablets around the resting place at the top of the ascent. But though the words have gone, their magic still remains in the steps, mysteriously inspiring the pilgrims to raise their voices in confident rejoicing.

Under the vibrant influence of their singing, many of the pilgrims press on, hastening ever faster, straining to gain the holy summit and observe the glorious view. Those who are wise will pause long enough to turn aside and read the inscription on a large, upright stone beside the way: "Who will go up to Mount Zion, and who will stand in this holy place?". The operative word of this challenge is "Stand". Who will be wise and patient enough to stay a while, to rest and meditate and refresh his bodily and spiritual powers, so that he may gain the greatest good from his pilgrimage and lose nothing by his haste?

Rabbi Zanwill "improves the moral and adorns the tale". He tells us: "Once upon a time, a rash and hasty man was driving his chariot and horses up a steep and winding mountain-road, on one side of which was the face of the rocky hillside and on the other, a sheer drop down into the abyss below. Impatiently, he lashed his horses on, sparing them nothing and recking naught of the steep incline nor of the rough stones of the road.

Bathed in sweat, the horses gallantly stumbled on until at last even their foolish master saw their exhaustion and realized he must give them breathing-time. Still in anxious haste, he climbed out of the chariot But scarcely had the horses time to feel the rein loosened from the guilding-hand, when they collapsed. Down into the abyss plunged the chariot, dragging the poor, over driven beasts with it... Alas, also, for the charioteer! Now, too late, he saw his folly and how his mad and senseless haste had lost him everything. In vain, he lamented and bewailed first his loss and then, even more sincerely, his own faults of impetuosity and stupidily; on both counts, a hard and bitter lesson to learn.

"So it is with us all," concluded the Custodian. "We must learn to climb wisely, with our souls as well as with our bodies. Haste will avail us nothing and may even cause us infinite loss. Steadfast patience and endurance, meditation and thoughtfulness, these alone must guide us, to be swift only where it is prudent and cautious only where it is necessary. Only time spent quietly in prayer and in true assessment of the object and progress of our journey, will bring us that maturity of judgment which we must offer both to our Creator and to our fellowmen.

"Let us therefore, pause in our speeding upwards and stand in contemplation of Mount Zion, the Holy Place."

THE SONG OF THE LEVITE

When the flames of fire leaped forth from the burning Temple and all seemed lost, the Levites went forth in fear and trembling. Tearing their garments and taking off their shoes, they placed their harps on their shoulders and went about sad and depressed in captivity, together with their families. They journeyed on and on to the most distant places, finding rest nowhere.

Wherever they passed through, they were entreated by their conquerors to regale them with some of Zion's songs, but their heart was paralyzed and their harps muted. They could not make them produce even one note or chord. All they could do was to utter before their tormentors, in a note sad and plaintive : "How can we sing the Song of the Lord on strange soil ?" Yea, Song itself was paralyzed and silenced.

164

One of the most aristocratic of the Levite families that had ministered in the Temple, wandered from place to place until it came to Toledo in Spain. There, a son was born to them, whom they named Judah, and he was the only son to his father. R. Samuel, of Castille. The muse of song stirred in the heart of the child, its spirit beating its wings on the Lord on strange soil ? They hoped for redemption and Judah also was all aglow with expectation. His heart hummed with abundance of song which, in turn, broke forth from his throat; yet he only expressed all his limbs. He soon became a poet, composing and singing sublime hymns. The elders, who treasured in their hearts and conscience the Songs of the Levites in the Temples, recognized in his Songs the tunes of the Levites and called him Ha-Levi; and Judah Ha'Levi, the Levite has remained his name to this day.

Trembling seized the elders of that generation. What ? The Song of a small fraction of the boundless melodies within him. Deep in his heart, they remained.

Both the poet and the people knew why song had been muted. Was it not because Spain was a strange land ? So the poet decided to leave Spain and settle in Jerusalem, there to treasure its earth and pour out his soul on holy soil. Leaving behind all his earthly possessions, he sailed in a ship towards his destination. Throughout the journey, his heart, full of the song of the Levites, kept pounding with the humming of the waves.

Many months did he sail on the wide seas, his heart full of melodies, beating time with the roaring and dashing of the waves. He passed through Egypt, where he tarried some time and thence wended his way towards Jerusalem. As soon as he reached it, he made haste towards Mt. Zion. Taking off his harp from his shoulders, he seized it with trembling hands, standing at the foot of the mountain while wending his song heavenwards. "Zion, why dost thou not enquire of the fate of thy captives ?".

His harp stirred to life and became as bursting with melody as was his heart within him. Song simply burst forth from him in its fulness.

165

causing a mighty storm in the world. The question asked was : "Has the time now dawned ? Has the end arrived when the harps can begin to play once more ?".

But the generation was not ripe yet, nor had the time arrived. The Song had been awakened before its destined time. The Levite had come before he had been called and before the Temple platform had been restored to its place.

For days on end, did the Levite remain standing at the foot of the Mount, finding no place where to go and sing. The time had not yet arrived. Thus he stood and sang at the foot of the Mount until an Arab chanced to hear the Song. Understanding its content and terrified at its implementation, he trod on the Levite who sang so divinely, with the feet of the camel on which he rode, trampling him to death in the very place where he stood singing.

His completed song could now be heard wafting across the mountain. Those who pass by the vicinity in the stillness of the night, listen intently to the Song of the Levite, prayerfully hoping for the day when all the Levites will return to their pristine function in the Temple.

THE BROKEN CHORD

R. Gershon was one of the most famous Hazanim of his time. When he conducted a service, his magnificent voice charmed all nearers. Some of them came from far and near to enjoy his rendering of the prayers. Especially dear to him was his chanting of Kol Nidre. This added to his great reputation. Many months after, people still went about humming to themselves some of of his strains. Latterly, however, when his heart became weak, he had to give up regularly conducting the service. He remained in the Ghetto, but his visits outside his home were infrequent, as such visits were often fraught with danger.

But a retired Hazan is soon apt to be forgotten. When the Solemn Days were approaching, memories and yearnings of past years began to assail him. The heart-rending tunes of Kol Nidre filled his weak heart, strengthening his effort to chant them publicly once again. Possessed by this determination, he ventured out into the streets of the Ghetto to ascertain whether an underground Kol Nidre service had been organized. To his joy, such a service had been clandestinely arranged. He approached those who organized it, offering his services free.

Among those who arranged this service, there were some who remembered R. Gershon in his prime, and were glad at this renewed opportunity of hearing him. "Walls have ears", and soon word of this reappearance of R. Gershon got around the masses. When the eve of Kol Nidre arrived, crowds filled the assembly-point. People, who had been confined to their homes, owing to fear of the enemy, were only too delighted to meet old friends with whom they could exchange tales of experiences and at the same time entreat for Divine mercy. Outside the temporary synagogue, guards were placed to report immediately on every suspected move and sound of the enemy around.

No sooner were the candles kindled on the eve of Yom Kippur, when R. Gershon came to the assembly, attired in his white Kittel and his gold-embroidered Tallit. Donning his large black hat, he drew nigh unto the Reading Desk. Each one held his breath in admiration when the same magnificent voice of previous years which had charmed them always, seemed to have lost none of its pristine glory. The man and his genius of song seemed to have lost nothing with the passage of years.

Kol Nidre — he began softly and slowly, climbing up the ladder of song, rung by rung. At the second repetition, R. Gershon's voice assumed even greater proportions. As in former years, it captivated and shook the hearts of all who listened to him. Mouths were opened in amazement. Yes, it was the same powerful voice that moved the mountains of admiration in years gone by. The sweet, haunting sounds made them forget their bitter tribulations and the dangers which lurked for them all around.

As he was reciting the Kol Nidre, fear and trembling also began to

167

take hold of those who had organized the service. What if the sounds could be heard outside the building by the Nazis? Would this not be the signal of certain death? In fact, one of those who kept guard outside soon came in to warn the Hazan to lower his voice, for its strains were beginning to fill the street outside. "Lower your voice", he peaded with the Hazan : "God can hear your voice even when you pray softly". But when he tried to lower his voice, his voice assumed even greater proportions. The congregation was greatly alarmed. "Silence, silence", they pleaded. But the poor-Hazan, trying as hard as he could, just could not lower his voice, at first. After some renewed efforts, he managed to stifle his voice until it became an inward gasp. Those present seemed to see the death of a voice. It was a painful, heart-rending sight to behold R. Gershon, standing open-mouthed, praying inwardly, wtih tears flooding his eyes and rolling down his cheeks and not a sound escaping his lips.

When he could no longer contain himself, R. Gershon burst forth in a mighty, piercing voice the words of the Kol Nidre — "from this day of Yom Kippur, to the day of Yom Kippur about to come to us for good". No sooner did he come to the last word "le'Tovah", when the chord of his voice and his heart both seemed to have snapped. He feil in a faint and was soon removed quietly and secretly to his home.

R. Gershon did not leave his bed after this. For weeks he lay paralyzed, his eyes wandering all around, his lips murmuring inwardly and his heart beating faintly. Gradually, his heart began to burn dimly as a candle about to reach its end, until it was extinguished completely one cloudy morning in Marheshvan. As he was being carried to the grave, those accompanying his mortal remains murmured softly : "It was not in Marheshvan that he died, but on Kol Nidre night. It was only the tune of Kol Nidre that kept him alive a full month afterwards".

THE THREE WHO FORGOT

In his kindness, God endowed man with the power of forgetfulness. For had He not done so, none would be able to survive long. Why do you think that it was fated for the dead to be forgotten-soon? For were this not the case, none would be able to survive long. May it not well be that one of the reasons for the Four Cups of Wine during the Seder was to make us forget the bitterness of the Marror, symbolic of the tyranny of Egypt? The thoughts and hopes of Redemptioh should make us forget the bitter experiences of past Jewish history throughout the protracted night of the Exile. Having convinced his hearers of the philosophy of forgetfulenss, the Reb Zanwill told his listeners three incidents of people who forgot.

THE SCHOLARLY R. NISAN

R. Nisan was a scholar who never ceased to study. Even when he had no books before him day and night, he would turn over in his mind all he had learned. One day, he was seized by the Gestappo in the streets and dragged off to the Polish Sejn to clean out the lavatories and remove the rubbish heaped up there. Many Jews were lined up in a row and each had to hand to the other the dust-bins of filth while the Nazi guards stood by jeering at them. When it came to the turn of R. Nisan, he was so deeply immersed in his thoughts of Torah that he was not conscious of what his task was. When one of the guards noticed this, he struck R. Nisan such a mighty thud with the butt of his rifle that he awoke to consciousness and fulfilled the task allotted to him.

When this went on several times, he was taken out of the queue and given such a beating that he fell exhausted to the ground with the blood flowing freely from him. On his recovery, he was again placed in the queue with the stern warning that if he persisted in his folly, he would be shot like a dog as a warning to the other cursed, lazy Jews. It was then that it was decided in Heaven that R. Nisan forget all his learning. As a result, he stood in the queue and carried on the work as all the others did.

On his return home, he could no longer sit and study for he had forgotten all his learning. When he could no longer learn, he sat weeping beside the open Gemara until he passed on High. Legend says that when he soared heavenwards, angels came to greet him bearing aloft scrolls of learning which he had thought of during his enforced silence. The Gemara in which R. Nisan learnt was brought to Mt. Zion. To this day, those who study therein discover lights of learning not found elsewhere.

THE MASTER OF PRAYER

So sweet and full of inspiration was the manner in which R. Jacob recited his prayers before the congregation that he won world-renown. Each word he uttered from the prayers, with such grammatical clarity and clear diction sprang to dynamic life and became clothed with new meaning. He swayed the whole assembly and each worshipper merged into one swaying congregation devoted to him body and soul.

In the waggon in which he and hundreds of others were transported to Treblinke, he hummed prayers all night long in such ecstasy, that all forgot their plight, being cheered by his prayers and tunes. So it went on all though the night. The waggon was transformed into a holy assembly of worshipping angels. It was only night which fatigued them and sleep silenced R. Jacob and his charmed co-worshippers.

When the rays of the sun pierced the waggon the next morning, the general request was made for him to begin his prayers anew. When he was about to do so, he discovered to his dismay that he had forgotten how to pray. Despite the constant requests that went up all around him, he remained dumb. It would seem that the night before had exhausted all his stock of prayers and he had none left to offer now. Full of pained surprise, he remained dumb until he was brought to Treblinke where he was cast into the furnace — another burnt-offering for hallowing God's name. Cabbalists add that when his soul fluttered to Heaven, he was thus greeted by the angels: "R. Jacob, why did you cry so bitterly that morning in your prayer?"

R. ISAAC — THE MINSTREL

R. Isaac was one of the most famous of Badhanim in the Warsaw Ghetto. No wedding was so joyous as the one in which he officiated, accompanying his witty and often audacious witticisms with the aid of a flute. He was the "one-man-band" at all joyous functions and his services were always generously appreciated.

When he was transported to Auschwitz and asked what was his trade, his reply was: "A musician". Thereupon he was placed in the camp orchestra whose function was, among others, to play for the amusement of the Gestappo officers and also to drown the cries of the tortured inmates. But when he was asked to do the latter, he forgot how to play. Weird sounds proceeded from the flute, to the amazement of all. The guards threatened him with death if he did not play as he once did. All R. Isaac could mumble was: "I have forgotten how to play." Saying this, he fell into a faint. A guard soon came up and pierced him through with a gun.

When he ascended heaven, says a legend, he was handed a new flute on which he would play and accompany the souls of all those who were burnt in the camps, on their way to their eternal place in Heaven.

THE STORY OF THREE CHAZANIM

So weak was the Cantor who conducted the Rosh Ha-Shanah Service on Mt. Zion, in the synagogue facing the Chamber of the Holocaust

171

that year, that his voice could only be heard with great difficulty. Besides the weakness of his voice, he lacked personality, giving the impression of a poor, dejected soul. In short, neither he nor his prayers stirred any feelings of emotion or respect among the worshippers.

All were surprised at the choice made by R. Zanwill for this important place and occasion. What qualification did he detect in this Cantor, if so he could be called? Many approached R. Zanwill and voiced their resentment, asking him : "Why did you not appoint one far more prominently suited for such an august occasion? Surely, you could find a Reader whose prayers could be heard, his voice pleasant and who possessed a more endearing personality?"

The Custodian retorted : "The possession of a "still, small voice" for this occasion, far from being a disadvantage, is even a great qualification. In the most solemn prayer of Rosh Ha'Shanah, its author stresses that "a still small voice is heard and the Angels hasten when they hear this Small Voice". So you see, the possession of a weak, unimpressive voice is far more opportune for this occasion than a loud, bellowing voice."

"As regards the Cantor himself, let me tell you the following story. My grandfather happened to find himself a few days before Rosh Ha'Shanah in a certain village and wished to arrange services there for the Holy Days. They searched for a suitable Reader, for one who would be fit to conduct services at which the renowned Rabbi of Warsaw could be one of the worshippers. His scholarly friend Rabbi Ezekiel, on learning of his Rabbi's need, himself undertook to act in the capacity of Hazan for the Yamim Noraim and left his home to come out to the village itself.

The Hazan of Warsaw, Berel by name, who officiated at the former Nalevke Synagogue, was also desirous of acting as Hazan on this occasion. Both these aspirants were of good and sound repute and both appeared eminently fitted for the task. Just prior to the Festival, however, a poor man came to the Rabbi, pleading to be appointed as the Cantor. He seemed poor and ailing, his voice was cracked and his

172

knowledge of the meaning of the Hebrew prayers he was to recite, of the scantiest kind.

In short, he was a typical, poor Jew, of whom there were not a few in the Polish towns and villages.

Touched by the poverty of this man and his crying needs, the Rabbi sat with him and patiently taught him the meaning of the prayers which formed the liturgy of the Yamim Noraim. Moreover, he gave him his own Tallit and appointed him as the Hazan for this occasion. Needless to say, all that the man seemed good for, was to weep; and this he did all the time. All could see and feel that these tears welled not only from his eyes, but also from the innermost recesses of his heart. When the Congregation, at the end of the service, approached their Rabbi and asked him to explain his choice, thus overriding the claims of the celebrated scholar R. Ezekiel and the renowned Hazan Berel, his reply was : "Because it is my considered opinion that the best Hazan is a poor man. There are 150 Psalms : steps on which the worshippers can scale to the heavens above. Three of these Psalms are guide-lines to the choice of a Hazan.

First, man himself must pray. To aid him in this exercice, comes the Hazan. The first Hazan represents Psalm 17, the sinner — "A prayer unto David". He leads man up to Psalm 90. (A prayer unto Moses), who leads him up to Psalm 102 which deals with the broken-hearted. It is the latter Cantor who conducts the individual worshipper to the seventh heaven by the aid of his tears. It is the last, poor Hazan that my grandfather selected for the Yamim Noraim. In choosing, this poor man, I have followed in the wake of my grandfather, of blessed memory. It is with the help of the warm, heartfelt tears that we recall, in pious memory, the two thousand communities destroyed by the Nazis and are grateful for the approach of Redemption in the miraculous establishment of Medinat Israel.

173

THE SIXTH GATE

THE CORNER OF THE JEWISH CHILD

Faithful to his assignment of linking the pangs of messianic birth and the sufferings of Jews during the Nazi holocaust with the beginnings of the "Redemption" which we have been privileged to witness in our own day, Reb Zanwill has allotted on Mt. Zion a special corner dedicated to the child. In this corner, will be displayed symbols of the heroism and the creative instincts which Jewish children have contributed towards the renaissance of our people and the re-establishment of our national Homeland.

This assignment he has commissioned to the veteran Kindergarten teacher, Mrs. Wolfson, who has been responsible for the education of two generations of children during her half-century activity in the sphere of Jewish culture and tradition. During all these years, she succeeded in establishing the absorbing interest and ready co-operation of her young pupils in the strenuous and heroic efforts which went into the establishment of Medinat Israel and into the absorption of the various aliyot (immigrations). She succeeded in helping her numerous pupils to give articulate expression to their emotions and abilities both in song and literary composition in legend and in actual events.

A BITTER TEST

Life in the Ghetto was harsh and tragic, and the thought to escape from it all gave no rest to Reb. Yeruham. For he was absolutely convinced that the diabolical enemy — could massacre all the Jews

174

of his village, as they had done in the surrounding area. Throughout the long nights, he would lie awake, his ears glued to every sound of the approaching enemy. At every suspicious noise, he would jump out of bed and gently awake his wife and their two little children — their precious hostage to fortune.

Meticulously, he had thought and planned how best to effect their rescue, should danger confront them. So far, all his plans to do so had come to naught, frustration meeting him at every turn. He was not so much concerned about his own safety. His sole concern being how to save his wife and children whom he loved more than his own life itself. While it may have been possible for an odd individual, here and there, to translate the thought of escape into successful action, it was almost beyond the bounds of possibility to succeed in rescuing an entire family from the talons of the wild Nazi beasts.

The gates of the Ghetto were barred and strongly locked and the wild Gestappo dogs, guided by their Lithuanian menials, kept a lynx-eyed viligance on all sides. The Angel of Death could be heard fluttering with his all-embracing wings on every side. Like one who had been poisoned and was seeking escape from the sure talons of death, Yeruham left no avenue of escape unexplored. At long last, a daring brain-wave flashed across his mind. True, it would involve the severest of risks and entail much self-sacrifice, but nothing was too great where the rescue of his dear ones was involved. His prayers were answered, and his bold plan to rescue himself and his family was crowned with success. But this success was, however, limited because of an unexpected event.

As he was extricating his wife and children from the jaws of danger, one of his small children burst out into loud weeping. No sooner did the human beasts trace the source of these cries, than they pounced upon the innocent child and brutally put him to death. Broken-hearted and shaken from head to foot, Yeruham stole during the night into the big Polish forest, renowned for its deep quagmires and dangerous swamps.

175

Holding his wife's hand, with his only surviving child bound to his shoulders, he set out deeper and deeper into the dark, forbidding forest. His aim was to be as far removed as possible from the neighbouring villages and hamlets, being afraid lest even a human shadow flit across his path, thus forboding danger. Yeruham knew only too well that in those perilous days it was rare to come across a man endowed with human, merciful feelings towards Jews. He realized far too well the dangers awaiting him in his path through that dense forest. Yet what other alternative had he, than to wander on and on, deeper and deeper into the danger-laden forest? His only hope was that he might eventually encounter a partisan group to which he could attach himself and help them to fight for their own lives, as well as for those of himself and his dear ones. Their sole food on this perilous journey consisted of grains of wheat, chaff and grass. He also trained his little boy, Yossele, not to cry aloud, for so to do spelt sure death. Was it not because his dear little sister Bruntchele had raised her voice in bitter weeping, that the murderous Nazis had so brutally massacred her?

Yossele turned out to be an apt pupil, learning how to cry inwardly, never raising his voice in lamentation. For many long days and nights, did Yeruham and his wife and child, tramp through the labyrinthine paths of the forest, keeping their body and soul together by munching the grass and roots they pulled out of the ground, while filled with grave concern at every suspicious sound that fell on their ears. Indeed, many were these sounds. At times, they proceeded from the barking of fierce dogs; at others, they were sparked-off by the whistle of the bullets, triggered-off from the rifles of the enemy.

Yeruham hopefully marched on, invigorated by the thought that he would eventually come across some partisan group that had hidden from the surrounding nests of Nazis, dotted all over the forest. But the more he marched on, the less trace did he come across of partisan existence. It would seem that, for safety reasons, the partisans had gone very far into the innermost recesses of this never-ending forest.

176

So he decided to trudge on and on, in and out of those perilous swamps and quagmires with which the forest abounded. His solitary hope consisted in discovering the partisan hold-out; a faint hope, indeed, but one that was better than nothing at all.

After what appeared interminable days of wandering, absolutely fatigued by endless marching, they were, at long last, surrounded by a group of partisans who persistently and tirelessly cross-examined Yeruham and his wife. The fears of the partisans, from bitter experience, was lest this couple be 'stooges" of the cursed enemy. sent to trap them. After much searching, the partisans assured themselves that they had nothing to fear from this pathetic trio of man, wife and little child. and helped to save them from the wild beasts on two legs that prowled the forest, waiting to pounce upon and tear their human victims to pieces as the ferocious beasts do in the jungle. They reluctantly told Yeruham, however, that they could not enlist anyone into their partisan group who was not the possessor of a rifle or any other means of defence, crude though this might be.

The partisans told him that it was the armed weapon that was actually the member of the partisan group, not the human being himself. Accordingly, they advised Yeruham to remove himself far away from their lair; for what especially filled them with trepidation was the fear lest the little Yossele would burst out crying. and thus reveal to the Nazis their hiding-place. They further sympathetically told him that a real partisan does not come armed only with a child! Moreover, they told him, "a real partisan leaves his child behind when he joins his group. It is the rifle only that becomes his child then."

Yeruham heard their words with hot tears welling in his eyes. Turning to their spokesman, he asked : "Then what shall I do with my child? Murder him, as the Nazis did my little girl?" These words found a deep response in the heart of the leader of this band of partisans. Actually, he was one who possessed a warm Jewish heart, but this had been hardened by the bitter experiences he had been forced

177

to undergo. Yet this hardness of heart was only an external crust; for inwardly, when all is said and done, a Jewish heart remains a Jewish heart despite all efforts to change it into one devoid of all human feeling. The leader, very sympathetically and with deep devotion, endeavoured to explain to Yeruham that partisans dare not include small children in their fold, lest their cries endanger the existence of the entire group.

Yeruham protested. "No! On the contrary, we will all be saved just because of my dear, little son. For Yossele has been taught not to cry out aloud. Just try him and see for yourselves that what I tell you is absolutely true."

His entreaties had their effect and Yossele was put to a most painful and dangerous experiment to ascertain whether he would cry out aloud. He was beaten by the men almost mercilessly, yet no loud cry escaped his lips. The tears of the little, beaten child endlessly flowed from his tortured eyes, yet no sob or cry was heard.

When the child was finally extricated from the savage beatings which had rained upon him from all sides, his entire face swimming in tears, he whispered in a voice which only his father could hardly hear: "Daddy, why do they torture me so?" When his father heard this pathetic question, he could not restrain himself from weeping and lamenting in loud tones, but Yossele continued to hold his peace and bear his suffering in silence.

The child had passed the severe test and had emerged therefrom with flying colours, so much so that he was unanimously admitted as a full member of the partisan group. Not every member of this brave partisan group remained alive to be able to tell his tale of courage and endurance, for most of them succumbed to the dangers always lying in their path. Yeruham, however, survived, not so much by his own endurance, but by the example of his brave little Yossele. Yes, it was mainly due to his courageous example that they miraculously survived the perils set by the Nazis with which to meet their untimely death.

THE ANGELS WEPT

On the day set aside to commemmorate the anniversary of "Holocaust Day" (Yom Ha'shoah), Reb Zanwill ascended Mt. Zion. Approaching the large cellar which houses many tragic relics of the six million Jews who were martyred in the hellish concentration camps, and which is haunted by poignant memories which defy description, affixed on a wall near it in the "Tears Fountain", in memorial of the Jewish children who perished at theh ands of the Nazis.

The Tears-Foutain was the gift of Dr. Frauenglass, himself "a brand plucked from the fire" who had witnessed and experienced the satanic tortures meted out to those who alas! are no longer in the lands of the living. The memorial took the shape of a large Magen David of the kind that the Jews were made to have attached to their clothes to mark them out for ridicule, and worse, in the camps and torture-chambers. From each end of the memorial emblem, which also served as a prayer column, drops of water flowed. These were to symbolize the tears shed by the innocent children when they were made to suffer at the hands of the inhuman monsters.

There is also a huge statue of Mother Rachel symbolic of the loss of twelve hundred thousand children, who met an unumely death at the hands of those wild beasts in Nazi unform. The Statue has been erected by Dr. Frauenglass. Tears flow ceaselessly from the fountain reminiscent of our Matriarch Rachel who is forever weeping over the fate of her children in the Golah, refusing to be comforted until they return to their ancestral Homeland (see Jer. XXXI, 15-16).

Our Sages relate that during a year of exceptional drought prayers, that almost tore the heavens to shreds, were uttered beseeching Heaven to pour down the precious rains so necessary for the preservation of man and beast. When these supplications availed naught, R. Akiba advised the addition to their orisons the words: "Do it for the sake of the school-children", the petition we include to this day in our Selichot No sooner were these magical words uttered, than the heavens opened

179

and poured forth rain in abundance. It seemed that these words were a kind of "Open Sesame" which burst open the barred gates of heaven's stores of rain.

The merit of little, Jewish children has always been great, especially great is that of the 1,200,000 innocent ones who were made to embrace death al Kiddush Ha'shem. Hence this Tears-Fountain would ever serve as a prayerful memorial and as a perpetual spur to the thought that it was largely due to them that the first signs of Jewish, national redemption began to emerge on the horizon.

On the great day of Revelation, when God was about to present His chosen people with the greatest gift that could be bestowed on mankind — the Decalogue, a great tumult and commotion broke out in the corridors of heaven. Many of the angelic hosts were up in arms at the Divine proposition. Approaching the Throne of Glory, they protested. "Is it fair that the most precious possession we have in heaven should be entrusted to fickle and wayward man?", they demanded of God. "What guarantee have you that the Torah will be observed on earth ?". "For what is man that Thou dost remember him, and the son of man that thou thinkest of him ?" But G-D thought otherwise. Despite these protestations, the Torah was assigned to mankind rather than be kept as a treasure trove stored in heaven. Only one stipulation was made: it was necessary that guarantees be given of their determination to be loyal to its teachings and to honour all the commandments in the observance rather than in the breach.

But there was the rub : "What kind of guarantors were demanded and where to find them ?" Many brain-waves flashed across their puzzled minds. Some suggested thut they produce the three patriarchs Abraham, Isaac and Jacob as guarantors, only to be told, however, that these were not acceptable. "These themselves", was the Divine rejoinder, need to furnish guarantors that they will be faithful to the commandments." A similar rejection was given when they suggested that the Prophets(according to the Talmud 48 in number) serve as guarantors. Other would be guarantors were the earth, sun, and moon. All were spurned as not good enough. The Angels, who objected to the Torah being given to man on earth, were beginning to feel elated. The prospects were good with all these rejections, and it seemed set fair that the Torah would, after all, be preserved in its celestial abode.

Their elation, however, soon received a nasty and unexpected shock. For they were then shown the vision of Hannah and her seven young sons being put to death, one by one, by Antiochus Epiphanes (the ilustrious", who was nicknamed by the Jews as Epiphanes, "the madman"), for not agreeing to bow to the idol he had placed before them.

They were also shown on this kaleidoscopic screen of the future how Russian Cossacks snatched young Jewish children from their mother's arms, in order to train them as soldiers for the armies of the Tsar. The scenes of heroism and endurance on the part of little, Jewish children seemed endless, but "the last straw that broke the camel's back", as the proverb has it, was when they were afforded glimpses of our own times. when they beheld the devilish tortures of the Nazi Reich and how 1,200,000 innocent little children of sunny appearance and eyes sparkling with innocent joy were killed in cold blood. Bowing before the Throne of Glory, they chanted in unison : "Heavenly Father, we will be the guarantors that our parents will be loyal to the Torah you are about to give Israel".

The Angels could not resist their mocking derision. "Fine guarantors ! Look at them !" Their laughter was soon stilled and a look of pained dismay covered their faces when they beheld God rising from His Throne. With outstretched arms, they solemnly declared that He-accept them as guarantors. At their word, the heavenly Torah would be handed over to men.

To silence the angelic murmurings, God enabled them to cast a fleeting glimpse at the screen depicting the history of the Jewish people, past and future, and the part the Jewish child has played therein. He showed them Abraham as a child hidden for ten years by his mother in a dark cellar in order to escape the murderous intent of Nimrod to kill him because he made fun of his father Terah's idols. Innocent children were cast into burning gas-chambers of camps like Auschwitz, Treblinka, etc., The angels could then no longer restrain their pent-up emotions. Tears began to well from their eyes. With remorse and humility, they turned to God agreeing that no better guarantors could be found anywhere in the whole, wide world than these little, innocent children.

Grouping themselves in serried procession, the Angels went out to receive the souls of these innocent, young, martyred victims of the Nazi holocaust. They now realized only too well that the heavenly Torah will safely be preserved by these young, staunch defenders of the Jewish faith. Yes, the Throne of Glory will not totter as long as it is supported by a phalanx like that of Jewish children.

PHARAO'H BLOOD BATH

King Rameses of Egypt was a pervert and evil man. He considered himself God of the world and he bore aloft and arrogantly the name of Pharaoh. Pharaoh, the king, is god of Egypt, sire of the Nile! He was extremely vicious and sadistic. Indeed, he was Satan incarnate! His heart was replete with poisonous snakes, and his brain with horrible thoughts constantly seeking new victims.

He delighted in doing evil. This was the essence of his life, from early dawn till late at night. Right at daybreak, he used to put to death some of his servants and he could not fall asleep unless he had in effect planned a few more murderous feats. His sleep was disturbed if he did not hear the groans of the condemned men. Even all this, did not put his mind at peace. All the time, he walked about grumpy and cross, seeking new victims. The baseness was unmistakeably reflected in his venomous eyes. It also gave rise to a skin-eruption.

He was afflicted with leprosy and his doctors told him that the disease stemmed from his raging and foaming blood. Furthermore, the blood was to be calmed only when it had been appeased. The leprosy was a clear indication that the blood was discontented.

The doctors advised the king to satisfy his blood. Pharaoh, heeding the the advice of the doctors, set out to kill every day a few servants of his household. Jews, unable to put up any resistance, were the special target of his murderous designs. He compelled them to perform the most difficult tasks, casting them to snakes and wild beats and hurling them from high towers. He also used men still alive, mostly Jewish children, as mortar to keep the bricks together.

Horrible was the suffering of the Jews under Pharaoh's yoke. Their cries gave the king great satisfaction and calmed his blood, but his propensity for more blood was ever on the increase. He looked for more victims and concocted new methods wherewith to torture then and to hear their cries.

There are limitations, however, to man's ingenuity. His counsellors could not conjure up any more new decrees, aiming to inflict more punish · ment on innocent people. Pharaoh became ill-humoured and irritable. The rash on his body now appeared also on his face. Angered at this further disfigurenent, he asked his doctors and counsellors to devise new sadistic methods wherewith to torment his innocent victims.

At length, one magician advised the king to bathe in the blood of small children. Accordingly, Pharaoh issued a horrible decree ordering small, Jewish children to be captured and kept imprisoned in the deep cellars of his palace. Pharaoh's servants hence swooped down on the Jewish community in Goshen and, wresting all small children from their mothers' bosoms, brought them to the palace and kept them locked-up in the cellars.

Every day, the servants used to fill a bath with the bubbling blood of these children. Their blood satisfied Pharaoh's venomous blood and healed the sores on his body and face.

The cry of the children's blood ascended to the hight heavens and, reaching the steps of the Holy Throne, stained then.

The angels in heaven, seeing blood-stains on the Holy Throne, began to wipe them; but far from succeeding in their task, the blood-spots got increasingly larger.

There are no stains on High, however, where everything is immaculately clean. Hence were the stains transformed into shining spots, like bright starlets, and they bubbled, beamed and radiated to God, blessed be His Name, and reminded Him of the promise to Abraham. Isaac and Jacob to liberate His afflicted and unfortunate people.

The Almighty accordingly, fulfilled His promise by sending Moses, one of these children whose mother kept him in hiding for three months in a dark cellar, like the other children were kept. She then threw him into the waters of the River Nile leaving him to God's mercy. His tears turned into beaming starlets, reminding God of His promise.

It was this very Moses whom God sent to redeem his afflicted people.

THE POWER OF CHILDREN

It was on account of the children that God first spoke to mankind and it is due to their merit that He continued to speak to our Sages throughout the corridors of Time. When these Sages found themselves perplexed by some problems, it was to little children that they often turned for a solution to their difficulties. They would stop a child on his way some from Heder and confront him with the question: "Tell me the verse your teacher explained to-day". It was from the verse cited, that they would almost invariably find the key to burst open the lock of their dilemma and the children thus proved in be trusty counsellors.

Popular legend records that it was through the agency of children that God spoke to Moses, and that even the Torah itself was given with their aid. Support for this belief was found in the first verse of the Book of Leviticus: "And the Lord called unto Moses".

Moses used to go over each lesson with the children of Israel four times and he also taught their offspring. The school-house which served

184

as his place of instruction was in the vicinity of the Tent of Meeting, the seat of his rendez-vous with the Shechinah. Whenever the Heavenly Voice reached him from there, he hurriedly entered the tent, eager to hear the message.

One day, so the legend proceeds, when Moses sat and taught his young pupils, they suddenly got up from their seats, shouting excitedly : "Tea cher, teacher, God is calling you", In surprise, for he had not heard a sound, Moses stood up, all ears for the sound of the now familiar Voice. The children were right. It was God, who was calling him from the Tent of Meeting, but from which spot exactly he was completely unaware. Did it proceed from the Ark in which the Scrolls of the Law were kept ? Or from the Altar on which the sacrifices were offered ? Or from the ceiling, or from the sides of the tent ?

After turning to all sides, it dawned upon him that the Voice was proceeding from the two Cherubim which topped the Ark. Looking closer, he beheld that their appearance resembled the faces of two young children, each facing the other happily and lovingly. It was then that he understood why God was calling him from there, for it was due to the merit of children that He spoke unto the Lawgiver and it was through their mouth, as it were, that He communicated His divine truths unto His trusted servants and Prophets. That is why we read in the Bible the words : "Speak unto the children of Israel and not "Speak unto the people of Israel".

The story of the Voice, explained Reb Zanwill, finds support in the verse "and the Lord called unto Moses". The last letter of the Hebrew word Va'yikra is smaller than the other four letters of which the word is composed. Why? To teach that the Heavenly Voice came to Moses only because of the merit of little children. And just as God spoke to His Prophets through the mouth of the children, so the Shechinah departed from Jerusalem and accompanied the children who were exiled together with their elders from the Holy City. As long as the children still remained in the city, although the Temple had already been destroyed and the leaders had been led into captivity, and although even the Sanhedrin had been banished from the Hewn Chamber in the Temple in which they sat, the Shechinah still lingered on, clutching as it were the hems of the garments of the children. When the children were taken into captivity, the Shechinah decided to accompany them in their wanderings.

God abided by His promise, sending Moses as the Saviour of His children from the Egyptian bondage, himself a little, innocent child whom his mother had succeeded in hiding for three months in a dark cellar, not unlike many millions of children in our own day and age, due to the inhuman Nazi persecutions. When she was no longer able to hide him, Jochebed, the mother of Moses, had no option but to cast him on the waters of the Nile in the hope that the bitter cries of the child would arouse the mercy of heaven. The tears of the child were each converted into glistening, sparkling tears which corruscated like diadems in the canopy of the heavens. God recalled the promise of Deliverance He had made to the patriarchs, waiting for the child Moses to grow up into sturdy manhood when He would appoint and charge him with the sublime command of being the deliverer, Lawgiver and teacher of the people of Israel.

THE LITTLE LETTER 'ALEPH'

"Speak with the children of Israel !" the Lord commanded Moses at the beginning of Leviticus. In the old days, this was taken literally. Those who taught the youngest classes started them off with the Third Book of the Bible. This Book of Leviticus was specially reserved for the little ones, for a most endearing reason. There is a pious mitzvah which every devout Jew hopes to perform; that is, in assisting to complete a new Torah Scroll, by himself writing therein one letter. Jewish children are fondly encouraged to perform this privileged duty, in which they naturally take great pride. The letter each one writes, is always the one which will help to complete the Book of Leviticus.

186

The choice of the Third Book for the instruction and encouragement of children has a charming legendary source, that of the Little Aleph. God chose the Little Aleph to equal the capacity of the childish heart Now it happened that a new Sefer Torah for "Klal Israel' was being written on Mt. Zion, and many pilgrims sought the honour of having a letter in this Sefer, Parties of children were also organized. For them it was to be a day of proud and joyous happiness to be led to Mount Zion and there, under the kindly and watchful eye of the Curator, to inscribe each his own letter in their own special Book of Leviticus. But alas ! when the great day arrived, one little boy was ill and could not go. Fretted and fevered with disappointment, he gave his mother no peace until she went herself with the other children and explained the sad circumstance to the Curator. Urged on by mother-love, she besought him that somehow the Scroll might be brought to the bedside of her little son, so that he might not miss the beautiful mitzvah of adding his own letter. The Curator, however, said this was not possible. Though kind and sympathetic, his refusal was firm and brooked no argument. The poor mother turned sadly away, wondering how she might soothe and comfort the sick child at home.

That night, the Curator had a vivid dream. All the letters of the Scroll whirled before his eyes, bouncing up and down as though teasing him to lay hold of them. But the one he set his heart on grasping was the Little Aleph. Evading and escaping his hand at every turn, it spoke to him very severely, refusing to come near him because, it scolded him. God had made it of a size and simplicity just right for the understanding of little children. The Curator, however, had not entered into the longings of a small boy's heart and had deprived him of the enormous joy of writing his very own letter in the children's Book of the new Sefer Torah. The Little Aleph told the Curator that, for all his authority and important office, it could give one puff and all Mount Zion would vanish... And in the Dream, it did give one puff and the mountain did vanish !

Next morning, the Curator was sorrowful and conscience-stricken.

187

Humbly, he took to heart the lesson the Little Aleph had taught him and, reverently wrapping up the new Scroll with care and love, he carried it himself to the home of the sick child and helped him to inscribe on it his own letter. The little boy's heart was filled with happiness and joy, because he knew that only one letter so written, has the same value as all the others in the whole Torah put together.

WHEN ROSH HASHANNA WAS KEPT THREE DAYS

Those who lived through the terrors of the concentration camps were convinced that Hitler's downfall would be due to the merit of the little Jewish children who together with six million others, were brutally massacred by the cursed Nazis. They arrived at this conclusion on Erev Rosh Ha-Shanah 1943, called by them the "Rosh Ha-Shanah of the children." It was that year when Rosh Ha-Shanah was kept for three days.

Our sages tell us that when Rosh Ha-Shanah is about to be observed on earth, the Angels enquire of God: "When is Rosh Ha-Shanah?" This they wish to know because it is their assignment to make in heaven all the necessary preparations for the days of Judgment in order to bring before the Heavenly Throne the Books of Life and Death, to summon the Accusing Angel, as well as the defenders — the Good Angels, as well as all the souls of those still on earth in order to arrange Judgment before them. By way of answer, God tells them to descend to earth in order to find out the exact date; for it is not He, but they, whose task it is to assign the exact date.

The angels did so and alighting in Jerusalem, they ascertained the time fixed. With this information, they soared back again heavenwards in order to make all the necessary preparations for judgment day.

This was the year 1943, when the Day fixed was Thursday. It so chanced that a day before, when one of the Angels happened to be flying over the world, he heard the haunting melody associated with

188

and assigned exclusively for, the prayers of Rosh Ha-Shanah. The Angel was surprised : How could it be that these prayers are offered to-day when they were told in Jerusalem that Rosh Ha-Shanah is on the day following ? Did the Angels hear in error ? So he descended from his flight above and alighted in Jerusalem, only to find that all shops were open, business proceeding as usual, people buying and sending off the usual New Year Greeting Cards. Nobody seemed to be engaged in reciting the New Year prayer. No, the Angel had heard correctly. It was only Erev Rosh Ha-Shanah; So whence did those soft, haunting medolies he had heard above, proceed?

He circled the earth in his flight to find out the source of these prayers till he came to Europe from which the voice proceeded. But how could that be ? Have not the Nazis snatched almost the whole of that continent into their talons?Did they not burn almost every synagogue there and clapped the Jews into concentration-camps? Who could that be whose prayers sounded so sweet and touching ? He flew over Rome, Greece, Yugoslavia, Albania, but all was quiet there, not a sound not a prayer. So he circled further, until he soared above Nazi Germany from where the voice seemed to come.

Amazed that it should come from there, above all places, he flew all over Germany till he came to Cologne, through whose grey clouds the sweetest of heavenly strains came through. Struck with wonder at their sweetness- but amazed at their source, the Angel flapped his wings, not knowing what to do next. He did not wish to descend lower into that cursed Cologne, even wondering whether he heard aright. Could it be possible that prayers so heart-rending could proceed from that cursed place? The voice, however, did come from there and from the most unexpected of all places-from the Gothic Cathedral there. For some time, he stopped his flight above it in amazement : — "How could this be ?" He covered his face with his wings, closed his eyes, entered unperceived into the cathedral, following the sound of the prayers. Through corridors and crypts, he glided along until he arrived at a small chamber hidden, in the lowest crypt.

Guarding its entrance, stood a small child clad in church uniform, whose duty it was to give warning to those within should he hear the slightest suspicious shuffle of a footstep towards the door. The angel was dumbfounded with amazement as he paused in that dark corner, with darkness enveloping the whole place. All he could see were twenty eyes of ten small children, large dreamy eyes they were and their owners were clad in church uniforms. It was they who sang so heart-rendingly, so pathetically, so sweetly. "Remember us for life O King who delightest in life."

The Angel could no longer remain silent and he was spell-bound. Who were these children, and what was happening here? He then learned that these are Jewish children whose mothers, in order to save them from a certain death,brought them to this church as an escape. But the children, young as they were, stubbornly clung to all the Jewish customs and observances they could remember.When it came to the fixing of Rosh Ha-Shanah of that year,difference of opinion broke out between them, but since the majority were convinced that it was to-day and not to-morrow — and access to the Jewish world without was impossible, as well as fraught with death — they decided to observe it. Choosing the most secluded room in the Cathedral, they chanted the few passages they still remembered by heart. Here they now stood before the Heavenly Father, praying. "And rule Thou alone, O Lord", imploring Him to tell His faithful people when that day would dawn when He alone would rule over the whole earth.

Moved to the depth of his being, the Angel collected their prayers and soared with them aloft before the Heavenly Throne, pleading before God : "The children in that cathedral, decided that to-day is Rosh Ha-Shanah, so let it be so. Does not the world exist because of the merit of little suffering Jewish children?".

At this plea, consternation broke out among the heavenly hosts. When is Rosh-Ha-Shanah, to-day or to-morrow ? Is it the day decided upon and consecrated by the Beth Din of elders. or that decided upon by little, innocent children ? Whose authority is in this case more binding ?

190

None could decide among the angels, until a compromise was arrived at : Let Rosh-Shanah this year consist of three days, the one day decided upon by the children and the other two those arrived at by the adults. The Angels, thereupon, made all preparations for Judgment there and then and summoned the Defending Angel (Suneigar), who brought the Two Books of Life and Death, and also summoned up to heaven the souls of the children to be arraigned before the Judgment Throne. The Accusing Angel, though summoned, would not appear, mockingly laughing at this "Kinder-Shpiel", of a Rosh Ha-Shanah, as he ridiculed the idea of children fixing such an important Day, feeling in *infra dig* to be present.

Heaven thought differently, however. The day was most solemnly regarded as a Day of Judgment. The prayers of the children eclipsed all others in sincerity and fervour and it was they who easily won their case. It was on this extraordinary Rosh-Ha-Shanah, which was kept for three days, that Hitler's doom was sealed with an impending miserable death and that the Nazi Reich, which he boasted would exist for a thousand years, would be ignominiously brought to its knees by the victorious Allies. All this, and more, because of the prayers of those little children in the German church and whom the Accusing Angel had ridiculed.

Others opine that it was on that day, that the "beginning of the Redemption" was fixed, starting from the defeat of the modern Gog and Magog and continuing with "the ingathering of the exiles", scattered the world over, until the foundation of the Jewish State — The Third Jewish commonwealth.

TO THE HEAVENLY FATHER ABOVE

One day, some hundreds of people had been rounded up in the Town Square, formerly the Public Gardens — and under a leaden sky, they awaited that "selection which would choose those who were still able to work."

Those who were considered by the Nazi officers as, "still capable of working", were given a yellow card, and grouped together on the right side of the Square before being sent to their different destinations. Every married man among this group had the right to take with him, his wife and one child. All the rest who had no yellow card, were forced over to the left of the Square. Everyone knew what That meant — Death!

Through the deafening noise of screams and cries, shouted orders and the weeping and wailing, a little child ran backward and forwards, sobbing and beseeching those who had been given a yellow card, "Oh, please, please, take me with you... Tell them that I am your little boy.. Say that you — are my Papa...". But all his anguished pleadings were in vain. Most of the people already had their own child. The others had already been registered as single people, or else childless. But always hoping for a miracle, the child besought one couple after another with his desperate and heart-rending cry. Everybody looked at him, their sad, compassionate eyes taking in only too well the child's tragedy; but not one among them could do anything to help him.

When it was his turn to come before the German officers, the child ran to the group on the right — those who had managed to get a yellow card. But the brutal executioners seized hold of him, beat him with the butts of their rifles and flung him down among those on the left.

Next, it was the turn of an old man and his wife who had with them no children. Desperately, the little boy threw himself into the arms of the old man and implored him, choking with sobs : "Take me with you... Oh, take me... Save me... Save me..." Instantly, one of the officers set his dog on the frantic child and drawing his revolver, shot him through the heart. As the boy crumpled in death, his dying cry still lingered, "Oh, please, Please... be my Father..."

The old man and his wife were thrust away to the left and patiently accepted their fate, But in moving away, the old man picked up the little body of the dead child and nestling it in his arms, he whispered in the lifeless ear : "Yes, come with me. Soon you shall have a father. Our Father, Who is in Heaven above... come with me, and we will go up and find Him together..."

There is a legend that Satan, when he saw this incident, felt his heart so moved, that even he broke down and wept. And leaving that place, Satan ran to God and said : "I can stand no more of this..." And thereafter, even Satan abandoned Hitler... and salvation shone upon them **again.**

THE LETTER

Some people have an impression that when David took up his harp, he had only to pluck at the strings expertly and it sang the harmonies of Joy and Praise. But as the Psalms make it clear to us, his music was often discordant of lamentation and pitiful wailing. Not only in the authoritative field of the Psalms do we find this, but also in the beautiful Land of Legend.

"A voice is heard in Ramah, lamentation and bitter weeping; Rachel weeping for her children. She refuseth to be comforted for her children, because they are not..." In many western countries, it has become the custom to keep "Mother's Day" when loving tributes are paid to individual mothers; but in Israel it is to the great and dear "Mother Rachel" to whom all children pay annual tribute on the eleventh day of Heshvan. This fond celebration, called Yahrzeit, has been throughout countless years the object of a devout pilgrimage to the Tomb of Rachel on the outskirts of Bethlehem (where she died after the birth of Benjamin).

During the nineteen years of Arab possession (from 1948-1967), it was no longer possible for the children of Jerusalem to visit the actual Tomb of Mother Rachel. So a Memorial was made to represent her grave in a small part of the Chamber of the Ashes set up on Mount Zion, in order to keep alive in Jewish hearts the hideous evil of the Holocaust This place of Mother Rachel was made holy by placing therein the Menorah and Parochet (curtain) from her grave in Bethlehem. It was to this shrine, that the children came to honour her every year on the eleventh of Heshvan.

A beautiful custom arose, that during this visit each child should write a little, loving letter to his, or her mother. Special writing-paper was given to each child and they were asked to remember that just as they honoured Mother Rachel at her shrine, so should they honour their own mothers.

On one of these Yahrzeit days, a young boy was observed at the shrine who was not writing, although all the other children were so occupied. Moreover, he even angrily and resentfully refused to take a piece of the paper provided. Very kindly, he was urged to write, but shook his head obstinately. Very gently, he was questioned, but only turned his back in bitter and silent misery. Only at the end, when the others were getting ready to go, did he suddenly steal quietly over and take the paper to write upon.

It was nearly a week later, that a letter was put into the hands of the Reb Zanwill, simply addressed to: "Zipporah, Room of the Ashes, Mount Zion". No one could find a clue as to who Zipporah might be. Intensive inquiries were made, without result. Finally, Reb Zanwil had a penetrating thought. He tenderly took the letter and laid it on the ledge above the Urns which held the Ashes of the Holocaust Martyrs that were recovered from thirty concentration camps.. Perhaps the unknown Zipporah had found a last refuge here.

A few days later, the letter was discovered on the floor, somehow dislodged from its resting-place. Once again, was it brought to Reb Zanwill. This time, he felt compelled to open it to see if there was anything that he could do. It was a pitiful letter from a young boy Yoshke to his mother. He told her that he had never forgotten his promise to write to her but that he could never find her or hear news of her. Now, perhaps, she was here among the Martyrs' Ashes... If she was, she

would hear him and know that he had kept his promise at last...
Though he still missed her, with all his heart, he was now happy and
she must not be troubled about him being still alive.

"Could this", thought Reb Zanwill, deeply moved, "possibly be the boy
who would not write at the Yahrzeit ?" He would try to find him.
Inquiries were made here, there and everywhere, for a thin, black haired
young boy named Yoshke, whose big dark eyes were set in hollows of
sadness. For a long time, even in the most unlikely places, efforts were
made to seek him out. At last, after much searching, he was found, a
student in a humble, little-known Yeshivah.

With infinite tenderness and gentleness, Reb Zanwill talked to Yoshke
and drew out the bitter pain and sorrow from his heart: Zipporah was
his mother. One day, "They" had come and "taken her away..." As she
was torn from him, his mother had turned and cried to him : "Write
to me, my son — promise me that you will write !" His sobbing promise
was the last word he ever spoke to her. Many times did he urge the
friends who cared for him to help him to keep his promise, but they
always put him off with vague answers (knowing all too well he would
never be able to keep it in this world).

Finally, Yoshke was brought to Israel, always mourning and wondering
about his mother. Then, when at the Yahrzeit he had seen and under
stood the meaning of the Urns of Ashes and the piteous sorrow of
Mother Rachel was in his mind, he had known that now here, at ast
he could keep his promise. Despite the anguish which tugged at and
seared his heart, R. Zanwill gave the boy the complete assurance that
his mother had received his letter. She knew he had kept his promise.
Above all, she would now be filled with a great rejoicing that all was
well with her son and that he had found courage and happiness in his
new life in Israel.

"For the Lord hath heard the voice of my weeping," softly sang David
to the muted tones of his harp. "The Lord hath heard my supplication
The Lord receiveth my prayer..."

GUIDED BY THE DIVINE HAND

The week, during which the first Sidra of Leviticus is read, is assigned
on Mount Zion, in the "Cellar of the Holocaust" to the imperishable
memory of the countless, innocent Jewish children who were slaugh
tered during the cursed Hitler Nazi regime. Kaddish in their memory
is recited, memorial prayers chanted and some account of the manner of their death is read from the enormous volumes in which they
are recorded and preserved in that haunting cellar. As an illustration
of the kind of stories told therein and one which is characteristic of
the death of those young and innocent little martyrs, the following
told by the Director of the Mount is very eloquent and heart-rending!
In one of the Orphans' Homes outside Jerusalem, you will find one
child, Isaac by name, who was snatched from the jaws of death that
were ever open in the devilish concentration-camps and was brought
to Israel by his widowed mother. Yitzhak'l, as he was called when a
little child, is now parentless, for his father perished in the notorious
Camp of Auschwitz and his mother outsoared the shadows of human
life soon after she had arrived in Israel. His early years were spent in
the concentration-camps. Yet despite this terrible early background, he
has grown, thank God, into a bright and strong young man. He is the
strongest of all the children and enjoys the respect of them all; and
when a fight breaks out between them, it is he that divides them with
a mere wave of the hand. He is always well, never even catching a cold;
and it is said of him that this iron constitution of his was forged in
the concentration-camp.

Regarded from every angle, Yitzhak'l is a most remarkable child. For
though the possessor of strength which inspired fear of him in
the hearts of other children, yet he was never known to smile at any-
body. He may have been seen on occasion to raise his hand as if to
strike, but none has ever seen this hand to descend upon anyone. It
once happened that another boy wished to engage in a fight with him,
an incident which is not too rare in a Home for children. Both were

196

locked in a fierce combat on the floor, and the other boy was mauling and pummelling Yitzhakl on the face. Several times, he raised his hand as if to smite back, but each time he dropped his hand lifelessly. The children who stood around watching this one-sided combat, shouted : "Yitzhakl, give him one back ! Teach him a lesson he will never forget". Being all on his side, they clapped their hands and banged with their feet to spur on Yitzhakl to retalliate and knock the aggressive boy out with a decisive blow. Yet, all that Yitzhakl did was to protect his face with his hands and push-off his antagonist brusquely aside, but he did not hit back. This reaction of his, in the face of violent blows, caused consternation and surprise among all who witnessed this unusual spectacle. How came it that their strong Yitzhak'l should not resist, even with one knock-out blow, the boy who was slogging away at him, right and left ? Those who were Sabras (born in Israel), especially could not understand such a one-sided spectacle. "How comes it ?, they asked of one another ?

This fight became a talking-point in the boy's Home and the Principal tackled Yitzhak'l many a time to explain his passive, non-resistance attitude; but each time his question met with a blank refusal to answer Yitzhak'l remained silent, his face turning both red and pale in reaction to these probings. It did not take long for the Principal to understand that he was treading on most delicate ground here and that the at titude of the boy may be due to some psychological experience in the concentration camps. He, therefore, bided his time for the opportune moment to arrive when the boy would explain all. When that moment came, the following was the story the boy poured into the ears of the sympathetic, fatherly Principal.

The beastly Nazis had killed his father and, while still hiding in his mother's apron, they were both transported to one of the labour concentration camps in Skorzhisko. After a while, his mother was whisked away from there to another place and he remained all alone in the camp doing his very best to escape the unwanted attention of the overseers of the camp. His sufferings during that period can better be imagined than described. For many days he hungered, seeking each time another hiding-place; and as he was not included in the official list of inmates, no rations were allotted to him. All he had, were the tiny morsels of food the other inmates would mercifully spare from their own meagre rations, for this poor and lonely little soul. All these physical sufferings paled into insignificance besides the mental anguish which was his. He could not drive his mother's face out of his mind, and his yearnings for her were excuciatingly painful. During the day, and especially during the stillness of the night, he would see her face staring pitifully into his eyes and crying out bitterlv : "Come to me, my child". In response, he yearned for her endlessly and the hot, salty tears rolled frequently from his eyes. How could he be restored again to his dear mother?

Alas ! no way was in sight. The camp was fenced in with electric wires and closely guarded by murderous guards and wild, ravenous dogs. From such a camp, who could escape ? Every time he made a desperate effort to escape, he met with failure, till one day his chance came. He hid himself in one of the huge dust-bins which the cleaners of the camp emptied each night into the open fields outside the camp and so he found himself outside that hellish prison-house of a camp. Picking himself up from the dirt, with which he was pitchforked into the open space wtihout, he felt a sense of freedom and happiness as he breathed once again the unsullied air of a world God created in which all men should live peacefully and happily. But where was he ? He did not know. One thing, however, he did know. This was, that he must run away as quickly as possible from this dreadful place and come to his mother who is so yearningly waiting for him.

The night was starless and exceptionally still and dark. Escape into the thick forest which surrounded the camp was the only alternative facing him. He began to walk and run, run and walk, not knowing whither his steps were leading him. What spurred him on was the interminable cry of his mother ringing in his ears : "Come to me, my child". He imagined that an unknown hand had grasped his and was leading him along, helping him to jump over little hills and deep pits and miraculously aiding him to avoid crossings that were dangerous. For five nights he thus wandered, not knowing whither he was destined and during which his sole sustenance was the grass, wild fruits and berries he picked on his way and drinking of the melting snows. His heart was pounding with a quick beat, but he was strengthened in the belief that it was his dear mother's hand that was leading him and that eventually he would fall into her open, welcome arms.

On the sixth day, he came across a group of wood-fellers who worked in the forest not far from Lublin where his steps had now led him. He was taken in by these Jews who had been mobilized by the Nazis for this back-breaking labour and after being given food and drink, was asked to recite his story. He was advised to sneak an unobtrusive entrance into the womens' labour camp adjoining. Perhaps his mother was there ? This he did and, miraculous to relate, there was his mother ' There she stood, as if she were waiting for him all the time. With a joyous cry, he fell into her loving arms. Pressed against her heart, ne could feel his own heart and hers beating in joyous, anxious unision, while both her eyes and his welled and streamed forth with tears.

Yitzhakl told her the story of his wanderings throughout the many nights across that fearsome forest. As he finished his tale, he burst out · "You, dear mother, made it possible for me to come to you; for it was your hand that led me here and that grasped mine tenaciously throughout, not letting me fall on the journey and guarding me from every pitfall and lurking danger."

"No, my darling",replied his mother, as she caressingly patted his head. "It was God who led you, not I. It was His hand that guided you, Happy art thou, my son, that He has guided you to me. May he do so in the future, too".

When he finished, Yitzhak'l turned to the Principal of the Home saying : "These were my mother's last words to me and, as you can see, her blessing of divine protection has been fulfilled ! For it is His hand that has guided me through all the dangers that encompassed me on the way to Eretz-Israel. How can my hand, which His once clapsed saving me from all perils, be lifted up to strike any one, even those who attack me? A hand once clasped by God can only be held out with love towards all and malice towards none."

THE INFANT HAZAN

The Vilna Ghetto was preparing for Yom Kippur, despite the dangers lurking around the holding of religious services on that day. Guards were placed at the entrances of such streets where services took place to give instant warning of any suspicions aroused by the Nazis.

R. Isaac Vaholol was responsible for the service to be held in the hotel in Shpitolma street. Prayer-books were collected, readers appointed. and a Scroll of the Law was hidden in a tumble-down house in a dark alley not far from the hotel. In one of the rooms of this tumble-down house, there lived a shoemaker, Moshe Yerahmiel by name, with his wife Hannah, and young child Hezkeleh. Yerahmiel was one of the few remaining residents who refused to leave the Ghetto. When "the selection" was made for Jews to be carted-off to the camps, efforts were successfully made on his behalf to receive a certificate as shoemaker whereby he would be left alone. Thereby, three lives were saved — his own, that of his wife and that of his baby son. While he sat the whole day repairing shoes, his wife would roam the streets of the ghetto to obtain food with which to keep alive her family and, especially with which to obtain medicinal cures for her ailing child.

On Erev Yom Kippur, R. Isaac came to Yerahmiel and requested him to conduct the service in Shpitolma. Giving him a Mahzor, he also gave him the password whereby he would obtain entrance to the underground service. Yerahmiel agreed to conduct the Kol Nidre service. In the early hours of that Erev Yom Kippur day, his wife Hannah wended her usual way around the Ghetto streets to obtain food. She went to the smugglers and "blackmarket" quarters to try her luck there. She knew all the secret alleys which led to and from the Ghetto.

Just that day, word had reached the Gestappo of what was going on in that quarter. With guns crackling away from all sides, they swooped down on the place, arresting all whom they found. Among those who were thrown into armoured cars was also the hapless Hannah.

Full of foreboding and anxiety, Yerahmiel sat in his workshop, one hand clasping a shoe in the process of repair, while his eyes were glued to the Mahzor in preparation of tunes he would sing to-night at the service. He sat and mumbled the refrain which would accompany his rendering of the opening words of the service : "With the permission of Heaven and the congregation, we are permitted to pray together tonight with those who transgressed". He sat and pondered . "There are no transgressors these days. Every Jew is holy and pure, and there is no need for such permission to be obtained. As he continued to hum the tunes, his heart began to pound with anxiety. Why was Hannah so late in returning? But he tried hard to allay the fears by assuring himself that her return would not be unduly delayed.

Meanwhile, little Hezkelah was lying in a corner of the broken bed, weeping bitterly, "Mother, mother". He was hungry and cried for food. His father did his best to soothe him and hummed the tunes he was practicing for the service. But in Yerahmiel's heart anxiety was tormenting — What had happened to Hannah? It was nearly four o'clock, when the time for the meal before the Fast was due. When would she return ?

He tried hard to soothe the weeping child. Picking him up, he pressed him to his bosom, and assured him that his mother would soon return. with plenty of food. "You only be a good child and wait." He will search for his missing wife. But all her usual haunts knew her not. It continued to cry out bitterly for his mother. Fear and trembling seized the whole of Yerahmiel's body. What had happened ? Why was she such a long time in coming ?

Leaving the weeping child alone in the room, he decided to go out and see."All will be well yet, my darling", he comforted him. But it was only in the smuggler's quarter that he learnt the bitter truth. Hannah was among those who had been mopped up by the Gestappo. He could no longer contain his grief. With a bitter cry that pierced the heaven, he cried : "Hannah, where art thou ?". Weeping bitterly, he wended his heart-broken way slowly homewards, as one from whom all reason had flown. He no sooner reached his room than he fell in a dead swoon on the floor.

After a long time, he was awakened to his senses by the piercing cries of Hezkele who kept on his lament for "Mother, mother". The child had crawled down from the bed upon his father's body, striking his unconscious father and crying in his ears : "Mother, mother",Gradually, Yerahmiel regained consciousness, looked around him and realized all that had happened. With a renewed effort, he took the child into his arms and sought to stop his weeping with the comfort that soon his mother would return. What to do till she returned, he knew not. Food there was not in the house. His heart was broken. He sat on the bed and the child in his arms wept. Both of them now wept.

Meanwhile, the large congregation in Shpitolma Street had assembled in eager anticipation for the arrival of Yerahmiel. Why was he so long in coming ? "What could have happened to him ?", was the thought which worried them all. It was so late already and they could not wait much longer. Some even were of the opinion that they should start without him. But then the only one who possessed a Mahzor was Yerahmiel and nobody present could conduct a service by heart.

So it was decided that R. Isaac Vohalal repair to the home of Yerahmiel to learn the truth of what had happened. Imagine his pained surprise at what he beheld ! Father and habe were both sitting on the bed weeping bitterly; the child crying "Mother" and his father seeking helplessly to reassure him that his mother would soon return. R. Isaac drew nigh and sought to appease the father. "Yerahmiel", he pleaded. "the entire congregation is now waiting patiently for you to begin the service."

Yerahmiel raised his eyes as on awakening from some painful nightmare. "What, they are waiting for Kol Nidre ? Right, here we go". Turning to the infant, he wept : "You hear, my child, the congregation is waiting. You are also waiting. I am also waiting. Oh, Hannah, Hannah! Where are you ?" He then made a manful effort to tell R. Isaac, all that had transpired. The latter did his best to cheer him, knowing only too well that his words had no solid foundation. They were only used to give him hope and courage for the present. But Yerahmiel decided to take up the child in his arms, and proceed to conduct the Service. Who knows? Perhaps God would have mercy on his helpless, ailing child left motherless ?

When he came into the assembly, many could not face the sad figure with the weeping child in his arms. Yerahmiel donned his Tallit, opened his Mahzor, his whole appearance as one demented, With the child helplessly clinging to him, he began. After all, what had he left in the world, beside this weeping child ? The congregation trembled at what might happen. Should he be allowed to conduct the Service ? Who knows what might happen ? They decided to wait patiently and see what transpired.

As Yerahmiel began to tune the Kol Nidre quietly, the child in his arms began a piercing cry : "Mother, mother". The entire congregation made an effort to silence him by shouting : "Shah ! Shah !" Also Yerahmiel tried hard to soothe him by saying: "She will soon return". When the child still persisted, the father then turned to it and said : "You know what, Hezkele, you act a Hazan. Here is the Mahzor, look into it, and cry "Mother, mother!". Like one demented, Yerahmiel kept on pressing the child to act as Hazan and cry "Mother, mother". Why should he cry to me! Let him cry to God! "The child did so, crying to God for his mother. The whole assembly wept with the child So did the Walls of the Synagogue; so did the whole of existence with him.

BERELE'S SIDDUR

During the services of the Children's day in the chamber of the Holo-caust, the entire congregation prayed wtih great fervour. Each one stared intently at the words in the Siddur in front of them. There was one old man among those praying who attracted attention. Wrapped in a long Tallit, he was swaying backwards and forwards, praying with great emotion, but though his lips were moving, one could not hear a word he was saying. In his hand, he had a piece of paper which he kept tossing into the air. It was certainly a puzzling sight.

At the conclusion of the service, a young fellow, approached him with a gay smile and asked :

"What is this piece of paper ?"

"Piece of paper? It is possible that you saw it and yet you do not know what it is?", said the old man in astonishment.

"Tell me", said the fellow seriously.

"This folded piece of paper has all twenty-two letters of the Hebrew alphabet. This is the Siddur of the Silent! It is called "Berele's Siddur".

Berele's parents, in order to save his life from the Nazis, were forced to send him to a convent. Before little Berele went to the convent, his parents instructed him several times; "Berele, Berele, don't forget, you are among non-Jews. Remain a Jew in your heart and with your soul! Be a Jew, but be careful so to act that people will not suspect it and report you to the authorities. These are dangerous times. Since we are commanded to keep alive, be a "silent" Jew! Berele listened to his parents and obeyed them. He carefully disguised his origin from every-one. Even though there were in the surrounding area a few scattered Jews, Berele never came into contact with them.

One day, Berele heard people talking of a trainload of Jews, wrapped in their traditional garb who had passed through his little town on the way to a concentration camp. The same day brought news of the capture by the dreaded S.S. of a group of Jews who were caught praying in a secret underground synagogue. This had happened on Yom Kippur ! The Nazis packed them into waggons headed for Auschwitz.

It was the members of the monastery who had seen the trains pass by and discussed it lightly among themselves. Such events had become routine, making sensitive people callous to the fate of others. Berele's heart was breaking, and he wanted to share the fate of his doomed brothers. However, he heard his father's voice in his ears and remembered his advice. Yet he had to express, somehow and in some way, his deep, turmoiled emotions.

When he was alone in one of the tiny cells of the monastery, the idea occured to him to pray, unseen by anyone except God.

He wanted to pray as a Jew, but he did not know any Hebrew prayer by heart and, obviously, he did not have a Siddur. He remembered that his father once related a story of a poor little boy who wanted to pray but did not know how, because he was never able to go to school. He entered the synagogue and recited all that he knew — which was only the alphabet. But he recited it so fervently and with so much meaning, that God gladly accepted it. He gathered the letters lovingly together and formed prayers from them. With this story in mind, Berele took a piece of paper and wrote the letters — as many as he remembered — on it. He, too, prayed that God should combine them into proper prayers. When he finished, Berele folded the paper, closed his eyes and prayed to God : "O Heavenly Father, you know that I am not accustomed to praying, but I recited all I knew. I hope that it is acceptable unto Thee", and with that, he threw the paper heavenward.

Three times daily, Berele prayed in this same way. At the conclusion of his prayer, he would always throw the paper with the letters skyward. He did this during his entire stay at the monastery.

Berele was saved from the monastery at the end of the war. Three American soldiers were sent by the victorious armies to investigate the situation at the monastery. One of them was a military chaplain. He came to take Berele away with him. He promised to make arrangements for Berele's emigration to Eretz Yisrael. Berele was as happy as could be and quickly changed into the clothes that were brought for him. Suddenly, Berele remembered his Siddur which he kept hidden in one of his pockets. He began to search through the pockets of his old clothing. "Did you forget something", asked the director of the monaste ry. "My Siddur", Berele replied to everyone's astonishment. When he found it, he showed it to them and they looked at it with admiration. Later, this Siddur was sent to the archives of Mt. Zion where things relating to the destruction of Jewry by the Nazis are preserved.

"This is the Siddur of the Silent", concluded the old man.

THE FEATHERS OF THE HUMMING BIRD

A young man, of lean and pale appearance, once approached Reb Zanwill with the request that he would like an exclusive interview will him. No sooner were they closeted together in the privacy of the Director's office, when the young man carefully took out of his wallet four feathers wrapped in paper, handing them over to Reb Zanwill. These once belonged to a young boy, Moshele, who had died in the monastery in which he and the boy were taken for safety to escape the destructive talons of the Nazi beasts. This he did in a kind of shame-faced way. With lowered voice, he began to tell the following tale :

"The home from which Moshele came, was one that was very Jewish in spirit. Not only was it Kasher in every sense of the word, but it was also a kind of rallying-place where the elders of the city would come to sweeten counsel together with Moshele's parents, especially concerning Eretz Israel. During such meetings, they would often chant chapters of the Psalms and sing glorious Zemirot describing the beauties of Eretz Israel. Moshele's mother possessed a humming-bird that knew the songs they sung and which would accompany them with chirping and twittering whenever they sang.

When rumours came that the Nazis were going to capture the children of the Ghetto, Moshele's mother was very perturbed as to how to save her five-year old child. Yes, there was only one way. Her former Christian maid would take custody of the child for a sum of money to be paid to her and place him in a monastery as a Christian child. and thus save him from certain death. At first, they were reluctant to have recourse to such a painful act, but when danger was imminent, they complied. For this act, they even received the approval of the Rabbi of the Ghetto. His reasoning was that since the intention of the Nazis was to destroy the body rather than the soul, it was permitted for us to try to defeat his devilish object by any means possible, by hook or by crook, even by crook.

When his mother handed him over into the care of the monastery, while the tears flowed freely from her eyes, her last words to Moshele were : "Always remember, my child, that you are a Jew. I give you to guard this humming-bird which will always remind you that you are a Jew, and that I am your mother. See that you remember not to forget what I am now telling you." Young in years as he was, Moshele was advanced in knowledge and emotions, as all Jewish children were in those days of Nazi extermination. When his mother turned to go, he placed his hand in that of the Mother Superior and with tears welling from them, he followed her.

He was led, together with his humming-bird, into the monastery, the hiding-place of many Jewish children. How he longed for his parents and his own home ! As time went on, one could hardly tell he was a Jew, so self-possessed was he. The bird continued to trill the Jewish melodies Moshele had heard in his home, though it was obvious how strange it felt in such alien surroundings. The hymns, the food, the whole place made the bird restless. It ceased to eat of the food laid before it; it became listless and lost all inclination to hop about from place to place. It was only towards evening, when Moshele returned from school, that the bird seemed to spring to life and twittered the parental melodies so beloved of them and which served to link the child with his parents and ancestral faith. As the bird went through all its repertoire of song, including such well-known hymns as Adon-Olam, Shabbat Zemirot, the tunes of the Yamim Noraim, Hatikvah, and so on, Moshele stood in front of the cage with rapt attention and breathless admiration. These tunes which the bird trilled and to which he hearkened, tied them both in bonds of inseparable friendship.

When morning came, Moshele went off to his studies and the bird returned to its solitary and muted confinement. It was obvious to those who looked after it, that despite the luxurious titbits so beloved of other birds with which they fed it, that the bird was inwardly pining so they decided to give it up as a bad job. Not so Moshele, however. For hours on end, he stood near the cage, doing all he could to persuade it to eat, but the bird heeded not even him. As a last resort, Moshele sang the song he heard so often at home.

"On a golden tray, food is offered,

And in a silver cup, drink is poured,

Why do not you eat ?"

All the response the bird made was a twitter so weak, that soon it ceased altogether.

The pale young man continued unfolding his tale to the Director. "One Shabbat Eve, the bird appeared listless, almost lifeless, with no strength left to hop about or to trill even weakly. Moshele watched it with sad heart, singing to it in German the above ditty he had heard at home. "Why are you so sad, my beloved bird?", he weepingly pleaded. "As I recall this scene," continued the narrator," my eyes still weep and my heart is torn. That very night of Shabbat, the bird died. Broken-hearted, Moshele buried it near his little room and placed its feathers in his pocket as a perpetual reminder.

"From that night onward, Moshele became a changed being. His longings for home and parents grew so painfully strong, that he ceased to study and eat and was confined to his bed with his strength wasting away. It became clear to those who looked after him, that his tenure of life was peacefully drawing to its conclusion.

"Although he and I never spoke about our Jewish origins, it became clear to me, as I sat at his bedside during those last days, that he never ceased being a Jew. For he would hug to his heart the feathers of the dead bird and quietly tune prayeful melodies. I understood, but said not a word. Like a candle, the light of Moshele's life waxed more dim. For hours on end, his eyes were riveted on me in silence. It was clear that he wished to say something but could not for fear. When my patience became exhausted, I whispered to him : "You are a Jewish boy, so am I. Say what you wish to tell me". His face waxed red. Seizing my hand, he kissed me, saying quietly : My name is Moshele". Saying this, he entrused me with the feathers of the bird, entreating me to take the greatest care of them, as if they were of some fabulous treasure. He added: "Perhaps you might meet my mother one day. Then, please give her these feathers". No sooner did he utter those words, than he breathed his last.

"To this day," continued the young man, "I have not met his mother. According to reports which have reached me, no trace of his family has survived. As I cannot be responsible for these feathers, to whose safe care can I entrust them ? So I decided that the safest place is the Cell of Destruction on Mt. Zion. Perhaps to this sad but holy spot, members of Moshele's family will one day repair and will think of the tale of the little boy and his beloved bird."

THE UNIVERSAL SONG

Reb Zanwill continued the tale. "These feathers belonged to the bird of the last Levite who participated in the Temple Songs". He then proceeded to narrate to them the tale told him by R. Shabbetai, one of the first pioneers of song which was his absorbing interest night and day. It was he, also, a devotee of Cabbala, who weaved these feathers into the harp of David.

At first, he explained, there were only the four feathers which the pale

209

youth had brought. One day, it was noticed that one feather was missing from the glass-case in which they had been placed. Seek where they could, there was no trace of the missing feather. Of what use could it be to the one who had taken it? It seemed as if it had vanished into thin air. At the termination of one Shabbat, a man came to me with the message that R. Shabbetai wishes to speak to me. When I hurried to him, I found him in a room, every corner of which proclaimed his poverty.

He then told me that the missing feather, together with others, was in his possession. Noting the look of surprise on my face, he exclaimed: "First let me tell you something about the nest of song; later, I will solve the mystery of the missing feather. You will thus solve all that is puzzling you now."

"The whole world is full of song to God. The Torah is one long song to Him", he continued. "But what is the source of this Universal Song? Well, tradition has it that it was Adam who first burst into song. It was Erev Shabbat when he was created and the first words which burst rapturously and musically from his lips were the words from which David later composed one of his favourite Psalms, "a Psalm for the Shabbat day". So pure and limpid was the song, that it resembled a well of living waters flowing from the Garden of Eden. This was before he sinned. After that, the world darkened for him, his rapturous melodies became sad and muted. The well of song dried up and the gift of Song was taken from him.

"But once song came into the world, it could never disappear altogether. So it was clothed with wings and flew heavenwards towards the Ministering Angels who were jealous of the gift of song possessed by mortals. A compromise was made. For the six days of the working week the bird of Song would remain on high, but on Shabbat it would descend to cheer man. This is why each Angel has six wings, for it uses one wing of Song for each day. At the dawning of each Shabbat, the Angels appear before God with the petition to grant them another wing. The reply they receive is: "Yes, I have another wing with which song can be flown to me, but this cannot come from you. "For from the wings (corner) of the earth, have we heard the song".

Adam grieved all his days because Song had been taken from him during the week, because of his sin. Jealous of the Angels, he complained: "What is the use of Song or of the Torah to them ? It is we mortals who need such support on earth. Are the angels prone to old age, physical ailments and the alternate moods of joy and grief ? Of what use to them is song, which reflects moods of which they know not ? Song must be born of earth and of mortal man. Does not the earth itself proclaim: "I declare Song: "Unto the Lord is the earth and the heavens thereof". Adam was not appeased until David appeared, after had he made full repentance. The world, hereforth, became full of song, as it was before Original Sin came though Adam's disobedience of the first Divine Commandment.

"As you know", continued R. Shabbetai, "the soul of David is part of that of Adam who, self-sacrificingly, donated to him seventy years of his own life. It was David who, with the aid of his harp which played and renewed itself each hour and, especially, each Shabbat and Yom-tov of its own accord and which filled the world with harmony Like the Song at the Well, which overflowed its banks and at which our ancestors sang "Rise up, O Well", the Song of Israel fills the whole universe. It is this act of Song which makes mortal man more beloved of God than His angels. For whereas the latter sing unto Him only once a day, some even say only once a week or once a month,or once a year, or once in a Shemittah, or even once during a Jubilee, the Jew is always full of song and praise.

Moreover, angels on High only burst into Song when they hear mortals sing below. Does it not say: "The sons of God sing together with the morning stars ?". This song was dedicated by David to the service of God entrusted to the Levites for the service of the Temple; only those who have the right ears can hear the mysteries of song". The old man then confided to Reb Zanwill two of the secrets of song

211

which he had heard from his father R. Abba, who had journeyed all over Israel with ears always open.

When R. Abba came to Kinneret, he noticed that its shape reflected a harp, like that of David's. Looking deeply into it, he seemed to see the Well of Miriam emerging from it bursting with song, as if in response to the music proceeding from this harp of David. When R. Abba came to Mt. Zion and sat in the little copse of trees near the Tomb of David, it appeared to him that the boughs of the trees seemed to form themselves into a huge nest. Peeping into the nest, he beheld wings of burnished gold instead of withered feathers.

As the wind soughed through the trees and gently touched the feathers, they burst forth into song, a song so haunting that R. Abba never ceased to hum it all his days. He died before Shavuot, the traditional day of the death of David; and it is believed that his soul, which was lived in purity and died in purity, will await the messianic age while it remains nestled in the trees.

A MOTHER'S PROMISE

Together with her sole, surviving daughter Malkah, the widow Rebecca lived in a dark and dilapidated room in the Warsaw Ghetto, as lonely as a stone. Her child was her only treasure. The cursed Nazis had murdered her husband and her children and her she guarded as "the apple in her eye". Despite the squalour and poverty in which they were forced to live, mother and daughter encouraged and comforted each other, until the sad day arrived when the Nazis made swoops on the remaining survivors of the ghetto, with the primary object of snatching away all young children for enforced slave-labour — and even worse. The end of such inhumane action was the slaughter of one million two hundred thousand little children, whose innocent death and cries pierced and darkened the blue heavens above that beheld this bloody holocaust.

Rebecca did all in her power to save Malkah's life and succeeded in persuading an old Christian woman who had once worked for her to hide her chlid in her home and look after her. But the child refused to leave the mother all by herself and pleaded : "I will not go; I do not want you to be left all by yourself. What will happen to you, will also happen to me", she pleaded.

The mother spent hours in trying to convince this child of the imminent danger which threatened her life, but the more she pleaded the more adamant the child became. When nothing else availed, the mother burst into loud weeping and adjured her child in the name of her dead father to comply with her wishes. She swore a solemn oath that she would be present at her wedding. This she did, in order to calm her daughter that all would be well in the end if she only listened to her. "You will see", pleaded the mother, "God will help us to survive these wicked tyrants and then we will both sing joyous songs at your wedding". After this, the painful parting took place. Mother and daughter tearfully separated and Malkah was taken over by the kind-hearted Christian woman.

Years passed, years of suffering and torture, cremation and concentration-camps in which six million Jews met a cruel end. Rebecca died during one of these indescribable "transports", but Malkah managed to survive. When the war was over, Malkah began a frantic search from one concentration-camp to another for her mother. Did she not promise her that they would meet after the war was over ! Though her search was not of the slightest avail, do what and search where she could, Malkah did not abandon the hope that her mother lived and would one day be present at her wedding to sing the joyous song she had promised.

In one of the camps, Malkah met and fell in love with Samuel who proposed marriage to her. The heart of the girl was saddened with the thought of her mother and Samuel told her that he would join in this search. When their combined search proved unsuccessful, they both decided to go on hachsharah, with the object of fitting themselves to take up permanent residence in Israel. They were taken on an illegal, immigrant-ship and managed to smuggle into the Land There, Samuel joined a Kibbutz and Malkah a youth settlement. Their love for each other could not keep them apart for long, but Malkah persisted that she could not think of marriage before she found her mother. "My mother is still waiting for me", she pleaded. She was impervious to all pleadings of her friends that her mother was no longer alive and persisted that her mother would abide by her solemn promise to be present at her wedding. No, she would not get married without her mother. Samuel heard her with saddened heart. He understood and was sympathetic. To himself, he observed : "A dibbuk (spirit) has entered her heart — her mother's promise".

Again, the years rolled on and Malkah still clung to the promise of her mother that she would be present at her wedding-nuptials. Out of true, abiding love for her, Samuel also decided to wait despite the appeals of relations and friends and even of Malkah herself not to wait and wed another. No argument availed; not even the fact that as the years passed, Malkah would get older and become less beautiful and attractive. Her friends also entreated Malkah to forget about her mother's promise and to get married to Samuel whose love for her was of such a rare kind. The day came when she could no longer resist their entreaties and tearfully she consented to marry Samuel. In a lucky hour, the time and place of the ceremony were fixed.

The day previous to the wedding, Malkah ascended Mount Zion to pour out her heart in the "Cellar of Destruction", as was the custom of those who had survived the dreaded camps. They regarded this pilgrimage as equated to a visit to the graves themselves, for in this cellar are deposited the ashes of many of the victims. It was also the custom of brides before their wedding to repair to the graves of their parents and invite them to their weddings. This, Malkah now did with prolonged sobs and endless tears. She asked her mother's forgiveness for not waiting for her, but invited her to be present in spirit at her wedding the next day. When she left the Cellar, she felt easier at heart and more prepared to face tomorrow's Huppah.

The visit of Malkah to Mount Zion caused a stir in the heart of Reb Zanwill and his followers, for as soon as she entered the Cellar of the Holocaust, the atmosphere became surcharged with a strange tension. All those present at the time remained tongue-tied, staring at her with eyes glazed in wonderment. The Superintendent of the Cellar sensed that something extraordinary had occurred. Reb Zanwill himself experienced the burdening sensation of gloom which now prevailed in the Cellar. The bitter weeping of Malkah shook his heart to its very foundations.

According to his usual practice when he beheld such heart-rending grief, Reb Zanwill stood beside her and began to speak to her words of comfort and encouragement. Synpathetically, he enquired as to the cause of her lamentation, promising to be of as much help to her as lay in his power. Malkah, however, brushed him gently aside, shook her head sadly and heaving a very deep sigh, said with profound sorrow : "What can you possibly do to help me ?", and continued with her heartrending sobbing. Her ceaseless tears streamed down beside the cupboard wherein were deposited the jars of earth collected from the hellish Nazi crematoria of the Concentration Camps, mingled with the ashes for the charred bodies of their victims.

The atmosphere of the Cellar became more and more oppressive and heavy to endure. Reb Zanwill was much preplexed and sorely worried. It appeared as if something concealed from his sight and extraordinary in its effects, was troubling his heart. It apeared to him, in his imagination, as if all the jars of earth and ashes assembled in the Cellar wished to break out and burst open from the cupboard wherein they were in the Cellar.

What suddenly caused this violent unrest and ferment among the ashes gathered in the jars and urns, giving those present the impression that the cupboard had suddenly become too narrow, too cribbed. and confined to contain them? A bleak, cold atmosphere had always prevailed in the Cellar; but Malkah had brought in with her, so it seemed, an even more deadly chill — a cold breath as of death itself. All present shivered, as the deathly spell congealed their blood and laid icy fingers round their hearts. All eyes were on Malkah and Reb Zanwill observed with silent, fascinated amazement this solemn and terrifying sight of the passionate ferment and revolt of the ashes in their jars and urns.

At first, he thought to himself that his eyes had deceived him. Afterwards, when he enquired of many of the Elders of the Mount if what he had beheld was reality or a chimera, their replies confirmed his conviction that the very Ashes were in a state of feverish protest, seeking to break forth from their confinement. Even after Malkah had left the Cellar and had descended Mount Zion, the troubled atmosphere prevailing in the Cellar did not depart with her. It continued and remained as oppressive as before, and the jars and urns did not cease to tremble and shake violently.

Profoundly disturbed, and his own limbs shaking with tension, Reb Zanwill paced up and down the Cellar frustrated and searched for some kind of explanation for this extraordinary occurrence. Sadly, however, all his attempts to solve the riddle ended with no glimmer of light. All his thoughts seemed chaotic and crying "Havoc!" in his mind.

On occasion, the Elders of the Mount would hearken intently to the "Song of the Mount", and shape the course of their minds and actions according to its mystical sound and melody. There was a tradition current on the Mount that the strings of the Harp suspended above the Sepulchre of King David are bestirred to play each night. Those trained in such esoteric music claim that with it, it is possible to be apprised of mysteries and things concealed from the usual gaze of men. The claim made on behalf of this melody is not only that it can lay secrets bare, but that it can also solve seemingly impossible problems and dilemmas. Very often does Reb Zanwill tarry on the Mount until the late hour of midnight, waiting with loving expectancy for the melody to commence, just as it did in the days of King David when the northern wind rippled across the strings of his Harp, awakening him to pour out his deathless Hymns of Praise and Supplication to his Heavenly Father.

That night, after Malkah's appearance, the melody was early in its arrival, breaking out in tuneful strains almost with the appearance of the stars which kindled the darkling sky. Reb Zanwill was seized with fright when he heard, as an accompaniment to the melody, a sigh so deeply laden with grief that if tore at the heart of any who heard it. Quickly, he turned in the direction of the sound, striving to pierce the darkness in order to find the person who was emitting such tokens of overwhelming sorrow; but not a soul was in sight. While engaged in looking on all sides to discover the source of these sighs, he continued to hear them but could not trace their cause. Horror and distress produced a faintness and a growing terror as he listened.

Gradually, some of the Elders of the Mount came to his side and kept vigil with him on this lonely midnight. They, also, had heard the mysterious sighing, now prolonged for hours, and the mysterious music, beginning as though sounded by a shrill Shofar and gradually being transformed into a symphony of sighs and groans, wailing and lamentation. With their leader, the Elders gave vent to their curiosity. What could be the meaning for the Melody of the Harp to have begun in the early hours of the evening ? Could it have beeen some figment of their imagination, or had they heard it in truth and reality ?"

They then resolved to follow in the wake of the sounds. These led them quickly to the Cellar of the Holocaust, to the very spot where the jars of Ashes were preserved in remembrance of the Six Million Dead of our glorious martyrs. Yes ! They could hardly believe their senses when they realized that the sighing came, in a profound accumulation of grief, from the Urns of Ashes themselves. They beheld the same unmistakeable revolt stirring the Ashes in their containers, almost throwing off the lids which held them down. From within each urn, the sighs escaped sounded like a lament impregnated with wild

217

grief and pain. **Reb Zanwill and the Elders** remained rooted to the spot, riveted by amazement and awe and terror. Was it a miracle which their eyes beheld — a mystery to which they could find no solution ? Their souls became charged with fear and their limbs trembled. They yearned inexpressibly to know the cause and thus ease the anguish of this agonized sighing and yearning.

According to the accepted custom prevailng among the Elders of the Mount, such mysterious happenings were finally explained by the discovery of the source from which such sounds originally emanated. Leaving the Cellar, they still heard — when they had regained the outer air — the combined melody and sighs leading them as before. They followed it by a direct route to the new dwelling-places of Jerusalem. It finally led them to an isolated house in Emek Rephaim (formerly known as the German Colony). It was at this lonely house that the melancholy will-o'-the wisp stopped and drew them no further.

When they entered the house, they found themselves in the presence of many men and women clothed in festive garments. There was also an orchestra of musicians. It would appear that a wedding ceremony was about to take place. The Elders could not suppress their exclamations of surprise at this scene. What connection was there between this happy celebration and the heartbroken sighs heard on the mountains ? But in accordance with the usual procedure in such cases, they kept their amazement to themselves, for they had learnt from experience that there must certainly be some close association in such a matter between this house and the mysterious sighs of grief.

The assembled guests were equally surprised at the sudden appearance of the delegation from Mount Zion. All eyes were turned upon Reb Zanwill and his band of followers who had apparently come uninvited to participatee in the forthcoming ceremony. What had prompted these honoured and distinguished guests to take the trouble of coming to participate in a wedding which would make man and wife of a bride and groom quite unknown to them ? However, they received their guests from Mount Zion with great respect and joy, placing them at

218

the head of the table as was befitting for such guests of distinction. The latter accepted the honour given to them while waiting inwardly with baited breath to see what would transpire.

Long did they tarry there with those assembled for the wedding-ceremony; not knowing whether or not to wait for a scene which seemed to be delayed so long in materializing. What were they to do ? To leave the house and proceed further, they could not because the music and the sighing had definitely ended here. Yet they tormented themselves with the question; "What link, if any, could there be between what was happening here and the Song of the Mount ?" So they decided to stay where they were,chained by their silent wonder, and so find out what would eventually happen.

While they were sitting at table lost in thought, one of the relatives of the bridal couple approached them, full of apologies for keeping them waiting so long in suspense as to when the ceremony would eventually take place. He, also, was surprised, he told them, at this delay, for the wedding should have taken place two hours ago. All was ready except for the bride, who still delayed her appearance and without whom it was obvious the marriage could not take place ! He went on : "We have sent messengers to her but the men came back with pale faces and very upset, telling us that the bride was not yet ready to appear here. Then, with lowered voices, they went on to tell us in confidence that the bride-to-be is sitting in her own room, weeping bitterly without ceasing. She explained, with eyes bathed in tears, that she is waiting for her Mother to come to her wedding. There seems no other explanation to us but that the poor girl has gone out of her mind. This ghost (Dibbuk) of a promise made by her Mother has penetrated into her heart. Who knows how the matter will end, or whether the wedding will ever take place at all ?"

When the uncle of the bride heard all this, a profound sigh escaped him and he muttered, as if to himself : "How wretched and miserable is this poor orphan girl ! Alas, she is waiting for her mother to come

219

and participate in her wedding — ceremony — little knowing that she perished in the Nazi Crematoria".

When Reb Zanwill and his followers heard the sorrowful sighing of in the "Song of the Mount" and hurriedly rose from their places, they asked those present. "Where is the bride ? We wish to go to her at once. Perhaps we can succeed in explaining to her that, in accordance with the law and practice of Israel, it is a religious duty to try to forget the dear ones who have departed from our midst and to continue our way of life as heretofore. Please tell us her exact whereabouts. Who knows? Perhaps it is for this reason that the sighing and the sobbing on the Mount has led us here !"

All the assembled wedding-guests replied with deep and heartfelt emotion : "Let us hope and pray that this is the very reason that has brought you to us".

Without further ado, or loss of time, Reb Zanwill and those with him were conducted to the house of the bride-to-be. The wedding-guests who accompanied them on the way, asked themselves at every step as they looked with trembling expectancy on those whom they led : "Will they succeed in their aim, we wonder ?"

All the way, from the house in which the wedding ceremony was to be held to the house of the bride-to-be, Reb Zanwill and his disciples could not help but hear, the still, lament inherent in the "Song of the Mount". They thus knew that they were on the right track. Soon, they arrived at the home of the bride and quickly ascended the stairs to the room in which she sat, surrounded by her relatives, all in sad and hopeless mood. For they could not persuade her to go with them to the house where the Huppah (wedding-ceremony) had been arranged. No sooner, however, was the door opened to let in the visitors, than he bride joyously leapt from her seat and cried out with sparkling excitement: "Mother ! Mother ! Oh, I knew you would come — knew that you would keep the promise you made to me !" She, thereupon, invited her Mother and her entourage, Reb Zanwill wished to take his leave from the bridal couple, but the bride refused to grant him leave to depart.

At first, the latter were dumbfounded at hearing the bride's words. The first conclusion they came to was, that they had before them a tragic case of a girl whom despair had driven to insanity. The near-by relatives wrung their hands in sheer agony and deepest pain. The face of the bridegroom went as white a chalk and he called out to his bride in a voice full of despair : "Malkele, do calm yourself now. Those who have just come are our friends from Mount Zion."

The face of Malkele, however, was illumined with dazzling joy. She alone, of all the people in the room, remained calm and composed while the others were thrown into perplexity and confusion. She then announced with happy exaltation : "Yes, yes ! Of course I know that they are the friends of my Mother and that she has come with then from the Mount ! Accordingly, let us all now go to the wedding-ceremony". She accompanied these words while hastily donning and arranging her bridal veil and urged all those around her to go with her, at once.

The others, however, all remained rooted to their places, as if they had been visited by a paralytic stroke. Reb Zanwill's eyes, however, soon became illuminated with a look of comprehension and tender sympathetic understanding which immediately inspired confidence in all around him. Realization had come to him, all at once, as to who the bridal pair were and he began to explain his discovery to the others. Turning to his disciples, he said : "This is the same girl who prayed this very morning, with heartbroken weeping, before the Urns of the Ashes. We have brought her Mother as the "bridesmaid", as it were, to her daughter's wedding. By doing so, we have exorcized the "spirit" (Dibbruk) from her daughter. Indeed, we have withdrawn her Mother from among the Ashes. Her daughter realizes that this is what has happened; for this reason her joy knows no bounds !"

All then went gladly to the wedding-ceremony, the bride walking all the way in silence but with steps of joyous confidence. Her bright eyes,

now and then, gave a sideways glance, as if to reassure herself that
her Mother was walking beside her. A smile of the purest happiness
shone on her face. Yes! After all, her Mother did keep her promise
to come to her daughter's wedding !

Those who were present at that wedding-ceremony, continue to tell
of the remarkable things which happened there. Thus they assure their
listeners, that when the bride was led to the Huppah (Canopy) by
women carrying lighted candles, they beheld two bright, burning,
candles suspended from above,borne by no visible hand, but surrounding
the bride with a brilliant aureole. When the ceremony was over, Reb
Zanwill wished to take his leave from the bridal couple, but the bride
implored him to stay. When, in the sweetness and insistence of her
request, he also heard the sigh which had issued from the "Song of the
Mount", he immediately decided to comply with her request and stay
on. This he did not only for "a little while longer", as she had asked
him, but for much longer than that, passing the pleasant hours away
engaged in conversation both with the newly-wedded couple and with
the other guests. He remained and was the last to leave!

The other guests constantly threw surprised glances in his direction,
for they simply could not understand why he was so interested in this
wedding, above all others ! Moreover, what "Niagras" of eloquence
had he poured out in order to persuade the bride to come to the
Huppah in the face of her previous reluctance to do so ? As if this
question were not enough, why did he tarry such a long time here,
seeing that it was the custom among very distinguished guests to fulfil
their obligation in such instances by appearing just before the commencement of the ceremony and taking leave of those assembled soon
after its termination ! The whole thing presented a real puzzle to
their understanding.

It was at a late hour of the night, when Reb Zanwill begged leave
of the bridal pair to depart. On doing so, he blessed them with the
usual prayer of the Mount "situated amidst beautiful surroundings, and
the joy of the whole earth." He blessed them with the greeting of

Mazzal Tov (Good Luck) and abounding happiness and then took his leave, accompanied by his elderly followers.

The bride, however, still kept on urging him to stay yet a while longer. When, in her voice, he could no longer hear the sound of that sigh which had accompanied the "Song of the Mountain", he realized that that the time had finally come when he might depart.

It has been suggested that while she was engaged in her persistent requests for Reb Zanwill to remain, the bride heard the voice of her Mother speaking to her; "Malkele, my darling, you see I did come to your wedding, as I promised you I would. Now, please, be a good girl and listen to me ! Forget all about me and devote all your best attention to your home, your husband and the children that will be yours in the days ahead. In one year from now, I promise that I will return to you again — not as your Mother but as your daughter !"

So it transpired. At the end of a year, a daughter was born to Malkele and her husband. The name given to this "feather of love, plucked from the pinions of marriage and dropped into the lap of motherhood" was Rebekkah, as her Mother had been called.

On the morrow, following the night of the ceremony, Reb Zanwill came to the couple with a present in his hand. This was a Tallit which had been saved from one of the Nazi Concentration Camps. As he gave them this gift, he said : "A Tallit was the usual present given by the bride's parents to their new son-in-law. I have asked permission from the Mount's Custodian to hand you this traditional present. The thirty-two threads of the Tallit symbolise the beatings of the heart (the numerical value of "Lev", a heart" in Hebrew, is thirty-two). It is the Heart of the Mother who promised to be present at your wedding which she has now brought you, as her wedding gift !"

THE SEVENTH GATE

THE LIGHT OF THE MENORAH

On the summit of Mt. Zion, at the commencement of the path which leads direct to the tomb of the "sweet singer of Israel," the mountain Menorah raises its branches proudly aloft. The crowns with which it is adorned and embellished sparkle like pure gold when the rays of the sun beat upon them — symbolic of the Kingdom of David and the anointing of a scion of his dynasty in the Time ahead, the era assigned for the appearance of the Messiah — the righteous son of David.

Light is the symbol of the Mount, as well as its ultimate target. For Mt. Zion raises itself like a flag, hovering over the residents in Eretz Israel to lighten their way through the labyrinthine entanglements through which our present-day and age have, to fight their way. This fight is meant to supply them with strength and persistence, by the aid of which they will be enabled to prevail over the dangers which terrify them. Our generation is in need of the light that comes from above, a light intended to penetrate our very being. It is our responsibility to liquidate the diaspora and to plant within all hearts the permanent duty of love for Israel and its ancestral Homeland.

In our daily Prayer-book, we recite a passage preceding that of "With abounding love" which links together the love which should burn in our hearts for God and Israel and for the Land He promised to our patriarchs, with that of Light : "Thou wilt kindle a new light on Zion, so that we may all merit to witness its light speedily." Does not this prayer intend to teach us that before we can hope to be filled with love for our fellow-beings on earth, it is indispensable for us to be surcharged with light from Heaven? For it is only by this harmonious symbiosis of love and light, that we will succeed in our aim to gather

224

together into Medinat Israel all the scaterred and farflung members of the House of Israel.

One of the legends clinging to the Mount, relates the preparations made in Temple times before the Menorah was kindled. It was found necessary for the Menorah to undergo a thorough cleaning daily. Why ? Legend is not short of an answer. It once happened that the Menorah would not function, despite its having been supplied with the usual wide and regular supply of oil. After careful investigation, it was discovered that in one part of the Menorah the wick did not come into contact with the oil — hence the blockage.

Our generation possesses many supplies of oil, metaphorically speaking, for the rekindling of the spiritual Menorah. The trouble, however, consists in the fact that this supply of kindling matter has not yet come into contact with the wick. Hence is the light still buried in the Mysterious Universe. It continues to burn, yet its flames are not visible. It is still in the sky aloft. It is our assignment, like Prometheus of old, to snatch down this heavenly fire and rekindle it on earth. Adam — the first man — had to knock two stones against each other before he could make sparks fly therefrom. Similarly, ours is the task to remove the stones and rocks from our Homesland, in order to flood it with spiritual light.

Mt. Zion is admirably suited for this task, since we pray to Him to light "a new light on Zion." This light must not be identified with God Himself, who is "the Light of the World." What this new "Light" can do is to enable us to see more clearly our Heavenly Father — the Light of mankind.

THE STORY OF THE LIGHT

When R. Hayim became inwardly aware that the sands of his span of life were reaching their lowest ebb and that the time was fast approaching for him to be gathered unto his people, he was assailed by many

225

deep and disturbing thoughts. What will happen to that Light which he had tended with such devoted and meticulous care throughout his life, after he had closed his eyes on earth, awaiting for his soul to be borne aloft to the eternal realms above? Will it be extinguished?

Will the Menorah be relegated to the limbo of forgotten, discarded things? Or will it continue to dispel darkness and banish ignorance with its powerful, illuminating rays?

R. Hayim called one of his most faithful disciples and made him promise that he would take over the guardianship of the light. The disciple took the Light and locked it very safely in a secret recess, to which only they had access. The Light shone for him alone; in fact, he himself became the Light which always paved the way for him.

That light continued to shine during the whole life-time of that disciple and continued to do so even after he had breathed his last and had gone the way of all flesh.

The light then began to pale, not knowing for whom it would now give forth illumination, after he who had tended it so devotedly died.

R. Hayim, still alive, saw what would happen and he implored another of his faithful disciples to become the new guardian of the Light. This time, however, he charged his disciple with this message:

"My son, roam throughout the world and shed light whithersoever thou goest.'

The disciple took the mission to heart and implemented it, wedding deed to creed, thought to action. Wherever he found a group of men dwelling in the darkness, he brought the light near unto them.

When the light became too powerful and too dazzling for them, they began to murmur and grumble and even to revile grossly the bearer of the Light, till finally they extinguished the light he held in his hand. The Light was now enveloped in darkness, saddened and pained by what had happened to it.

Saddened also was R. Hayim at what had transpired. How would darkness be banished without light? Pained by this nagging thought, R. Hayim, who had been struggling against death since he first handed over the light to his disciple, who had since died, became desperately ill. This time from sheer worry. What would be the fate of his beloved light?

When the festival of Hanukkah approached and his disciple brought the Menorah near his bedside, so that he could kindle a light on each of the eight successive days of the celebration, R. Hayim performed the ceremony with a blessing and asked his disciples to place the Menorah at the entrance of the house, as is prescribed by the halachacha "In order to spread the miracle" unto those outside.

It was then that he had a "brain-wave." and his face sparkled with joy.

"Children", he cried out rapturously, "I have now realized that the only and best thing to do with the Light I inherited from my ancestors is not to hand it over to an individual, but to place it outside for the whole world to see."

This is the procedure followed by R. Zanwill. He has placed the Menorah on the Mount at the entrance of the path leading to the very top, so that it may cast its rays from there to every part of Israel and from Israel to every nook and cranny of the vast world.

Our present generation has been summoned to emphasize two fundamental revelations: the revelation of the light which was kindled with the establishment of Medinat Israel, and the other revelation of the Light which will eventually and gradually see the liquidation of the diaspora. It is a case of Light versus Light — the Menorah which faces David's tomb confronting the Menorot of the Golah. In good time, both lights will blend in wondrous perfection, ready to usher in the Messianic Light. which will be sevenfold as strong as the light of Creation. The evolutionary process towards this millenium will be the breaking of old vessels and the supply of new vessels, to contain the wick and flames of the Menorah.

LIGHT FROM DARKNESS

Some men of the Mount make a habit of walking on very dark nights, in order to catch the rays of light which suddenly shoot through the gloom. These sparks of light are not larger than grains of sand or the mustard seed. They collect these fleeting rays, one by one, into their lanterns which, when placed together, compose such a bright light that those who view the sigh rapturously exclaim "Barkai", "It is light". The Scribes on the Mount have recorded these words in white fire on books of fire.

The story of the collected sparks of fire began to circulate on the Mount on that strange evening, during which the conversation circled around the topic of the Light which had been hidden and the scattered light which the righteous will have to collect for themselves. It was on a night of Hanukkah when Reb Zanwill and his close associates were gathered around the various Hanukkiyot that had been brought from the Golah and which burnt with a dim light. It seemed as if these flickering lights were whispering secrets and relating wondrous stories about the "Invisible Light," which will one day again be revealed to the world.

The evening began with a talk from Reb Zanwill concerning this Hidden Light which was created simultaneously with that of the first man, but which was hidden away after thirty-six hours. So powerful was this light, that its ray enabled one to see from one end of the world to another. Under its sheen, everything blazoned and corruscated like the brightness of the firmament, with nothing able to impede or block its penetrating brilliance. The whole world was charged with light, even covering the corners thereof. But when God realized that this light would spur on men to sin even in the hours of darkness- and that mankind would not be able to withstand the temptation ushered in by this light, he reduced it in size to its present proportion. The Midrash records the following in the name of R. Elazar: "The light created by God on the first day of creation was so powerful,that Adam could see, with its aid, from one end of the world to the other. When the Holy One, blessed be He, tourned the pages of the future generation of the Flood and the generation which witnessed the separation of the races and saw how they had corrupted their way on earth, He decided to hide this light."

A similar story was told by Reb Zanwill concerning the great light of the Moon, which will be restored sevenfold in lustre when the Messianic Age dawns.

In the beginning, the sun and moon were both equal in size and in the power of the light they cast on earth. Of this, the Bible assures us: "And God made the two great lights." It was soon after their creation that the moon lodged a complaint to God, protesting: 'How is it possible for two kings to have only one crown between them?" God was displeased with this question and His retort was: "As a punishment, go and reduce yourself in size." From that day, the moon appears much smaller than the sun in size.

Since the moon accepted its punishment without demur and in pious resignation, it was endowed with many qualities; one of which is that it would renew itself, in the course of time, to be of the same size as it was at Creation. Moreover, Israel shares the same fate as the moon; for it, too, would be renewed after the protracted and bitter night of the Galut had been eclipsed by the light of the Messianic Era. Apart from the overtones of light which we can still see in sun and moon, there are also mystic undertones; for the "Invisible Light" can actually be seen by the "Eye of faith' in the world around us. Though it is concealed from the outer gaze, it is enshrined in Torah and good deeds, which flash forth brightness in endless array. As the Book of Proverbs has it : "The precept is as a lamp, and the Torah spells light", (Torah and Orah sound alike). The light which is enveloped in the Torah is perceived and known by those who conscientiously study and fulfill its commandments.

Every good deed and creed displayed by man, helps to bring out this concealed light from its sheath, in which it has been deposited. The

Ba'al Ha'turim, (the famous compiler of the Four Turim on the Laws and Customs of Israel and the commentator in the Bible whose characteristic is to find numerical values in the Scriptures), points out that the numerical value of the Hebrew words: "And God saw that the Light was good", adds up to 613. Thus implying that the light is folded-up in the 613 Torah precepts.

The whole world and the fullness thereof is the sheath of this light, its sparks glimmering throughout every part of the universe. This light has been stored away from the rest of the world, but it is right here for the use of the upright and noble of men who pace life on earth with dignity.

Accordinging to popular tradition, each generation possesses thirty-six righteous men, dotted the world over, on whose merit alone the world continues to survive. No one knows who these are, not even themselves.

Who really are they ? What qualifications do they possess and in what pursuit are they engaged: Is it at all possible to be a perfect Tsadik, when nobody is any the wiser for his existence? Would it not be far better if they were known as such to their generation so that they may be paragons of righteousness and models of perfection to those around them whom they could influence to do likewise? Moreover, what significance, if any, can be attached to the number thirty-six to which their number has been strictly limited? What happens if they were a few less, or one or two more?

Generally speaking, people are blind with regard to the "Hidden Light." There are even those who love to minimize and disparage good actions, thus casting shadows upon the concealed brightness. On the other hand, there are those righteous who see in everything that which is unobserved by others; they see the spark and know how to attract it with a fraction of the Hidden Light, until the time will dawn when the world will no longer appear in isolated fragmentization. It is these "Thirty-six" anonymous, saintly personages that collect together the sparks, one by one, thus forging them into one mammoth torch of light.

These gatherers of the sparks are thirty-six in number, corresponding to the number of hours this "Hidden Light" shone at its Creation. It is they whose righteousness causes the world to survive and supplies it with a fraction of the Hidden Light until the time will dawn when all the sparks will have been gathered together and be restored to their roots. When this will be accomplished, the world will undergo a revolutionary reconstruction and the primordial light will brust forth in all ists glory, just as Dawn flashes the awakening of the morning with a rich pool of magnificent, dazzling colours, even excelling those of the rainbow.

"But where are these sparks? Is it at all possible to catch a glimpse of them?' were the questions which Reb Meshullam excitedly asked. To them, the reply of Reb Mendel was : "Yes, it is possible to see them, but their light is not comparable to other lights. For whereas all other lights shine from above down below, this "Hidden Light" does the exact reverse : it casts its sheen above from below. In other words, its lights proceeds from the darkness; it emerges from within and penetrates the outer world around it. "When I was in the concentration camp", continued Reb Mendel "I saw this light. Moreover, I actually managed to collect a few sparks of this magic light which I have since kept treasured in my chests where I keep the things most precious to me."

THE GIANT MENORAH

On account of the fact that R. Mendel had been interned in many concentration camps established by the devilish Nazi regime, the men of the Mountains usually referred to him as "the man of the camps". This name was not only due to this fact; for had this been the sole reason for this nomenclature, many others who had similar experiences and who still bear the marks of the beast tatooed on their arms and ingrained in their hearts, would have deserved this title. R. Mendel, however, was of the select few who managed not to allow his spirit to be crushed even when subjected to the most hellish tortures ever devised by barbaric and dieseased minds. From the flames of the cremation and the graves of their victims, he could see in his mind's eye, sparks of beauty and grief being triggered-off, all expressing defiance of their tortures and a corresponding brave hope in their ultimate salvation. These sparks of confidence and courage he collected, one by one, by which he himself became equipped with buoyant hope and thus enabled to offer the cup of consolation to his fellow-inmates. In a nutshell, R. Mendel was feet to the lame, eyes to the blind, health to the sick, hope to those in despair — a gracious benefactor unto all with whom he had come into daily contact.

The Hanukkah Menorah, which had been rescued from the Jewish communities which had been decimated and finally expunged from the map, had already been kindled on the Mount. By their flickering, whispering light, the residents on the Mount were exchangeing memories, experiences and tales they had heard from others concerning the life in those camps. Chief among the narrators was R. Mendel, who told his listeners of his many wonderful experiences, above all, emphasizing that during the tearful and tragic era of the Holocaust, the entire world was one flaming Menorah and the crematorium served as the lighted candles in this colossal Menorah. Although the exact number of these crematoria could not be stated with exact precision, yet they were popularly imagined to be 36, corresponding to the number of candles — not including the extra candle which served as Shammash (attendant) on each separate night.. that were made use of during the eight days of the Hanukkah festival. Hence the inmates of the camps referred to these crematoria as the "Hannukkah candles."

Those who now heard R. Mendel dilate on these things were held in spellbound amazement and admiration. They had cherished a totally different conception of these crematoria. To them, these spelt the chamber of Hell incarnate- to which it was impossible to attach the tiniest fraction of light and sanctity. No, they just could not swallow the words they now heard from R. Mendel, for they were beyond human comprehension. When the latter observed their lack of belief in his words, he endeavored to explain that it was possible to regard these crematoria from divergent angles and varying points of view. Thus it was possible to reflect on their existence from the physical and material angle, seeing them just what they really were — murderous cells of hellish tortures, Valleys of despair, Hades and its demons let loose, the Satanic realm; in short, the zenith and apotheosis of wickedness incarnated in the flesh and in the shape of human beast Although this was what they were, in reality, added R. Mendel, yet this estimate was very superficial, one which did not plumb the depths of reality.

Though R. Mendel usually conversed in a voice sad and restrained, he now began to talk in most enthusiastic tones. He gazed with his two large, dreamy eyes at those sitting with him and, looking intently at the various Hanukkah lamps that had been kindled, posed the question to them : "Do you actually believe that the camps were created only as general instruments of torture? Do you really believe that Povidence has, God forbid, been entirely liquidated on this earth below? Has everything absolutely become disorder and anarchy, at the whim of upstarts and at the beck-and-call of every scoundrel basking in ephemeral authority?" He went on : "Is it right to look upon the concentration-camps as branches of Hell let loose?"

True, Hell conducts those whom it had enmeshed in its tentacles to the Infernos below; but where there is Gehinnom (Hell), it is also possible to be afforded a glimpse of the Paradise (Gan-Eden) close by. One cannot exist without the other; both are two sides of the same coin."

Having delivered himself of this semi-philosophical reflection, which he voiced with the warmth of emotion but in sad tones, he went on to unfold the conversation he had held with R. Shlomo on the Hanukkah of 5702 in one of the labour camps near Birknau.

233

It was one very cold and dismal winter's day. As dawn flushed the sky, they were summoned to their various assignations while still in a state of semi-undress and hunger. "For hours on end, they wallowed through mud and snow, dragging their feet to a commanded pace and rhythm. until they had arrived at their allotted posts of work. It was strictly forbidden to pause even for a brief while on their journey, in order to take breath; for they were accompanied on this route march by police armed with pistols and spiked-sticks. Woe unto him who was caught not keeping step in those serried marches and who had side-stepped out of the routes, dragooned and marshalled with military precision ! For then, would he become the victim of deathly-blows and be left behind in the snow, wallowing in blood and trodden upon by other marchers that followed in his wake."

R. Mendel went on : "I dragged my feet along together with Reb Shlomo, speaking in secret, hushed tones of Hanukkah, as we slowly wended on our miserable way. Our main anxiety was: "How to fulfil the festive observance of Hanukkah while still being inmates in the camp? In his usual characteristic manner, R. Shlomo gave him encouragement, assuring him that, in such circumstances, Judaism emancipated one from the observance of all commandments, save the one of the preservation of life. According to him, this latter commandment took pride of place in the camp. It consisted of "Hallowing the Name" and to resolve to keep body and soul alive, despite the devilish machinations and the hellish wrath of the barbaric enemy who spared no cruel device to be used in order to destroy us and blot us out from the lands of the living.

The argument of Reb Shlomo ran as follows : "Those in the camps have been exempted from the performance of almost all the 613 commandments of the Torah. The Torah was given to mortals only because man is possessed with the Freedom of Choice and will know how to choose life. But does this Freedom of Choice exist in the camps, wherein their inmates have been reduced to a life entirely composed of abject slavery? What connection, if any, can there be

234

between the Torah and its Commandments and those whose every act is a violation of their own free-will and is against their very being?"

"At first", continued, Reb Mendel, stopping his narrative only to take fresh breath, "his words surprised and pained me. As we trudged our way along, walking in the snow and slush, weary and hungry to boot, I turned my face towards him and asked":

"And so, Reb Shlomo, has the wicked enemy truly succeeded to extricate the Torah from the hold both of the universe, as well as from us to whom it was originally presented? Have we now been left without any Torah? Has the whole of mankind been orphaned of God"s Word? Can one imagine a Jew without his Torah and Commandments? Heaven forbid that Israel and its Torah should have been totally destroyed!"

"I still vividly recollect this question," said Reb Mendel, "because I received my punishment for asking these tantalizing questions on the spot and without any further delay. As I only cast a side glance at the enemy marching with us, I received a thunderous blow on the head; but I girded myself with superhuman strength and bravely continued my march.

"When I regained consciousness from the blow which at first completely knocked me out, I continued my hushed conversation with Reb Shlomo and repeated the above question with which I had plied him before. He then replied:

"God forbid that the implications you drew from my remarks were correct. Certainly not. It is only the values which have changed. We ourselves are the Torah: the world, the camp, we ourselves — all are Torah.

"We ourselves have been transformed into precepts. In normal times, the Jew was wont to go to the synagogue, there to pray; in the camp, he himself has been metamorphosed into a synagogue, a prayer. Hence, is there still any need left for the Jew to pray in a camp? The Rabbi, Reb Bunem, (a famous hasidic teacher), when he came to the words of the Psalmist: "VA-ANI TEPHILLAH" ("And   as for me, my prayer"), he explained them thus:

"It can be compared to a poor man who had not eaten for three whole days and had come before the King begging for alms, with his clothes in rags and his poverty writ large all over him. Is there then any need for him to state the object of his appearance before the King? Does he not himself proclaim what he wants, even without the utterance of a single word?"

He continued his reflection: "In the camps, the Name of Heaven is constantly being hallowed. There, everyone suffers because of his Jewish affiliations, helping each other in hours of trial. All are transformed into an Holy Ark, in which is deposited the whole Torah, replete with its 613 precepts. For we, the inmates of these devilish camps are the agents of filling the entire universe with His glory and help to uplift in sanctity the Holy Name. This being so, there does no longer exist any need for individual prayer. The entire camp is one big synagogue and schoolhouse; it has become the embodiment of prayer and the incorporation of supplication. If, in addition to all this, the internees in the camps can yet fulfill an additional precept, such an act is regarded as the very summit and apotheosis of holiness.

"When we returned to the camp that evening, and the internees scrambled in order to snatch their sparse portion of despicable soup, Reb Shlomo took me by the arm and told me to follow him to kindle the lights.

"I pierced him with my eyes, lost in amazement. Was he bereft of his mind, all of a sudden? Where has he got candles with which to kindle the Hanukkah Menorah? I put this question to him: His reply was: "No I have no candles, neither is there any need for them. The commandment of Hanukkah is fulfilled by the act of seeing alone. Come, therefore, with me out of the camp, and we will see the lights burning in the Heavenly Menorah."

"We both repaired outside and we looked at the fiery flames leaping forth from the crematorium straight heavenwards. There are thirty-six such furnaces in the world, equating the number of candles used during the celebration of Hanukkah. The whole world is now ablaze like a veritable Menorah and is actually hallowing the name of Heaven (Kiddush Ha'Shem).

Reb Shlomo then looked long and in reflexive mood at these furnaces of Birknau, as his lips murmured inwardly in his heart the blessings recited over the kindling of the Hanukkah lights.

When Mendel was hard-pressed by his enthralled listeners to tell them how ke managed to collect these wonderful sparks of the fabled, mystic light, he unfolded before them the following story:

LIGHT OF BREAD

The general custom is to light the Hanukkiyah either with wicks dipped in oil, or with candles made of wax. Ordinary people view light as something tangible and natural; we in the camp, however, groping in the thick darkness, when we observed R. Shlomo kindling the lights, perceived in them something radically different. We regarded them as lights sparked-off from the darkness, as hidden and abstract lights, which the usual life of the ordinary man could not understand.

Since the 36 candles symbolized the 36 hours during which the light of Creation shone, Reb Shlomo himself brought out part of that "Hidden Light" which he revealed to those who shared his nobility of mind and uprightness of character. This is what actually happened:

"Very low, indeed, was the spiritual and ethical atmosphere in the camps. The unbearable conditions under which they were compelled to live were responsible for a slackening of the general, moral behaviour of the inmates. Each man began to care only for himself, living only for the needs to enable him to keep body and soul alive. The general motto appeared to be : "Sleep and eat, snatch and drink." Human instincts appeared to have been immobilized and petrified. There were, however, a few who preserved their more ideal instincts and instilled a modicum of holiness into the life of the camp. It was they who were greatly concerned that the living coals of humanity be not extinguished altogether.

It was the Eve of Hanukkah, and R. Shlomo spoke to his circle in the camp as to the meaning and traditional observances of the festival. He explained the way to light a candle. Obviously, his talk was not of ordinary candles, for these were not to be obtained in the camp; but he explained that since it was not possible to obtain light from without, the only alternative would be to derive it from within. How was this possible? The answer is : "Every noble thought, accompanied by a good action, causes the sparks to be triggered-off and soar upwards. As a proof for his words, he cited the words of the Ba'Al Ha-Turim, "the numerical value of the two Hebrew words Et-Ha'Or is 613, the number of the Torah precepts". He added that this was the way for them to kindle their lights in the camp.

Little wonder that following this exhortation, each one endeavoured to the best of his ability and possibility to fulfill this precept; with the result that each of their lights, when combined, became transformed into a mighty spiritual blaze. Naturally, the light kindled by Reb Shlomo excelled all others. So bright did it appear, that it seemed to have clothed its spirituality into tangibility.

One was always hungry in the camp, for the portion of bread given was of the most meagre kind and certainly not enough to appease ravenous hunger. The inmates began to dream of receiving their morsel of bread, being prepared to do anything and everything in order to receive it.

It was a real case of "saving the soul," for one could actually keep a person from dying of hunger by giving him a portion of bread. During the days of Hanukkah, Reb Shlomo took his parsimonious ration of bread and divided it into two equal portions; one of which he ate, the other, he shapped into a long candle. It was the "Bread Candle" that he gave to one even more hungry than himself. He handed this "Bread Candle" to the other, just at the time of sunset, when the halacha prescribes the kindling of the festive lights of Hanukkah. Reb Mendel continuing to unfold his tale said : "When the inmates of the camp observed what I was doing, they gazed in breathless amazement at this splendid sight. They seemed to behold a blaze of light surrounding a candle made of bread. It was a light which penetrated into the innermost depths of the soul, which suffused with splendour the entrails as well as the heart. It seemed as if they were beholding with their own eyes the "Hidden Light" which was the 36 hours of Creation. Yes, they rubbed their eyes in wonderment, for they were witnessing that "Hidden Light" emerging from its hiding-place and illuminating part of this "Vale of Tears" to which life on earth had been reduced. Yes, what they were now seeing was "Light from Darkness."

IN THE FOREST

"When I fled from the camp in the month of Kislev, it was a night of thick darkness. One could almost feel the massive columns of night, with the aproach of strong winds and tempestuous gales. As if not enough, a strong fall of snow began to dance wildly and which made walking almost next to impossible. My weary and bruised feet wallowed in the snow, dragging my tired body after them without knowing whither my feet were dragging me. It was only the fear of death, which stalked about in the camp which hastened me onwards, supplying me, as it were, with an inner reserve of strength of which I was not conscious. At each step, I tottered and fell but continued to wend my weary way around. My pain was great and the darkness seemed to grow apace with every faltering step.

Suddenly, a lightning flash appeared before my eyes from a great

239

distance ahead. I was still in the heart of the forest and I could not help wondering : "Whence cometh the light in this dark forest? And on such a terribly dark night? The mysterious light again flashed for a moment before my eyes, and I could not help observing that this light differed from all other lights. Moreover, it began to dawn upon me that this light was being flashed forth from another who, like myself, was trudging in the snow, but that he had a small child on his shouders. I girded myself with all the little strength I still possessed and approached the man. The latter observed me closely and with some apprehension, before he realized that he had encountered another Jew. We greated each other and then I asked him : "Where do you come from, and whither do your feet take you from here?"

His reply was : "Ten of us Jews fled from the camp this night. The thick mantle of darkness and the snowstorm miraculously aided and abettted our escape, unnoticed by our murderous captors. Our aim was to reach the house of a certain farmer, one who could be counted among "the pious of the nations," and one with whom we once had been on the friendliest of terms. Among the ten, there was a father who wished to save his little boy also. On account of the indescribable agony and ravenous hunger which we experienced that night, we were unable to continue on our way. Each of us began to fall down like so many flies, before we reached this forest. When we reached the forest, I realized that I was the only one left, for the other nine had perished on the way. I looked around and my eyes fell on a little child, apparently lifeless.

"I stood for a few moments, speechless and plunged in deep sorrow, for I did not know what to do next. Suddenly, a voice proceeded from the mouth of the child, and the words which fell upon my ears were : "My father has died, Please carry me to the spot where he now lies dead in this forest, so that I may breathe my last near him." I tried to calm the child : "My child, since God has spared you in life, you shall not die but surely live. Come, let us continue to trudge along together and Heaven will have mercy upon us." The child did not entreat me to take him with me. As for me, I was in the very depths of tiredness and my feet did not obey my will. But how could I commit this great evil and leave a little Jewish child alone in the forest? I girded my remaining resources of vitality, put the child on my shoulders and slowly, very slowly, continued my trudging and wallowing, step after step, falling but marching on.

"I wished to take the child in my arms, but to this he refused to agree; whilst I, bravely trudged on in the snow and threading my way through the labyrinthine paths of the forest, with the child firmly saddled on my shoulders. So I continued, weary and broken, but determined to use up even my last ounce of strength in this Herculean and prodigious effort."

R. Mendel continued: "That man was not aware that there danced an aureole around his head which lit up the darkness of the forest and that I had been walking by his light. So we walked on together until the light of day had dawned.

Having begun to narrate of his fund of experiences, R. Mendel continued: "I left the forest, thanks to the light flashed forth by him who was carrying the child, and I began to wander from one forest to another bruised and broken, in rags and almost barefooted, weary and hungry almost to the very point of death. In the course of my many nomadic wanderings, I kept on gathering additional sparks of the "hidden light" until, with divine help, I reached the Ghetto walls of the city. My luck abided by me even then, for I was successful even in sliding myself into the city during a patch of enforced labour, which kept the cruel barbarians occupied at their merciless task of supervising their hapless victims.

"A complete stranger did I feel, as I stalked along the deserted Ghetto. There was no place for me to enter, nor any man to turn to. My heart advised me not to seek assistance from the local Jewish Board, for I knew that wicked eyes were spying all around there. Like a lost sheep, did I wander about the Ghetto streets. All the dwellers

241

of the Ghetto appeared to have locked themselves in the miserable hovels which constituted their homes. It would seem that I alone was left in the street, haunted by the dread of death awaiting my capture.

In the meantime, while so brooding and wandering, night had arrived and the streets had become even more deserted. That day happened to be the one preceding Hanukkah.

Suddenly I beheld a Jew, with a Hanukkiyah in his hand, standing at the door of a room within his house. I at once understood that he was about to kindle the light of Hanukkah; so I girded my loins with strength and entered his house. He did not seem at all perturbed or surprised. On the contrary, he welcomed me with open arms. I now beheld him standing surrounded by his wife and children before a candle-less Menorah, chanting quietly : "These are the lights which we now kindle," as if he had actually kindled candles. I looked all around. There was no oil or candles to be seen anywhere, but a certain mysterious light seemed to be streaming forth from the Menorah, a light that flooded the entire room with its brightness.

I could not restrain my amazement and asked, him : "Whence cometh this light? Is that not perhaps sparks from the Hidden Light?"

"As for me, I was then received with great joy. The light which streamed therefrom, also illumined my entre being, giving me peace of mind and restoring my mental equipoise after wretched weary days of tramping.

Reb Mendel continued : "It was a wonder to me that the Jew was so delighted to see me, receiving me almost as if I were a messenger from heaven. He had always been accustomed to entertain guests at his home during Hanukkah, but he now felt sorry and apologised that his house and table had been emptied almost of the very necessities. For this reason, he could not entertain me as was his wont. He showed me every respect, asserting that I brought light into the house, adding : "Since I have no light for the Hanukkiyah, you will be deemed in my eyes as if you had been the light for the festival." His joy was of the rarest spiritual kind. For him, his narrow room now radiated with light, making it appear palatial. You ask : "Whence cometh the light?" It comes from within, my friend; It emanates from the heart of man and is sparked off from the "Hidden Light." "I gazed for a long time at this wonderful light, until I also became suffused with a joyous exaltation. I took hold of this friendly strange Jew, and gazed at the lights corruscating as dazzling stars, that shone intently from inside the aperture.

"I stood confused. Whence comes this bright light when all around is so pitch dark? I followed the gleam of this miraculous vision and fixed my stare in the direction of this fantastic light. All of a sudden, a shot cleft the air that seemed to come from the aperture in the wall. Immediately after this sound, I heard the cry of death coming piercingly from the hole in the wall and I saw blood flowing down and becoming intermingled with the scintillating light which shone from without. I furtively approached the aperture and beheld a Jewish child, lying wounded. Thereupon, I took him away immediately to a side, bandaging hss wounds and poured cold water upon him till I succeeded in restoring the pulse of life to the child. The mysterious light continued to emanate from his body and flood all around with the dazzling brilliance.

"As soon as the child came to, he moaned and began to cry : "Mummy, mummy, do forgive me, please. I cannot walk; I feel as if I were going to die". The mother of the child was bed-ridden in the Ghetto, fatally ill. She was all alone, lacking the barest necessities which would enable her to keep alive despite her broken state of health. The only comfort she still possessed was her child Yossele. He would look at his mother, suffering so much torture on account of her illness, helplessly, with eyes full of sympathy and longing.

"One day, he decided to go out and seek help for his mother, come what may. He tried to squeeze through the hole in the wall, in order to escape outside the ghetto boundary, there to seek some food for his mother. Since be began this adventure the first time he repeated this performance each night, successful in bringing a little nourishment for his ailing mother. All went well until that bitter night of which I now tell, when he was shot at by the guards who kept ceaseless vigil lest any Jew leave the Ghetto at night.

"I was not able to move from the improvised bed of the wounded Yossele. Day and night, I held a watching brief over him, hearing his struggles for life with the Angel of Death. Evening arrived, an ink like blackness enveloped the Ghetto when Yossele breathed his last and his innocent soul outsoared the shadows of this wicked world. It was then, that I suddenly observed a very strong ray of light, as if lightning had flashed forth from the bed of the dead child, winging its way constantly, upward. So powerful was this light, that I was compelled to close my eyes. I then knew that the pure soul of Yossele had flown to heaven. I then realized the exact meaning of the words in Provebs : "The soul of man is the light of God". Verily, this was a precious, rarefied light, the kind of light which is stored beneath the Throne of Glory, the Light which even the Ministering Angels cannot behold without blinking, or entirely shielding their eyes.

Reb Mendel concluded : "Though I was not able to stare at that light, I did manage, however, to gather some sparks thereof which I stored within my soul. From there, they still continue to shine like pecious jewels, illumining my way. They will, endlessly and for all time, brighten my path in life, as the stars in the splendour of the firmament."

One of the most absorbed in these stories of Reb Mendel, was Reb Shalom. On the morrow, he also went out to collect sparks of this rare light, pacing among the inmates of the camps, among those who gallantly fought "The Battle of Freedom" (1948) in the forests and roads. He came across many sparks of light on his way. These he collected and brought them to Reb Zanwill, so that he could file them in the "Book of Lights".

The story of Reb Meshullam gained wide popularity on the Mount, and many began to imitate his example of collecting sparks from the "Hidden Light". Mystics aver that it is this assembly of "Sparks", which will help in the restoration of the original Light which, in the pristine days of old, always shone from Zion and which will, in the Messianic Age, again illumine a world basking in eternal peace and righteousness.

THE EIGHT — FINGERED MENORAH

On a raised dais, in a corner of the room of the Ashes, there stands a Hanukkah Menorah which is *sui generis,* something unique of its kind. It is a glass window, apparently frozen over and adorned with flowers in the shape of icicles and snowflakes, and made to resemble a Menorah composed of eight kindled fingers.

This Menorah possesses great attraction for all who first behold it, for they realize that its symbolism has something unique to reveal. In fact, two are the legends which cling to this Hanukkiah, one is associated with R. Shabbetai of Auschwitz, the second with R. Ya'acob of the Warsaw Ghetto.

THE REB SHABATAI LEGEND

It happened late one night, about two years ago, just when they had finished kindling all the Hanukkah lamps on the Mount. Suddenly, there appeared an elderly Jew, lean of face and sad of expression, accompanied by a young man. Turning to Reb Zanwill, he expressed his wish to kindle a Hanukkiah which had been brought from Auschwitz.

The way the man spoke, as well as his strange request, both made so strange an impression on Reb Zanwill that he himself went to look for that Hanukkiah, the lights of which had already burnt themselves out. When found, he placed it before the visitor who wished to kindle

245

lights therein anew. With many expressions of gratitude, the visitor modestly turned aside and recited the appropriate blessings, in a sad voice choked with tears, before kindling the lights.

Then something extraordinarily strange happened. The two hands of the visitor only had two thumbs between them. Moreover, and this was perhaps more significant still, the eight holes left by the eight fingers that had been choped off, cast a shadow on the wall behind which the newly-kindled Hanukkiah was placed, and which resembled a Menorah, the eight missing fingers serving as the lights. Those present were seized with fear and trembling at this sight, and the silence, of the grave reigned in the room. Reb Zanwill realized that this phenomenon veiled some mystery. As if groping for some enlightening explanation, he looked in turn, first at the "Menorah of Fingers" on the wall and then at the hands of this strange visitor. As he gazed from one to another, he could not help being struck by the sad eyes of the man, a sight which caused his own heart to pound fast.

When one of those present sought to engage in some conversation with the man, and thus perhaps to find out some *personalia* about him the latter obstinately refused to be drawn into talking. Those present gazed at each other in blunt astonishment, deciding that it is best to maintain a dignified silence in this case. The man left the Mount, with an expression eloquent of suffering. Since that episode, nobody ever came across him on the Mount. This caused R. Zanwill much distress, for the event had given him much food for thought and had left many unsolved problems.

Two years had elapsed since this episode, when one Erev Hanukkah the pale-faced young man that had acompanied the man who possesed only two thumbs, suddenly appeared on the Mount asking to be ushered into the private office of Reb Zanwill. When this was done and both were alone, the young man began:

"You remember, of course, the kindling of the Menorah by my uncle two years ago, and that he was the possessor of two thumbs only."

"Of course, I do," Reb Zanwill replied with great emotion. "I certain-

ly remember. Please tell me what has happened to him? Is he dead?"
The young man replied : "He has asked me to tell you the story
of the Hanukkah in Auschwitz."
The heart of Reb Zanwill began to beat loudly. He shrank in his
chair, closed his eyes, all set to drink in with thirst each word that
would flow from the lips of the youth. The latter commenced his
quaint tale thus :
"My uncle, R. Shabbetai, was a native of a small place in Poland.
He was a man who enjoyed an honoured reputation as a great scholar
and a polished gentleman, a scion of the famous WORKA Hasidim,
Throughout his life, he was a meticulously observant Jew to whom no
precept was too hard to perform. Even when cast into one of the
concentration camps, he did everything possible to be strictly observant even of the lightest commandment, as he was of the most
difficult. In his eyes, the camp was just another "test" of his faith.
So he did his very best to emerge triumphant from this test.
His fellow-inmates told wonderful things about him, how he had
always endeavoured to live as a Jew, dedicating his days on earth
to the service of his oppressed brethren, doing his utmost to help
and support them in their bitter hour of trial."
The young man paused to take breath, sighed and continued his
account of his uncle.
"In the camps, they knew how to die as Jews, but not how to live
as Jews. For life there was so confused and entangled, that it was a
life without life. My uncle was one of the very few who knew how
to live as a Jew even in the camp. It was this which made him strong.
Knowing this, he was prepared for everything and armed against
every possible contingency.
His suffering was especially almost beyond endurance on the Shabbat
and Festival, when his imagination conjured up vivid scenes how
these "appointed days of the Lord" were hallowed in his parental
home and at the table of his teachers. The scene I am about to describe
transpired thirty years ago in the infamous Camp at Auschwitz. It

247

was the eve of Hanukkah, and my uncle paced about the camp as if he had ben bereft of his mind by some cruel fate.

When asked to explain the cause of his agitation, his reply was : "As it is Hanukkah soon, I am going around and around myself in imitation of the Trendel which children used to spin round during this festive celebration." The memories he had stored and the pain they now brought, gnawed and devoured his heart. When the midnight hour had struck and all the inmates were asleep in the five layers of hard and broken wooden benches which filled the room, my uncle descended from his wooden couch and approached the small window of the shed, which was completely covered with frost and ice and looked ruminatingly at the thick pillars of smoke which were being belched forth from the chimneys of the four crematoria which were situated at the far end of the camp. The shadows of death flickered from every corner, parachuting from the faces of those who were sleeping on the benches. This pitiful sight of broken and depressed spirits intermingled with the leaping tongues of flame and smoke which were escaping from the jaws of Moloch, that pagan deity with a mouth wide open, agape and athirst for the blood of his hapless and innocent victims. As my uncle beheld this tragic scene, he repeated to himself the words with which the Pesah Haggadah has familiarised us : "Blood, Fire and Clouds of Smoke".

"As he stood at the window, as if paralyzed by the scene, he was determined to implement his thoughts. He bent his finger into the shape of a lamp and placed it on the window-pane, coated over with frost and snow. He stood thus, glued to the spot for half an hour during the festival, adding each night another frost-bitten finger to symbolize the lights of Hanukkah. Throughout this time, he pressed his finger against the glass pane of this small window. The fire of the intense frost scorched his finger, giving him the sensation as if he had actually kindled a Hanukkah limp according to the minute regulations of the Din, even to the extent of "spreading and publishing the miracle" to the world without. This he did throughout all the eight days of the festival, adding each night another frost-bitten finger until the fingers broke through in the shape of candles in the glass facing the carpet of frost which had assumed the shapes of flowers and plants which sparked off their sheen from the window-pane each day. They were lost in wonderment at this fantastic apparition of a strange Hanukkiah in the camp. Surely, it was little else than a sign sent from Heaven to give them moral support. They were remembered in Heaven during this festival, and this gave them a feeling of confidence and support. The Hanukkiah of R. Shabbetai was looked upon as a miraculous phenomenon and soon became the talking-point of the camp. This incident, however, caused Reb Shabbetai the loss of his eight fingers; for these had became petrified while holding them, pressed tightly, against the frosted, window pane. After this prolonged and hazardous exposure of his fingers, each of his eight fingers fell off his hand and he was left just with two thumbs.

It was Reb Shabbetai's rooted belief that he had been saved from extermination in the camp on account of his improvised Hanukkiah. It was for this reason that he always made a pilgrimage on Hanukkah to Mt. Zion, there to kindle the festive light in the Menorah that had been brought from the Golah and before which to pour out his heartfelt supplication. His heart beat fast and strong as he kindled the Hanukkiah, from which the flickering light cast the shape of an eight-branched Menorah — symbolic and reminiscent of his eight frozen and numbed fingers which took the place of the ceremonial Hanukkah lamp during his stay in Auschwitz."

When the young man had concluded his tale and had taken his leave of Reb Zanwill, the latter moved around the various Menorahs for quite a length of time as if he were himself a Hanukkah "trendel". He went to the studio of the Custodian of the Mount, requesting him to place among the rest of the Hanukkiah Menorahs on the Mount this eight-fingered lamp, in order to publicize the

Holocaust tragedy, as well as the resplendent courage and daring manifested by suffering Israel during that period when, despite everything, Jews flagged not in their love for Torah and Mitzvot.

THE STORY OF REB YA'AKOV

Reb Ya'akob was in his youth in Poland dynamic in his efforts for Torah and manual occupation. Eloquent of tongue and pen, he was instrumental in firing the heart of his companions and others who moved in his circle, enthusing them with a love for Torah and the good life. A fire was kindled in his soul when he learnt of the "Eight-fingered Menorah" and he resolved that he, also, would bravely enter the fire of the crematorium, with his eight fingers ablaze as if they had been metamorphosed into a Hanukkiah. His body would serve as the Shammash-light for the Menorah, standing above and apart from the rest of the lights. What actually transpired was this :

At the instigation of the persecutions and decrees which were constantly being levelled and promulgated against the hapless and helpless, the activity of his organization had almost been liquidated. In the course of time, some early, some later, people fled withersoever they hoped to find an asylum against persecution and extermination. Soon, only a select few remained behind, among whom was Reb Ya'akob. These "faithful few" were determined to keep aglow the "spark of Juadism," that it be not extinguished entirely.

Reb Ya'akob continued his work for the movement of Torah V'avodah, supervising the welfare of its members, visiting the Joint, seeking counsel with the Elders of the community. and participating in the prayer and study-sessions that were still carried on despite all difficulties and hazards.

It was actually hazardous to pace the streets at this period. and not all who ventured forth bravely were fortunate enough to return safely to their homes and families. Nothing, however, daunted Reb Ya'akob; the work had to be carried on "by hook or crook"; and if it could not by "hook," then there was no alternative than to accomplish it by "crook"; that is, in the face of danger. He always left home with a hearty farewell to his wife and child, but his farewell blessing was always tinged with a tone of sadness. For who could tell what each day would bring forth? Tears stood in his eyes each time he closed the door on those whom he loved as dearly as life itself.

It was the eve of Hanukkah when he left home one day and when his young daughter asked him not to forget to bring home for her Hanukkah candles. Hearing this, he tenderly stroked her delicate and smooth cheeks and promised her that he would not forget to come home with her Hanukkah candles.

For a whole hour, Reb Ya'akob went from shop to buy candles, but they seemed to be a rare commodity. At long last, his quest was successful in a store in Lishnew street. He did not bargain with the rather stiff price asked for them, paying the sum demanded.

After all, what mattered it? The chief thing was that he got what he wanted. As he left the store, his heart became disquieted. He felt inwardly that he had spent far too much time away from home; certainly far longer than he had at any other time.

Indeed, the hour was rather late. He had hardly made a few paces, when he encountered a sadistic group that blocked his way and seized hold of him. They then placed him in a line with others they had similarly snatched, leading them to a dilapidated house and commanding them to remove the mountains of stones to which it had been reduced.

The captives were then made to march the whole way in a military step. The leader of this wild, Nazi gang marched them with an overwhelming arrogance. In German, he kept on shouting gruffly, "One, Two, Three" again and again, until they had arrived at the ruined building where they were to be tried for disobeying the Nazi rules prescribed for Jews. They were placed in a circle, each one being commanded to throw a stone at the one next to him and so on till the last in the row. This sadistic "sport" went on and on, much to the wild enjoyment of the barbarians who saw to it that in this cruel game no one cheated but went on with meticulous precision. Yes, it was a hideous, satanic sight. Each captive was forced to bend down and to cast stones on the other until blood spurted from the spots where they were hit. The air was filled with cries of pain and terrifying groans.

Finally the tragedy occurred. When the turn of Reb Ya'akob came to bend down, the bag of candles dropped from his pocket. He paled and hastily made an effort to remove them out of sight by shuffling them along with his foot in an attempt to cover them with some of the stones. Alas! it was now too late. One of the barbaric gang noticed the fallen bag and made a hasty dash at it, shouting wildly as he ran along to seize hold thereof:

"What have you got inside that bag? A bomb?" He began to swipe with his whip the head of the poor victim, demanding with arrogant fury: "What is inside this bundle?"

Reb Ya'akob muttered feebly: "Only some candles," and opened the bag to show that he had spoken the whole truth and nothing but the truth.

The other was far from convinced. "So many candles! For what purpose?" he growled. His voice now became a roar. "You jolly well know as much as I do that all these candles were meant with which to give illuminated signs to the enemy at night that they may know at which places to hurl their bombs".

Reb Ya'akob pleaded: "No, no. These are Hanukkah candles which Jewish tradition commands to kindle during the eight days of Hanukkah."

The other mocked in rising anger. "Eight candles? Hanukkah?" Ha. Ha. Are not your fingers good enough with which to fulfill this ceremonial? Let me show you how to kindle lights."

He thereupon seized hold of the two hands of Reb Ya'akob, soaked them in benzine and turpentine and applied a match to them.

At first Reb Ya'akob fainted because of the burns he had sustained. Soon, however, he quickly pulled himself together, summoning all the latent strength he still had within him. Running around and around, he called out merrily : "Fellow-Jews, it is Hanukkah to night". Running with all his might towards his home, with thoughts of the festival in his childhood vivid in his mind, he kept on his jubilantly calling out to his little daughter : "Here my darling, I have brought you the Hanukkah candles you had asked for and which I promised you to bring. These burning, holy lights are intended as signs that I have hallowed His Name."

As he said these words, his fingers kept on burning away, and he kept on shouting : "My darling, here are the Hanukkah candles you asked for."

The picture of his little girl in his mind spurred him on to run faster and faster, through the burning aches increased a hundredfold. Darkness had fallen while he was still dancing round in circles with his eight fingers aflame, his cries being accompanied by the piercing jubilations of the sadists. His fingers sparkled like kindled lanterns in the thick, shadowy darkness. His fellow-Jews were spellbound at this terrifying sight, as they gazed at from closed windows, out of the sight of their Nazi torturers. All who stood at their windows, could not help muttering to themselves :

"These are the holy lights of Hanukkah. Yes, this is the work of the Menorah, all of which was constructed from blood, tears, and heart'

THE LIGHT OF REBELLION

Among the many Memorial Lamps that burn on the Mount, there is one Menorah in the shape of a barrel. This is kindled only on the first night of Hanukkah. Near it, the torch brought from Modiin (the stage on which the Maccabean victory was first enacted) is placed).

It is generally believed that the Warsaw Ghetto rebellion broke out on Erev Pesach. This is quite correct; but every big revolt is preceded by a smaller one. In this case, the revolt commenced in the winter following Hanukkah and it was sparked by a certain incident, one that the troubled times have brushed aside almost from memory. from almost.

It happened in a small chamber, on the third storey of a house in Leshnah street, in the Warsaw Ghetto, wherein R. Sender and his wife dwelt in abject poverty. Hunger was their constant companion and heavy burdens were residents who made themselves "at home" there. It was their implicit faith in their Heavenly Father that made them accept their fate uncomplainingly. R. Sender well knew that the cause of his suffering could be attributed to the fact that he was an observant Jew who meticulously fulfilled the precepts of his Creator, whose Name he constantly hallowed.

Despite these hardships, R. Sender most conscientiously made an "all-out" effort to fulfill the commandments of Judaism even amidst the sufferings heaped upon the dwellers in the Warsaw Ghetto.

R. Sender manifested a special love for the kindling of the Shabbat and Yomtov lights. Prior to the Second World War (1939—45), he was very much attached to these lights, which he kindled at every festive occasion, not sparing their number. His Shabbat table literally radiated with lights, when no less than seven candlesticks adorned his table — four in each of the corners and three in the centre. These gave forth a scintillating illumination. He also had special lamps for each of the festivals, as well as for all meals arranged in honour of the religious command just observed — such as a circumcision, a Barmitzvah, an engagement, or a wedding ceremony.

When a shortage of candles began to be felt in the Ghetto, as well as the mounting danger inherent in kindling lights — and thus drawing the attention of Jewish enemies, R.Sender became filled with aching anxiety and his sufferings tormented him almost to distraction. He searched for all kinds of devices whereby to implement the precept of kindling lights; or at least to discover some suitable counterpart some *ersatz* to take their place. Thus, when no candles for Shabbat were forthcoming, he would place the empty candlesticks after having cleaned them thoroughly beforehand, so that they were dazzling in their brightness. His wife would then raise her hands with which she covered her face when actually lighting the candles, reciting over them the allotted benediction. As she did so now over the empty candlesticks, she wept inwardly, though outwardly in the presence of her husband, she very bravely carried out this "mock' kindling, as if she were really lighting the Shabbat candles. When she finished, she approached him with "Shabbat Shalom", despite the grim fact that the table was orphaned of any Shabbat delicacy and bereft of the sheen usually cast by the lights in the candlesticks. What mattered it, as long as the inner lights of the soul were burning brightly?

As Hanukkah began to approach, R. Sender made all preparations for the kindling of the festive lights. During the whole of that month (Kislev), he had been storing up, by devious ways, little quantities of oil and small stores of candles so that he be enabled to fulfill this religious ceremony, one that was so beloved of him. Even before the shadows of night began to lengthen at the close of day, he would place the beautiful Hanukkah Menorah in front of the window overlooking the street and kindle the lights to the cheerful accompaniment of the appropriate benedictions. This accomplished, he would jubilantly sing the special hymn "Ma'oz Zur Yeshu'ati", ("The Rock is the fortress of my Salvation"). In the rapturous exaltation he had experienced in having been enabled to fulfill this beloved observance, Reb Sender had completely forgotten the very existence of the Ghetto and the presence of the Nazis. It was then that the tragedy occurred.

As night drew on and the world was now plunged in darkness, the vigilant Nazi police who paced the streets of the Ghetto and the suburbs without it, soon espied the flickering candles which cast their sheen for miles around. They quickly summoned the Gestapo, asserting that "these cursed Jews were now plotting a rebellion." Soon, the clanking noise made by the armed cyclists of the Gestapo was heard all around the hitherto silent streets of the Ghetto. Their wild shrieks frightened the slumbering dwellers of the Ghetto like the most terrifying nightmares, and all scrambled to find the newest and safest shelters, in preparation for the terrors about to be visited on them. For this sudden visitation betokened evils to come. All felt that something terrible was about to happen and all hearts pounded with dread. The Gestapo soon surrounded Reb Sender's house, from which those simple lights shone so brightly. Their "goose-trot" congealed the blood in the veins of those who heard them and it seemed that their soul was about to flee from their body in sheer fright. With piercing yells, the Gestapo burst open the door of R. Sender's home and found him in the very act of humming to himself the Ma'oz Zur hymn and unconcerned at this unwelcome invasion. The infuriated Gestapo lost no time in reducing the whole room into one massive shambles. After having cast the Hanukkah lamp on the floor, they handcuffed Reb Sender, dragging him down the steps as if he had been a bound and dead carcass.

When he was outside the house, they began to torture him diabolically; their aim being to make an example of him which would deter others from doing likewise and act in defiance of the commands of the Gestapo. They brought a large barrel, filled it with paraffin and cast Reb Sender into it after having saturated him with paraffin and other incendiary liquid. They then applied a burning match to the barrel and its living occupant and both began to blaze. It took the shape of a Hanukkah Menorah, for whereas the body of Reb Sender was within the barrel, his head and neck protruded from without — like the Menorah itself.

R. Sender uttered not a cry or groan but went on chanting the words of the Psalmist, while his body was being brunt alive.

"Avenge the blood of Thy servants; for Thy salvation is long in coming, and there seems to be no end to the days of evil'. R. Sender was martyred, but he gave no sign of feeling his terrible suffering. His soul and body had become part of the rare light which had been shed by the rays of the Hanukkah Menorah he had kindled.

The Jews in the Warsaw Ghetto who had observed this terrifying scene from their windows, trembled with fright as they gazed at the barrel of parrafin, ablaze with its human flesh that burnt like a wick. Fear and trembling filled their broken hearts, as they could not help comparing the sight which they now beheld with that which must have taken place in the days of Antiochus. when the gallant Maccabeans snatched their resounding triumph from overwhelming odds.

Throughout that long night, the barrel burnt like a mighty torch, shedding its rays of revolt and drawing its strength from that blazing barrel. Thus did this flaming barrel become the symbol of the great rebellion, known in history as the famous Warsaw Ghetto rebellion, which broke out on the eve of Pesah when the Ghetto burnt but also kindled the rays of Salvation.

When the leaders of the revolt were debating afterwards when the rebellion actually broke out, one of the older mystics of that generation opined that "it was the Hanukkah flame of the living torch of R. Sender. He must have been the incarnation of the prophet Elijah, who also transformed himself into a flaming torch. According to tradition, it is he who visits Jewish homes during the Seder night of Pesah. Who knows the mysterious ways of Providence?

THE JOURNEY'S END

It was the last day of Hanukkah. Reb Mendel and Reb Zanwill remained sitting in the chamber where the Hanukkiot had been stored. The festivities which marked each night of the festival were

257

long over and, gradually, the candles in the various Menorot were burning low. Many of them had been extinguished altogether, but the two of them remained sitting, gazing dreamily at the flickering lights casting their shadows all around the chamber, yet shining as brightly now that they had almost brunt themselves out, as they had done when they were first kindled.

Reb Zanwill linked arms with Reb Mendel. Piercing him with a look, he observed : "Thank you very much, Reb Mendel, for your brilliant, inspiring exhortations. Your stories are very sad, yet they possess so much actuality and are so practical in purposes. Yes, they are endowed with a soul and they sparkle with an inner light. You do well in telling these stories, so that future generations may know and take heed. Yet I have an important question to ask you : "Why does this light always stem only from the abodes of thick darkness? Why? Why??"

Reb Mendel gave Reb Zanwill a piercing and almost terrifying stare. He answered him with an even more profound question : :

"In truth, why do the lights always emerge from thick darkness? Why are the lights hidden from the eye for all to behold? Is there, then, a shortage of lights in the treasury of the Holy One, blessed be He?".

At this, Reb Zanwill sighed as he replied : "Puzzling are the ways of Providence, which move in a mysterious way His manifold wonders to perform."

E N D

(Translated from the original Hebrew & Yiddish by S. M. LEHRMAN)

258